PATRIOTISM is not ENOUGH

PATRIOTISM

👉 IS NOT 👈

ENOUGH

HARRY JAFFA, WALTER BERNS,
AND THE ARGUMENTS THAT REDEFINED
★AMERICAN★
CONSERVATISM

STEVEN F. HAYWARD

Encounter Books
New York · London

First American edition published in 2017 by Encounter Books, an activity of Encounter for Culture and Education, Inc., a nonprofit, tax-exempt corporation. Encounter Books website address: www.encounterbooks.com

Manufactured in the United States and printed on acid-free paper. The paper used in this publication meets the minimum requirements of ANSI/NISO Z39.48–1992 (R 1997) (*Permanence of Paper*).

FIRST AMERICAN EDITION

LIBRARY OF CONGRESS CATALOGING-IN-PUBLICATION DATA
Names: Hayward, Steven F., author.
Title: Patriotism is not enough : Harry Jaffa, Walter Berns, and the arguments that redefined American conservatism / by Steven F. Hayward.
Description: New York : Encounter Books, 2016. | Includes bibliographical references and index.
Identifiers: LCCN 2016024177 (print) | LCCN 2016027479 (ebook) | ISBN 9781594038839 (hardcover : alk. paper) | ISBN 9781594038846 (Ebook)
Subjects: LCSH: Conservatism—United States. | Political science—Philosophy. | United States—Politics and government. | Jaffa, Harry V. | Berns, Walter, 1919–2015
Classification: LCC JC573.2.U6 H393 2016 (print) | LCC JC573.2.U6 (ebook) | DDC 320.520973—dc23
LC record available at https://lccn.loc.gov/2016024177

As this book is chiefly about Harry Jaffa and Walter Berns, naturally I'll dedicate it to . . . C. S. Lewis. Partly because Lewis's own moral philosophy was congruent with Jaffa and Berns, but also because he was not a stranger to confronting disagreements between like-minded men.

But what would I think of your Thomas More or of our William Tyndale? All the writings of the one and all the writings of the other I have lately read right through. Both of them seem to me most saintly men and to have loved God with their whole heart: I am not worthy to undo the shoes of either of them. Nevertheless they disagree and (what racks and astounds me) their disagreement seems to me to spring not from their vices nor from their ignorance but rather from their virtues and the depths of their faith, so that the more they were at their best the more they were at variance. I believe the judgment of God on their dissention is more profoundly hidden than it appears to you to be: for His judgments are indeed an abyss.

C. S. LEWIS, LETTER TO FATHER GIOVANNI CALABRIA, NOVEMBER 25, 1947

Contents

The First Rule of Straussian Fight Club Is . . .

I had great difficulty describing this book as I was writing it, which is usually a sign of trouble not only for the writer but also, especially, for the would-be reader. Normally you should be able to describe a book in one or two sentences, but my account of this book changed almost daily. I recall Norman Podhoretz once writing that he didn't know what he really thought about something until he wrote a book about it. Now I know what he means. This book is the result of a voyage of discovery.

It grew out of the remarkable coincidence that Harry V. Jaffa and Walter Berns died on the same day, January 10, 2015. They had been preeminent students of Leo Strauss, who raised a fundamental challenge to modern political science by reviving the classical tradition of political philosophy. It is astounding to consider the lasting influence of this slight, weak-voiced man whose highest ambition as a young man in Germany was to be a rural postal carrier and raise rabbits on a farm, while reading philosophy in his study in the evening. But he could not escape the meaning of

Trotsky's axiom, "If you want to live a quiet life, you picked the wrong century to be born in."

Jaffa and Berns each made a substantial mark in political thought, along different though parallel paths. But they carried on a bitter feud for many years. Alice Roosevelt Longworth once said that Theodore Roosevelt disliked the young Winston Churchill the one and only time they ever met because they were so much alike. Such was this personal feud. Both men were spirited and combative in similar ways. They wrote a lot about the same topics, such as Lincoln and the *Dred Scott* case, both with a lively wit and frequent sarcasm, usually arriving at the same conclusions but by different routes, which is where the trouble came in. Would Jaffa have still been Jaffa had he been less cantankerous and personal toward his opponents? Probably not; and neither would Berns. As Churchill liked to say, you have to take the rough with the smooth.

My favorite recollection of the Jaffa-Berns feud was the time, around 1985 or 1986, when the chairman of the Government department at Claremont Graduate School, George Blair, announced his retirement, and the faculty on the left swooped in to try to take over the department. One of our allies in resisting was the distinguished historian Leonard Levy, then chairman of the History department, and although Levy was an old school New Deal liberal, he was on our side in wanting to preserve the conservative character of the department. Levy sent a note to Walter Berns asking if Walter might be interested in becoming chairman of the department.

Walter's reply was succinct:

Dear Leonard:
Thank you for thinking of me, but I must decline the invitation. At the present time, 3,000 miles separate me from Harry Jaffa, and I'm not interested in diminishing that distance by a single inch.

Jaffa had been my principal teacher in graduate school way back in the 1980s in Claremont, and later I had the privilege of becoming a colleague of Berns at the American Enterprise Institute (AEI) in Washington, D.C., where, at length, we became friends. I wouldn't claim we were close friends, if for no other reason than the considerable age gap. Yet he did once invite me to join him at Chief Justice John Roberts's monthly poker game, where Berns was a regular fixture. I declined for the simple reason that, being a terrible poker player, I didn't want to degrade their game with my poor play. (The idea of engaging Charles Murray as a tutor didn't occur to me until later on.)

Along with others I grieved at the enmity between these two great men. John Agresto, who dedicated his most recent book to Jaffa and Berns, expresses the sentiment of many that "while they disagreed, I think not at the deepest level."[1] Michael Uhlmann relates an occasion when, during a walk together on Capitol Hill around 1990, Berns made a favorable comment about Jaffa's great work on Lincoln: "Harry really is Lincoln's poet." Given that Berns wrote that Lincoln was America's poet, the completion of this syllogism showed his residual regard. Sensing a possible opening, Uhlmann summoned up his courage and asked Berns whether he (Uhlmann) might attempt a rapprochement. After a long pause, Berns said: "NO!"[2]

I agree with Agresto, though this book is not an attempt at posthumous reconciliation; but neither is it a simple rehash of their disagreements. I wish to celebrate and extend something else.

I understood the arguments of each, but the issues between them receded from my view as a result of the comic misadventure of a twenty-five-year period of my career when I concentrated chiefly on environmental issues. This period did include a large detour for writing a two-volume chronicle of Ronald Reagan, a necessary diversion to prevent me from dying of self-inflicted wounds out of despair of the abyss of environmental nonsense. Even here, however, the unique teaching of profound thinkers like Jaffa and Berns provided an extra dimension to my policy wonkery, as I never tired of wondering how so many people who are concerned about understanding ecosystems and preserving the right order of wild nature could seem indifferent or hostile to the idea of *human* nature and the protection of human social ecosystems. My economist friends wondered how this perspective could possibly fit in with cost-benefit analyses of regulation.

Returning to the academic world a few years ago reopened all of the concepts I had studied and read with Jaffa and others more than thirty years ago, now more freshly urgent because of the continuing decay of the country. Making sense of what I wanted to explore about the legacy of these two great men and some of their wider circle of colleagues led inexorably to casting this work in the form of a personal memoir. I have a congenital dislike of writing in the first person or telling personal stories, but I think I'm reaching the age where I ought to relent. In any case, first-person accounts and impressions may be a better way of conveying the essence of men and ideas. And after all the theorizing is done, real politics turns out to be a first-person business.

I said this was a voyage of discovery. Among other things, I was surprised during background research to find some of my own very modest early work cited with some prominence in some of the ongoing arguments, including by George W. Carey in a preface to a new edition of *The Basic Symbols of the American Political Tradition*, which he published in 1970 with coauthor Willmoore Kendall. I had read this book as an undergraduate—it was in fact the first serious book on American political thought that I ever read—and found it compelling. I wrote my first undergraduate paper in political science on *Basic Symbols*, and though my liberal professor lauded the quality of the writing, he nonetheless gave me a "B" because of the approving viewpoint I took—my first experience of liberal bias in the classroom. Never in my wildest imagination did I think that my name might earn a reference in a future edition of the book, but there it is, in Carey's preface to the 1995 edition.

As I say, I found the Kendall-Carey book very powerful—until I read Jaffa's contrary perspective, which seemed much superior. How to sort this out? Graduate school beckoned. And the rest, as they say . . .

As already mentioned, Jaffa and Berns were students of the controversial Leo Strauss. I'm not sure who deserves the credit for coming up with the lightbulb joke for the followers of Strauss, but it works on several levels, just as Straussian hermeneutics would suggest: "How many Straussians does it take to change a lightbulb? *None*—the light is made conspicuous by its absence!"[3]

It's only funny if you get the joke.

Socratic irony is the heart of the Straussian interpretation of Plato, and it carries over perfectly to the way in which the Straussian community has never abided by the first rule of *Fight Club*, for no sect of supposedly hidden knowledge has ever been so bad at keeping its secrets. The Straussians are generally the most interesting people working in political science today, which is one reason they are so widely hated in the academy. The fact that most, though not all, are conservative is a bonus. I go further and assert that the Straussian community has, for two generations now, provided the most serious defenses against the deliberate degradations of the Constitution and the American character. "If Strauss's students have sometimes displayed an unseemly self-assurance," Herbert Storing, another of Strauss's leading students, wrote at the time of Strauss's death in 1973, "the source is not so much pride of truth as relief that they have not allowed political science to make them more stupid than they need to be."[4]

Trying to explain briefly the important sources of Strauss's legacy for our time is as daunting as the "Summarize Proust

Competition," the famous Monty Python sketch in which contestants are challenged to explain *Remembrance of Things Past* in thirty seconds. Most accounts of the Straussian world typically comprise three interrelated issues: reviving the battle between ancients and moderns; confronting the "theological-political problem"; and emphasizing esoteric writing, which makes them the Bletchley Park code breakers of academia. I'm going to violate all the unwritten rules of Straussian fight club, and not talk about any of these usual angles.[5] Instead this book will use Jaffa, Berns, and some of their like-minded colleagues and students to explore three topics: statesmanship, patriotism, and equality.

The mainstream of political science does not think statesmanship is a topic that can be studied intelligibly or rigorously. Storing writes that "statesmanship is not much respected. . . . [It] is almost un-American. The word has an elitist and obsolete ring."[6] Strauss and his students did not think so, and statesmanship is at the heart of Jaffa's and Berns's work. Both Jaffa and Berns saluted Lincoln and Churchill as examples of statesmanship deserving close study and emulation. Statesmanship is the point of contact between political philosophy and real politics. The central proposition here is bold: The statesman stands above the philosopher; practical wisdom is superior to theoretical wisdom, even if it rests on theoretical wisdom. Jaffa argued that "political science, properly so-called, would have at its heart the study of the speeches and deeds of statesmen."[7] Berns wrote that "theory depends (in part) on practice."[8]

I'll explore the title of this book—*Patriotism Is Not Enough*—more fully in chapter 2, but the short answer for the moment is this: America is different. Berns once said that "an American patriot is a better patriot than a Spartan who loves his country simply because it's his country and doesn't know anything else."[9] Patriotism is disdained in academia as a subject of inquiry, because patriotism is the root of nationalism, and nationalism is presumptively a bad thing these days among the cosmopolitan elites of the faculty club and the media. One of Berns's students from Cornell in the early 1960s told me, "Berns was living proof that one could be a well-educated brilliant scholar and still love America, honor the flag, respect religious faith, and defend the traditional family—all of which were already up for grabs at Cornell by 1962."[10] Berns's final book was called *Making Patriots,* and I have a hunch Berns felt more deeply about that short and accessible book than any of his other well-regarded works. The Founders, Berns wrote, knew that "the making of patriots could not be left to chance."[11]

It may be that just now is an important time to revisit the foundations of American patriotism, as the remarkable and astonishing campaign of Donald Trump has raised the issue of patriotism in the guise of nationalism and American greatness. At the other end of the spectrum are found the small but growing number of well-paid professional athletes protesting the national anthem before games, ostensibly on account of the nation's historic shortcomings. I suspect Berns would have found Trump appalling. In his very first book, *Freedom, Virtue and the First Amendment,* Berns worried about the demagogue "who plays on the vilest passions of citizens in order to win political power," and said that "loyalty cannot be defined as patriotism. In order that a nation deserve the loyalty of a good man, it must promote virtue."[12]

The shame of protesting athletes is that they are unable to make out a parallel between the exertions necessary for excellence on the playing field that command the loyalty of sports fans and the exertions necessary for excellence in a nation that commands the loyalty of citizens. Game plans, like constitutions, are not self-executing. Berns put the problem this way:

A regime to which a good man can freely give his loyalty does not come about accidentally, it does not just grow through the passage of time; in addition to good fortune, it requires the conscious and intelligent effort of men who are aware of the goal and of the difficulties to be overcome before the goal can be achieved or approximated.[13]

About the professional athletes disdaining the nation, Jaffa would point again to the example of boxer Joe Louis. Louis once answered the question of why he was willing to fight for a country that treated blacks so badly: "There ain't nothing wrong with this country that Hitler can fix."[14]

Jaffa and Berns can be seen as two sides of the same coin. Berns was vitally concerned about the philosophical ground of virtue in the individual, which was the necessary foundation of a decent regime. Jaffa was concerned with the philosophic ground of the regime, which he thought was the necessary foundation for individual virtue. For all of their sometimes bitter differences, their work complements each other's because of the reciprocal problem of regime and citizen.

It is commonplace now to say that Jaffa had a "second sailing," which will be explained in due course, but I think the same can be said about Berns. At length Jaffa would come to think of America as the best regime, in the classical sense. Though Berns never quite declared himself directly on the question as Jaffa did, he came to think something similar, but for reasons best captured in the old joke that an optimist thinks this is the best of all worlds, while the pessimist knows it is. Berns was more pessimistic about the nation's course for a long time, and who can blame him? Berns's love for his country went through a dark night of the soul, a period of understandable gloom based on his bitter experience of the shameful meltdown of Cornell University in 1969, when Berns's life was threatened by the student mob, which led for a time to his exile from America—a separation that was more than just a matter of geography. (Parallel lives: a similar racially based eruption occurred at Claremont Men's College at the same time, complete with bombings and arson fires, though with less media notice, and Jaffa received death threats for publicly opposing the student mob.) The fact that some of the student radicals who took up arms to sack Cornell had been students of Berns, and had perversely taken the wrong lessons from Berns's teaching about the possible limitations and defects of the American Founding, shook him to his core. While in exile at the University of Toronto in the early 1970s, Berns told more than one student that he feared constitutional democracy was finished.

Berns's exile from America—maybe the most salient aspect of his life—lasted a decade. While shedding none of his justifiable bitterness at the shameful cowardice of Cornell and what it meant for academia, by degrees Berns recovered his patriotic fervor. After this long period of pessimism, *Making Patriots* represents Berns rallying for his country one last time. Berns in no way surrendered his dismay at the plight of our republic, but, just as he said there was "no question" that he was going to join the armed forces and fight when World War II broke out, there was no question at the end that the necessity of patriotism would win out. The popular reaction to 9/11 made a deep impression on him. For all of the confusion and anti-Americanism of our cultural elites, it was clear to him that the great mass of the American people still cared about more than just their private concerns. Neither Berns nor Jaffa was Pollyannaish about our prospects. Jaffa, in one of his last interviews, said he was neither pessimistic nor optimistic—he saw grounds for both.

Equality, meanwhile, is the central obsession with much of the intellectual class, though it is understood in simplistic terms, measured quantitatively, and used chiefly as a cudgel against existing institutions and social structures. One of Jaffa's main ideas is that equality is a *conservative* principle, but arguing such requires considerable effort against the powerful tides of our time.

A common thread marks out Jaffa, Berns, and several of their colleagues from others even within the Straussian world: their intense political engagement. While some of Strauss's students turned away from or avoided political engagement (even though Strauss criticized what he called an "unmanly contempt for politics") in favor of cultivating their private gardens, Jaffa and Berns were not disposed to the pure ivory tower existence. Most of their scholarly work was directed at urgent current public controversies, rather than abstract esoterica or remote philosophical speculation. Jaffa, in particular, had contempt for the theoretical detachment of "pure" philosophy, once quipping that as "philosophy" means "lover of wisdom," a "professional philosopher" must be a professional lover, or a whore of the intellect. In one of his disputes with Berns, Jaffa wrote, "Philosophy may belong to the perfection of human life. But it is not the whole of human life. Moral indignation, under the direction of reason, also belongs to the perfection of human life."[15]

Both men wrote a large number of newspaper op-ed articles and blunt letters to the editor of major newspapers and magazines. Jaffa worked on Barry Goldwater's 1964 campaign, and wrote several speeches for Goldwater. Berns more than once suited up for a stint as a U.S. representative to the U.N. Commission on Human Rights, which he found less congenial than a root canal. But the Commission brought out his fighting spirit, which was just as morally indignant as Jaffa's. He delighted in ostentatiously walking out of the meetings when they went off on an Israel-bashing bender, and in a 1983 speech to the U.N. Commission on Human Rights, Berns called out the Soviet Union by reminding them of their common ideological roots with Nazi fascism, memorialized in a great article: "How to Talk to the Russians: Call Them Fascists."[16] Bravo!

By their thoughts and the inspiration that they imparted to two generations of students, Jaffa, Berns, and their like-minded colleagues teach us the nature of the American Founding and a robust basis for patriotism. In short, they show us how to think about America. They were more than just very smart professors.

They were great men—magnanimous men right out of the pages of the *Nicomachean Ethics*—because just talking with them filled you with courage, the first of the moral virtues. Thinking of them reminds me of something once said of Churchill: "Nobody left his presence without feeling a braver man." Harry and Walter had that effect, too.

PATRIOTISM is not ENOUGH

CHAPTER I

"A Little Touch of Harry in the Night"

*A teacher affects eternity; he can
never tell where his influence stops.*

HENRY ADAMS

DECEMBER 2014

"Is Walter Berns still alive?"

"Yes. He's ninety-five and in poor health, but I think Walter and Harry [age ninety-six] are seeing who can outlive the other as the last act in their long-running feud."

I offered that whimsical speculation the week after Christmas in 2014 at a meeting at the Claremont Institute. About two weeks later, on Saturday, January 10, the *Weekly Standard* magazine was the first to publish on its website the sad news that Berns had passed away that morning. Jaffa, also in failing health, had gone to the hospital the day before. He was slipping in and out of consciousness, but intermittently awake enough to make the standard complaints about the usual defects of hospital life. His family and visiting students were guardedly optimistic; he had overcome several acute crises and hospitalizations before. But he took a turn for the worse, and when he passed away a few hours later, the comparison to Thomas Jefferson and John Adams passing on the same day in 1826 became inescapable.

Jefferson and Adams had been bitter political rivals, culminating in the close and initially inconclusive election of 1800 that could easily have ended in the ruin of the still infant nation. Abraham Lincoln taught, as Jaffa never tired of reminding students, that the election of 1800 was the first to prove that ballots could replace bullets as the means of changing a government.

Adams and Jefferson reconciled in later years, chiefly because the two giants of the American Founding shared the same basic political philosophy, which slowly dissolved the rancor of personal ambition and party spirit that dominated their poor relations for the better part of a decade. Some of their political and constitutional disputes had deep theoretical roots, turning on subtle shadings of how republican concepts should be understood and practiced. Jefferson had some radical inclinations at times, like that "God forbid we should ever be 20. years without such a rebellion" musing he once made in a private letter, while Adams was the prototypical cautious conservative.[1] Arguing politely and respectfully over their differences in a long correspondence became one of their favorite pastimes in retirement.

Jaffa and Berns never contested each other for political office, but their arguments over the course of a decade took on the bitterness and personal invective of partisan strife. "In your present state of mind," Jaffa wrote in one public letter to Berns, "nothing less than a metaphysical two-by-four across the frontal bone would capture your attention." One of Berns's retorts began: "Who will rid us of this pest of a priest?" Unlike Jefferson and Adams, they never reconciled their intellectual differences, although the feud gradually burned itself out, and the two old giants did once sit together and talk cordially, if a bit stiffly, over lunch in Washington, a meal carefully brokered by the Claremont Institute around 2005. It wasn't necessary to confiscate the forks and knives. By then Jaffa had turned his attention to new feuds with other targets, and Berns was happy to pass the bull's-eye on his back to Allan Bloom, Robert Bork, Chief Justice William Rehnquist, and Justice Antonin Scalia.

Epic academic feuds are common, but are often about trivial or obscure matters. It is a mistake to explain the Jaffa-Berns quarrel as an example of the narcissism of small differences, or still less the simple pride or one-upmanship typical of most academic fights that have little consequence in the real world. But the differences between Jaffa and Berns and their allied camps that seem abstract or remote on the surface are connected to a serious question, perhaps the most serious political question of this or any time: What kind of country is America? What is the right or best basis for patriotism? Is democracy capable of being understood and conducted nobly? Above all, can these questions be answered without recourse to pondering deeply the nature and condition of the human soul?

As these questions unfolded into their numerous constituent parts, the arguments began to engage several urgent political issues, including jurisprudence (especially the frequent disappointments arising from Republican-appointed judges), the nature of individual rights, and how conservatives should contest liberals for the meaning of justice and equality. Like Adams and Jefferson, Jaffa and Berns shared the same basic political philosophy, and it is possible to compare some central passages of their writings and be unable to guess accurately which was the author. Each would grudgingly praise *some* of the other man's work.

Jaffa and Berns were among the handful of Leo Strauss's students who, unlike Strauss, devoted their attention chiefly to American politics. Both men decried the dead end of value-free social science and were unflinching about calling out the nihilism at the heart of the conventional modern mind. Both believed not that the Constitution was merely a legal document belonging to lawyers and judges, but that it should be expounded rigorously and philosophically by statesmen and citizens alike. Both men revered Abraham Lincoln as the highest practitioner of this kind of constitutional politics. Jaffa's scholarly work, especially *Crisis of the House Divided*, transformed modern perspectives on Lincoln and the Civil War. Berns's careful work on various aspects of virtue, jurisprudence, and other constitutional controversies are a model of applied political philosophy and found a wide audience. Countless passages in their respective works are substantially identical, and they were once friends. Berns's copy of Jaffa's *Crisis of the House Divided* bears the inscription, "To Walter, who waited impatiently, appreciatively and warmly, Harry."

How did they become so estranged?

Jaffa's critics thought he picked fights with Berns and others out of sheer obstreperousness or worse. He even picked fights with friends, students, and coworkers over their smoking habits, writing long letters about the evils of tobacco and the righteousness of antismoking measures. Charles R. Kesler, one of Jaffa's closest colleagues and defenders, admits that Jaffa could be "occasionally splenetic and vainglorious." Harvey Mansfield Jr. once complained directly to Jaffa: "What you do is stand behind the front lines, and point your weapon at the backs of your friends and shoot! And you're not even looking." Berns charged Jaffa with "frittering away your great gifts on petty, vain, and vindictive projects." Joseph Cropsey, a boyhood friend of Jaffa's, lamented that Jaffa's "fulminations reached new peaks of sulphur and apocalypse" because of Jaffa's "absolute conviction that what everybody else understands to be insignificant is the germ of universal calamity."[2]

Jaffa's friends and students occasionally tried to convince him that he was being too severe, at least rhetorically, with his former friends or allies, a list that included Berns, Irving Kristol, Martin Diamond, Edwin (Ed) Meese, Robert Bork, Allan Bloom, Antonin Scalia, and Robert Goldwin. It was to no avail. "Gentlemanly obfuscation may be indulged in all manner of prudential matters," he replied to one student who objected, "but not on the fundamentals." One person who received more than his share of acerbic Jaffa letters was William F. Buckley Jr., though Jaffa had a significant influence on changing Buckley's views on many subjects, including Lincoln and Churchill. (*National Review* had been indifferent or hostile to both statesmen before Jaffa began making the case for each in its pages.)

While Jaffa can be criticized for gratuitously giving personal offense in the conduct of his fights—was it really necessary to use "Robert 'Borky-the-Big' Bork" or "Billy Kristol" to convey his disagreement?—to attribute his stance merely to personal pique and unfulfilled pride is unjust. Yet time spent in his youth as a Golden Gloves boxer should be considered in understanding Jaffa's character; he couldn't resist the pugilistic delights of the sharp jab. He couldn't accept the intellectual equivalent of a technical knockout or scorecard decision; he could only be satisfied with a full ten-count knockdown on the mat, which is seldom attainable in intellectual dispute. He didn't direct his fire only at friends and fellow conservatives. One note to a liberal colleague at Claremont Graduate University included the less than cordial provocation, "I understand your major professional preoccupation is with garbage," before going on to conclude that said colleague was a "moral eunuch."[3] He was fond of quoting a medieval aphorism: *Solet Aristoteles quaero pugnam*—Aristotle is accustomed to seeking a fight. And if one looked beyond the personal angles, his letters often contained some of his most lucid arguments about the underlying issues. His students might groan in the classroom when Jaffa pulled out his latest letter and began to read it aloud, but they were effective teaching tools, as Jaffa's extended commentary about the issues involved was invariably enlightening.

For his part, Berns could be gruff, stubborn, and taciturn. Berns was much less gregarious than Jaffa. He would often declare his disagreement with something that had been said, but end with a great harrumph, as if to suggest it was a chore to explain why more fully. John Agresto once quipped of Berns, "Underneath that rough and gruff exterior beats a heart of stone."

No one who really knew him would think so. A more kind-hearted, even cheerful man seldom graced the hallways of Washington. But getting to know him was not easy or quick. Walter was more than a bit standoffish when I first arrived at the American Enterprise Institute in 2002. He had good reason to be. He knew that I came from Claremont and had been a student of Jaffa. He had called Jaffa a "pest"; surely it couldn't be good that a carrier of the pestilence was settling in down the hall. My first attempt at a "hi, nice to meet you" conversation didn't go very well. I'm not sure I'd say Walter was *rude*, exactly, but . . .

His deep baritone voice and his very direct manner of expressing disagreement with whatever nonsense he confronted certainly made it intimidating to approach him. But his magnanimous and delightful side soon became evident. And he had a great wit: when something amused him or met with his approval, his eyes would visibly brighten and a wry smile that started at the corner of his mouth would spread into an irrepressible grin. Like his nemesis Jaffa, he had a low tolerance for unsound thinking (of which there is no shortage), and it summoned forth his gravitas; his deep voice, when summoned to express disapproval, made you think you were hearing from Moses himself. During discussion periods at AEI events, there were comments and questions, and then there was Walter. You could make out a clear difference between the categories. I can only imagine what he was like in his heyday in the classroom. At Cornell, his students routinely applauded him after every lecture, not just after the final lecture of the semester as is customary. His Cornell students also tell me that he lavished extraordinary praise on Jaffa's *Crisis of the House Divided*.

One of his students from the early 1960s recalled a memorable classroom incident:

> Berns taught an early evening seminar on Locke in spring 1964. As the classroom in the Government and History building was not air-conditioned, the windows were wide open on a warm spring evening, when suddenly a deafeningly loud motorcycle drove by just outside, silencing the booming-voiced Walter. As only he could, he glared at the class for probably ten seconds but felt like an eternity, face growing redder by the second. Then he walked over to the desk and proceeded to kick a heavy wooden chair clear across the platform, and wagging his finger, he slowly growled: "If I ever catch you riding one of those things . . ." That bright, sunny grin and lighted up eyes were not to be seen that night.[4]

There are limitless examples of Berns at his blunt but clarifying best. My favorite is his summary judgment of Oliver Wendell Holmes Jr., who for some reason seems to have every would-be jurist bamboozled. Contrary to Holmes's popular reputation as the greatest judicial statesman since John Marshall, Berns wrote that "no man who ever sat on the Supreme Court was less inclined and so poorly equipped to be a statesman or to teach, as a philosopher is supposed to teach, what a people needs to know in order to govern itself well."[5] Boom! (My codicil to Walter's argument is that any potential GOP Supreme Court nominee who names Holmes as someone they admire—as David Souter and Harriet Miers both did—should be immediately disqualified for the appointment. Lots of grief could have been avoided if President George H. W. Bush had applied this simple screen to Souter.)

Although most students are rightly loyal to their principal teachers, fairness all around compels me to note that Jaffa admired many parts of Walter's work, and especially recommended to students Walter's bracing series of articles on the folly of world government—a bad idea that was popular during the early phase of Walter's academic career and that still returns to favor from time to time.[6] Jaffa also agreed enthusiastically with Walter's analysis of First Amendment issues and capital punishment. (Ditto for Thomas Pangle, with whom Jaffa quarreled strenuously in the 1980s. But in 1980, when Pangle was in the midst of a bitter tenure fight at Yale, Jaffa rallied to his defense, writing strong letters to the president of Yale protesting Pangle's shabby and politicized treatment.)

Accordingly, I was never ill-disposed toward Walter's thought. The Jaffa-Berns feud over how Hobbes and Locke should be understood in relation to the American Founding, while serious, seems less important than the many things they agreed about. In any case, Walter's wariness of me began to wear off initially through the solvent of single-malt scotch, for which we both made a beeline to the bar following early evening events at AEI. He must have figured that anyone who liked his single malts neat couldn't be all bad, if for no other reason than that Jaffa was a teetotaler (except on Winston Churchill's birthday) as well as a militant non-smoker. Walter enjoyed his tobacco as well as his cocktails—Churchill's "admirable vices." By degrees, however, between casual conversation and comments made in formal panels and events at AEI, it became apparent that we were throwing in with exactly the same point of view for the same underlying reasons. The initial wariness began to be replaced by nods of approval.

One day Walter called me on the phone to applaud my embrace and deployment of John Locke's doctrine of executive prerogative from the *Second Treatise of Government*, which happened to coincide exactly with Walter's muscular understanding of the idea, and which differed diametrically from our in-house champion of pure legislative supremacy, Norman Ornstein. Walter noted with enthusiasm my interest and periodic work on Churchill, and started regularly asking when the long-promised unabridged edition of *The River War* was ever coming out. (It still hadn't, alas, by the time of Walter's passing, though I often tried to shame the editor and publisher by saying "Walter is *waiting* on you guys, damnit!")

Soon I noticed that Walter was showing up for nearly every panel or conference I was on at AEI, and he was especially enthusiastic about the second volume of my *Age of Reagan* when it finally appeared in 2009. At the back of this interest was Walter's fundamental agreement with Harry Jaffa about the centrality of statesmanship for any serious study of politics. In my last personal conversation with Berns, over the phone in the spring of 2012 as I was preparing to leave Washington and reenter ordinary academic life, Walter said he hoped I would continue working on narrative political biography because it was a dying genre.

Walter did something else in that last conversation that stunned me: he apologized for having been rude to me a decade before. I never made anything of it at the time and had forgotten all about it, but it obviously had grown in Walter's mind, and this expression of decency and respect was humbling in the highest degree. No matter how old I get to be, or whatever my own accomplishments, I shall always think of Walter and my other great teachers and colleagues from the generation ahead as my superiors in every way, from whom no apology could ever be owed.

———

For all of the harsh and personal language that Jaffa sometimes used in his public arguments, his in-person demeanor was the polar opposite of Berns's. George Anastaplo, one of Strauss's rare students who remained mostly on the left, observed that "Jaffa has the charming characteristic of sometimes being considerably more prudent in private than in public." You could hardly find a professor more generous and dedicated to his students, more

cheerful in his greeting, and more patient with our errors, willing
to explain and instruct as long as you were willing to listen, even
on a street corner or supermarket aisle if that's where you ran into
him. Only in print did the irascible Jaffa appear.

William F. Buckley Jr. wrote that "If you think Harry Jaffa is
hard to argue with, try agreeing with him. It is nearly impossible.
He studies the fine print in any agreement as if it were a trap,
or a treaty with the Soviet Union."[7] (Though perhaps Edward
Shils's similar quip about Frank Knight is equally fitting: "Arguing
with him was like wrestling with an intellectual porcupine."[8]) Jaffa
thought that seemingly minor theoretical errors could have large
practical consequences over time—as Lincoln argued concerning
Stephen Douglas's doctrine of "popular sovereignty." Since Jaffa
was the author of Barry Goldwater's infamous line, "Extremism
in the defense of liberty is no vice . . . moderation in the pursuit of justice is no virtue," it should have surprised no one that
Jaffa would take an exacting stance against error. "The errors of
excellent men," Buckley continued, "are at once more instructive
and more seductive than those of fools. So the relentless Jaffa
logic pries at apparently trifling differences until they open like
chasms."[9]

Jaffa thought Berns and many other conservative thinkers were
insufficiently attentive to or dismissive of the essential connection
between the Declaration of Independence and the Constitution,
or that they had wrongly neglected or downgraded the Declaration altogether. Berns had criticisms of the Declaration, but as
time went on his view approached Jaffa's, as we shall see. But this
dispute in turn opened a controversy over how to understand the
sources of the political thought of the Founding, especially John
Locke—"America's philosopher," as Berns and others call him. I'll
come to this dispute in due course.

Although this account will make a generous nod to a number of the leading figures of what I call "renegade" political science, it must necessarily dwell more on Harry Jaffa as its central figure for the simple reason that it was my privilege to be more closely associated with Jaffa than any other. Any reckoning with Jaffa has to inquire about the long period after the triumph of *Crisis of the House Divided* in 1959. A sequel to *Crisis* had been promised, but as the 1960s unfolded . . . nothing. And the 1970s . . . still nothing.

Well, not quite nothing: Jaffa wrote that famous political speech for Goldwater—his first and last such speech, about which more in due course. He later liked to joke, to Jack Kemp among others, that he'd promise *not* to write any speeches for them if they'd act on his private advice. His feuds in the 1960s and 1970s seemingly diverted him from the prospective *New Birth of Freedom*, though this long quarrelsome period led directly to the gestation of new angles on the American Founding that are proving very significant. He also produced a flood of notable essays and lectures on topics as far-flung as Tom Sawyer, Fyodor Dostoyevsky, and William Shakespeare, which have been collected in several books.

Though I had read a few of Jaffa's disputations from this period before entering graduate school, I was still unprepared for the direct experience. Nothing could prepare you for the shock of hearing Jaffa in the classroom for the first time. It was not that his manner or words were shocking in the sense of transgressing conventions (though he was no respecter of conventions). From the first moment of class with Jaffa, you could tell that this was not going to be political science or political philosophy as it is usually taught. Above all, it was instantly clear that the course would involve engagement with the most serious political matters at the highest level. Practically the first words out of his mouth in the first class of the semester concerned "the crisis of the West." There was no pawing at the ground with methodological preliminaries, no "on the one hand, on the other hand." He plunged headlong into the assigned texts—Aristotle and Aquinas—whose themes and implications Jaffa illuminated with a peripatetic brilliance that ranged from Plato to Shakespeare to Thackeray; from architecture to drama, music, poetry, modern culture, and sports, all without a single lecture note. Above all, Jaffa said, the most fundamental political question is the nature of the human soul. *Political* question, mind you; not theological or psychological.

And that was just the first fifteen minutes.

His lecture was a dazzling vindication of the ancient claim that political philosophy is the queen of the sciences, and that the arguments among the greatest minds (among whom it became apparent Jaffa belonged) were not a matter of antiquarian curiosity or the mere history of ideas, but a live argument directly relevant to the problems of the here and now. My very first three hours in class with Jaffa cleared away years of half-learning, confused ideas, and superficially grounded opinions with a force that others who shared the same experience have compared to a religious conversion—just as Jaffa described his own first encounter with his great teacher, Leo Strauss.

My experience has been widely shared. At Jaffa's memorial service in 2015, Michael Uhlmann recalled his first encounter with Jaffa over a cup of coffee after a panel in Chicago in the mid-1960s:

> What a food of words and ideas! Whole paragraphs, pages, books, and libraries came tumbling out, on everything from the Goldwater campaign and the future of the Republican Party, to the virtues and vices of *National Review* and the burgeoning conservative movement, to Shakespeare as political thinker, to the centrality of natural right in the American political tradition, to the greatness of Leo Strauss, the American Founding, Abraham Lincoln, and Winston Churchill. I had never

encountered anything like this in my life. There was no finger-wagging, only an endless stream of learned reflections, for the most part gently delivered, one thought begetting another in a long chain of reasoned discourse, which, if one followed the links (which I was barely capable of doing), connected the condition of America circa 1965 to forgotten lessons taught by Aristotle.[10]

Michael Anton describes the experience in similar fashion:

His mind was a museum stuffed to the rafters with masterworks. Name any "great book" and he knew it cold. Books he hadn't studied for 50 years he could recall in detail, with total clarity. Montesquieu, Machiavelli, Marsilius . . . all of it. Wondering about an obscure passage in Shakespeare? Ask Professor Jaffa. First he would quote it in full, from memory, and then spend an hour explaining what it meant, in the context of that play, and in Shakespeare's corpus. The same could be said for Plato—a philosopher about whom, unless I am very much mistaken, he never published a word beyond a passing reference. And not just the *Republic* and the *Apology*—he knew all of the dialogues. He knew every book of the Bible. And he knew more about American literature than the English faculties of all our elite universities combined.[11]

The typical Jaffa class never got very far into the assigned texts. Every Jaffa student who took his course on the *Nicomachean Ethics* has the same story: by the end of the semester, Jaffa had failed to get us beyond the end of Book I (though by some miracle, the semester I had the course we actually got through several chapters of Aquinas as well as Book II of the *Ethics*). It didn't matter: at the end of that semester, everyone could read and comprehend the rest of the *Ethics* on his own.

This lack of normal progress through the assigned texts wasn't because of excessive focus on minutiae or pointless digressions. Indeed, half or more of Jaffa's classes consisted of digressions, often forty-five minutes or longer, which were always deeply interesting, after which he would say, "Where were we? Oh, yes . . . ," and he would pick up the main thread of his thought on the text exactly where he had left off. His phenomenal memory was best seen in his ability to recite long quotations verbatim.

One of the startling paradoxes of Jaffa was that such an argumentative and confrontational person could be so unfailingly patient and generous to students. He rarely had a sharp word for a student, even one who might be obviously far off track. Seth Leibsohn, now a conservative talk radio host in Arizona, recalls how Jaffa invited him to coffee after Leibsohn, as a left-wing undergraduate, had strongly attacked Jaffa in the student newspaper. Leibsohn recalled at Jaffa's passing: "Harry took my hand, started introducing me to a line of thought and reason I never even knew existed, walked me through everything he could teach me, and never let go. . . . He changed my whole life."

A long line of graduate students—an apostolic succession of sorts—lived in a three-bedroom house rented out by Peter Drucker, and when the phone rang the probability was that Jaffa would be the caller, even if you weren't enrolled in one of his classes that semester. Ken Masugi recalls that "A telephone call *from* Jaffa could be a blessing or a terror."[12] Jaffa gently upbraided me a few times for immature or ill-considered things I had written, but my experience was usually benign. What are you reading? Are you writing anything? Did you see that terrible op-ed today in the *Los Angeles Times*? Sometimes he'd give you a private mini-lecture, a tutorial on a particular thinker, and sometimes he might criticize you, always gently, for a mistake he thought you had made. I always wish I had kept a notepad by the phone for these calls. One I vividly recall sent me scurrying to my bookshelf to ponder the vital connection between Aristotle's *Ethics* and the *Politics*, which took him about forty-five seconds to explain, but which I was hard-pressed to recapitulate once I put the phone down.

A whimsical side of Jaffa seldom emerged in his writing but was frequently expressed in person. He could be quick with a laugh or quip, often spontaneous, but also referencing classic comedy, especially P.G. Wodehouse, whom he first learned about from Strauss. Early in his graduate student days with Strauss in the 1940s, Jaffa accompanied Strauss on a train trip for a lecture, hoping to glean more from the great teacher. Strauss was reading a Wodehouse paperback and, rather than entertain Jaffa's incessant curiosity about Plato or Aristotle, he curtly cut him off, barking in his heavy accent: "I am not *verking!*" Instead Strauss reached into his book bag and handed Jaffa a second Wodehouse novel from his stack.

Jaffa's humor was never far removed from his serious purpose. As Churchill explained: "In my belief, you cannot deal with the most serious things in the world unless you also understand the most amusing." Jaffa could be spontaneous in his wit, like the best improv comics. Perhaps his finest comic moment came when he was being questioned during *voir dire* in a jury pool:

LAWYER: I see from the jury questionnaire you are a professor of political science. As a professor, what is your attitude about expert psychiatric testimony?

JAFFA: Anyone who would put credence in the testimony of a psychiatrist ought to have his head examined.

Naturally it was impossible to stop Jaffa from explaining why—essentially Plato's division of the soul—after which the judge dismissed the entire jury pool, reckoning correctly that Jaffa's cogent explanation would bias potential jurors against the prospective expert witnesses. Jaffa was a very popular person in the courthouse that morning.

Jaffa's effectiveness in the classroom and in his writing was based chiefly on his ability to spot the innermost essence of an idea or problem and render the right way of thinking about the problem in simple and accessible language. This is not to say his teachings were simple or brief, merely that they were direct and sure. This was not always true of his great teacher Leo Strauss—or some of Strauss's other leading students—who could be obscure, ambiguous, or indirect much of the time. While Jaffa's teaching often involved difficult and profound subtleties, he was never turgid or obscure. Reading Jaffa is to be arrested with his remarkable aphoristic capacity—the way in which, after a long train of analysis, he renders the innermost character of a complicated or controversial matter in one or two sentences. It is hard to pick out a favorite. There's one on almost every page of his work, many of them highly prescient to the circumstances of the present moment—especially the many manifestations of philosophical relativism and the denial of human nature that are rampant at the moment.

Reason is ordered toward truth, and truth lies in an objective order of reality, an order external to the mind, as the moral law is external to the will.

Today, terrorism is a symbol of the fact that to avant-garde modernity not even self-preservation can be called a rational goal.

Man is not free to determine the human good on the basis of his subjective preferences.

Whether you want to belong to the human race is now a matter of personal preference.

The heart of post-modernity is the proposition that the sub-
jectivity of one's convictions matters more than their objective
validity.[13]

Jaffa's prescience was no better displayed than in a public lecture
he gave at the end of 1991, when the West celebrated the disin-
tegration of the Soviet Union and began believing that we had
reached the "end of history," which meant the permanent triumph
of liberal democracy and open markets. Jaffa would have none of
it, and correctly perceived that things would soon *get worse*:

> The defeat of Communism in the USSR and its satellite em-
> pires by no means assures its defeat in the world. Indeed, the
> release of the West from its conflict with the East emancipates
> utopian communism at home from the suspicion of its affinity
> with an external enemy. The struggle for the preservation of
> western civilization has entered a new—and perhaps far more
> deadly and dangerous—phase.[14]

I'll return this point at some length in chapter 9, but for the moment I only want to note that Jaffa would not have been surprised
by the renewed wave and intensity of campus political correctness,
nor the revived enthusiasm for socialism, for he knew, better than
most conservatives, that the crisis of the West was more of an
internal problem than a challenge from an armed enemy nation.
In this respect Jaffa always reminded me of Whittaker Chambers,
except without the pessimism, because he had the remedy, if we
had but open minds to grasp it.

———

Jaffa mellowed ever so slightly in his final years, often treating
some of those who disagreed with him with a little more generosity. While yielding nothing on the substance of his disagree-

ments or criticisms, he seemed less vituperative. Perhaps it was the natural lengthening of perspective as mortality approaches, but I think it had more to do with the undeniable triumph of *A New Birth of Freedom*, which finally appeared to wide notice and near-universal acclaim in 2000. Jaffa joked that the forty-year interval between *Crisis of the House Divided* and *A New Birth of Freedom* "corresponds closely to the distance in time that separated Plato's *Republic* from his *Laws.*" It was a typically impish comment, designed precisely to provoke his critics and embarrass his students. He added, "One can claim a resemblance to the great without laying any claim to their greatness!" In fact, the real meaning of this self-referential quip was a subtle acknowledgment that, like Plato's two bookend works, Jaffa's two works had an important difference in outlook—a difference that came to him slowly over the course of his three decades of feuds.

In his last decade, Jaffa's isolation dissolved into a growing acknowledgment of his achievement and importance. One prominent neoconservative (I won't name him since it was a private conversation, but he was among the large number who had been on the receiving end of Jaffa's critical gaze) remarked to me that Jaffa should be enjoying his vindication: "You know, even as late as Reagan's election in 1980 it wasn't clear what direction the conservative movement might take. It could have gone in a Friedmanite libertarian direction, or it might have gone in Russell Kirk's more traditionalist direction. But it really has gone more in Jaffa's direction—toward reclaiming the Declaration of Independence and the Founding as the core of American conservatism."

Jaffa wouldn't accept such an easy agreement, or think the cause had been won. But he was surely gracious when all of conservative Washington turned out for a Claremont Institute birthday dinner in his honor in 2011 at the Mayflower Hotel. Norman Podhoretz, who as editor of *Commentary* had rejected numerous Jaffa article submissions and received his share of sharp, complaining letters from Jaffa, rose with some trepidation to pay tribute, hoping that Jaffa would "unearth nothing heretical in this little tribute of mine."

> When dealing with what he calls the most consequential subjects, everything is at stake. And when everything is at stake, every detail counts. It is not enough to agree in general: the particulars, each and every one of them, have to be got right . . . to him it suffices that in this world these errors conduce to misreadings of the Declaration of Independence and the Constitution and the Gettysburg Address which then eventuate in harm to the gloriously blessed Republic to which the first two gave birth and then, after the carnage of the Civil War, the third gave a new birth—"a new birth of freedom" in Lincoln's words.[15]

Podhoretz needn't have worried. One might have expected Jaffa, when his turn came to speak last on the program, to say something along the lines of "I told you so," or renew his exacting criticisms. Instead, in a frail voice, he gave a charming—indeed moving—account of his early education at Yale and how he came almost by accident to Leo Strauss's classroom in New York in the 1940s. (A fuller version of this story appears in the first chapter of his final book, *Crisis of the Strauss Divided*.)

I can recall vividly the last two times I spent an extended period of time in his company. The first was in 2007, when he came to Washington for some function related to his great interest in Lincoln. Now close to ninety, he had not lost a step. Over lunch (appropriately at a restaurant on Thomas Jefferson Street) with a small number of his former students now perched in Washington, Jaffa enthralled us once again, as much as he ever had in the classroom. There was no beating around the bush. The fate of the world, he said, depended on the United States; the fate of the United States depended on the conservative movement; and the fate of the conservative movement depended upon the health and success of the Republican Party—unfortunately so, since the GOP could be so confused and faltering. The fundamental causes of the crisis of the house divided that summoned the Republican Party into being are still present now—the Democratic Party is just as intellectually corrupt today as it was in the 1850s. We had our marching orders.

Another day, around 2009, I was passing briefly—or so I thought—through Claremont and decided to drop by Jaffa's office at the Claremont Institute. He still went to his office every day, even though he had finally stopped teaching at the age of ninety. I had meant just to say hello for five minutes. I remained for two hours as he gave me a private seminar, a refresher course on the crisis of the West and what we needed to do to reverse it. He was reading, and disliking, Jacob Heilbrunn's new book on neoconservatism; what did I think of it? Although much of what he said was familiar, coming directly from him it still seemed like the first day of class all over again.

At one point he swiveled his chair around and paused to look up at his framed poster of Winston Churchill walking alone on the forecastle of the HMS *Prince of Wales* during the Atlantic conference of 1940. "The fate of the Western world depended on that single man, at that single moment," he said, going on with a few of his own firsthand recollections from 1940. "We need him again." Whether we get a Churchill again or not, Jaffa equipped a generation of students to know the difference, as Strauss put it, between mediocrity, however brilliant, and true greatness.

CHAPTER 2

"Patriotism Is Not Enough"

[T]he price of liberty is eternal intellectual vigilance.

D. W. BROGAN

One of Abraham Lincoln's less recalled speeches that both Jaffa and Berns celebrated was his eulogy for Henry Clay, the "Great Compromiser" and leader of the Whig Party, who died in June of 1852. Lincoln, then serving in the Illinois state legislature, took to the floor of the statehouse on July 6 to deliver a eulogy more than five thousand words long, probably running close to an hour of speaking time.

The eulogy was more than just a panegyric on Clay's career. Read carefully, it provides a description of the prudence of the statesman and a compass of the growing "crisis of the house divided" that would soon thrust Lincoln to national prominence. Whether Lincoln ever met Clay personally is not known, but Clay's influence on Lincoln is undeniable. He described Clay as "my beau ideal of a statesman," and a reader cannot come away from Lincoln's eulogy without wondering whether, had Clay lived another decade, Lincoln would have wished for Clay to become the leader of the new Republican Party and its presidential standard-bearer in 1856 or 1860.

Lincoln's eulogy notes the difficulty that honest differences of opinion, not to mention partisanship, present for the practice and understanding of statesmanship: "Taking a prominent part, as he did, in all the great political questions of his country for the last half century, the wisdom of his course on many, is doubted and denied by a large portion of his countrymen." Political life was ever such and ever will be.

The great question dividing the nation at that time was slavery. Lincoln distilled the essence of the problem, the dilemma that would soon define his own life, in a single sentence. Noting that Clay, a slaveholder, opposed slavery and sought its end, Lincoln reflected: "Cast into life where slavery was already widely spread and deeply seated, he did not perceive, as I think no wise man has perceived, how it could be at *once* eradicated, without producing a greater evil, even to the cause of human liberty itself." The problems of circumstances, public opinion, law, and violence at the center of political life overmatch most human beings who lack the perception, skill, and moderation to cope with such trials, which, to continue with Lincoln, "is probably the reason why such men as Henry Clay are so rare in the world."

Yet an even shorter sentence by Lincoln about Clay is crucial to comprehending and judging any American statesman—and America itself: "He loved his country partly because it was his own country, but mostly because it was a free country." Here Lincoln proposes a very different ground of patriotism, one that goes beyond loving your country merely because it is your place of birth and the home of your fathers. We can go a step further than Lincoln and propose that America deserves unconditional love because it is a free and *just* country. No country in human history was so self-consciously founded, and has publicly proclaimed itself so founded, on a comprehensive foundation for being a *just* regime. Its frequent failures to live up to those principles fully— none more massive than the obvious failure that caused the worst war in American history—are the source of most controversies in American politics right down to the present day.

American politics since the Founding might be said to be a continuous argument about how to live up to "the proposition," as Lincoln referred to the most famous axiom of the Declaration of Independence, "that all men are created equal." Has any country ever so publicly and consistently flogged itself for its imperfections and failures? (Does France obsess about how well it lives up to "liberté, égalité, fraternité"?) Do these imperfections mean that America is fundamentally *unjust*, or that it was falsely founded? The idea is widespread today that the answer to this question is *Yes*.

America's critics always seem to think that their insights into America's defects and shortcomings are a fresh discovery, but in fact these criticisms have a long lineage. Before the Civil War leading Southern partisans referred to the central proposition of the Declaration as a "self-evident lie." Progressive thinkers in the early 1900s, especially Charles A. Beard, J. Allen Smith, and Vernon Parrington, argued that the Constitution was essentially a fraudulent charter designed to thwart democracy and protect plutocratic wealth. Leftists have dined out on this critique ever since, while "progressive" liberals largely detach patriotism from the Founding and look to a utopian future for the ground of present patriotism—the country can be worthy of pride only after it is "fundamentally transformed," to quote a recent political figure of some prominence. For a very long time now, this orientation has disabled liberalism's ability to resist challenges from the far left. This was most evident in the supine reaction of liberals to the New Left of the 1960s, but a sequel is under way today in American universities and other cultural institutions that is just as appalling and threatening to the long-term health of the nation.

On countless college campuses the grievance industry against supposed racism, oppression, homophobia, and "white privilege" is met with groveling confessions of guilt from faculty and administrators alike ("We failed you," Yale's president Peter Salovey cringed before a mob). The best argument that can be mustered in defense of the liberal tradition is an appeal to free speech and academic freedom, which tacitly concedes the charges of bigotry and racism against American institutions.

A recent Black Lives Matter protest featured signs proclaiming "Lincoln was a racist," and demanding that Lincoln be removed from the five-dollar bill. This is not a brand-new charge. *Ebony* magazine in 1968 published an article titled "Was Abe Lincoln a White Supremacist?"[1] (answer: yes), and more genteel forms of this charge can be found in so-called mainstream histories and biographies of the figure we long called "the Great Emancipator," though we appear to be using that encomium less and less as time passes. About the first thing mentioned today whenever the name of Thomas Jefferson comes up is that he *owned slaves*, thereby vitiating the Declaration of Independence. In the impatience for complete "social justice" now, Jefferson's thoughtful ruminations on the problem in his *Notes on the State of Virginia* and elsewhere are waved aside, if they are read at all. In late 2015 presidential candidate Bernie Sanders said in a prepared speech at a campaign stop that "I will also say, that as a nation—the truth is a nation that in many ways was created, and I'm sorry to have to say this from way back, on racist principles. That's a fact."[2]

Sanders's view, very widely held today, represents a startling departure from how Martin Luther King Jr., let alone Frederick Douglass, regarded the *principles* of the nation. King and Douglass were able to distinguish the *principles* of the nation from its *compromises*, and knew how important it was to have those principles constantly in sight as the solid foundation on which to make progress toward a more just world. This distinction today is lost or deliberately confused amid the disgust over "white privilege" and other slogans of indignation and injustice, typically fostered or abetted by the defective modes of civic education in our high schools and universities.

The sum of these vicious currents renders America a country that is either fraudulent or hopelessly hypocritical. How can anyone love such a country? Is there a rational ground not merely in defense of the country, but for loving and celebrating it—for proclaiming it a good and just country, despite its faults and failures both present and past?

Harry V. Jaffa liked to say that "patriotism is not enough." Merely having a nation as one's homeland is an insufficient defense against enemies without and nihilists within. Walter Berns found common cause on this point. In *Making Patriots*, Berns noted that patriotism "is not natural, but has to be taught, or inculcated, or somehow acquired."[3] American patriotism is based on ideas, a fact best grasped by noting that, as Jaffa and Berns's colleague Martin Diamond pointed out, the terms "Americanism," "Americanization," and "un-American" have no equivalents in other countries. "This is not by chance," Berns noted, "or a matter of phonetics—Swissism? Englishization?—or mere habit. What would a Frenchman have to do in order to justify being labeled un-French?"[4]

Lincoln was the common denominator for Jaffa and Berns. It is astonishing to compare some of the aspects of Lincoln, such as Lincoln's interest in Shakespeare, and *Macbeth* in particular, that they understood in exactly the same way. While Jaffa disputed with Berns about how to understand the Declaration of Independence, in the fullness of time Berns came close to conceding Jaffa's essential view—maybe because he didn't really disagree with it that much in the first place. By calling the central idea of the Declaration a "proposition," Lincoln didn't mean it was speculative; he meant it needed to be *demonstrated*, just as a Euclidian geometric proposition needed to be demonstrated with proofs. The "proof" of democratic liberty, however, depends upon something quite a bit more difficult than mathematics. Walter Berns wrote: "Demonstration depended on the perpetuation of the institutions, and that, in turn, depended on a new kind of patriotism. The patriots of seventy-six were moved to do what they did by their attachment to the abstract idea of liberty, but Lincoln doubted that those who came after them were capable of that sort of attachment."[5]

The idea that patriotism is something that must be acquired or taught is at least as old as Socrates. How well are we doing this today? Not very. And the problem goes much deeper than the opportunists who leap to deploy the charge of hypocrisy or fraud for every shortcoming or alleged injustice that Al Sharpton can think up.

During the Cold War the principal challenge to the basis of American patriotism came from a rival creed. Communism and other radical utopian ideologies claimed to offer a theoretical account and practice that was more just than liberal democracy, and their claims attracted many adherents in the democratic West. They claimed to be not just superior but also *universal*, like the principles of the Declaration, which is another reason why coexistence was not possible from the point of view of either side. The eventual collapse of the gigantic Communist lie did not end the self-doubt or even condemnation of America from within. Today the challenge to the goodness of America comes from the successors and fellow travelers of Marxism, most of which share a common root.

Today the foundation for political and social thought is said to be "non-foundationalism," that is, a rejection of "universal truths" or "absolutes." This has been the dominant philosophy of Western political thought for about a century. The paradoxes and contradictions of this current are deliberately obscured with the jargon of postmodernism, which seems to create intellectual celebrity in proportion to its distance from intelligibility. (Think of Slavoj Zizek as the preeminent example at the present time.) The fatal defect of this view is that it reduces all questions of justice to power, a noxious idea one might have thought Socrates had dispatched forever in the fifth century BCE.

The rise of "non-foundationalism" is usually traced back to Nietzsche, who, as Allan Bloom famously argued in *The Closing of the American Mind*, has essentially replaced John Locke as "America's philosopher." Regardless of its exact nature and pedigree, and whether you prefer "postmodernism" in all its various forms to "non-foundationalism," today it is beyond the pale among liberals to champion the original meaning of the preface of the founding statement of America, "We hold these truths to be self-evident . . ." The best that can be said for our inheritance derives from Pragmatism, America's early homegrown response to the Nietzschean challenge: the Founders designed sturdy political institutions that we can adapt to our changing times so long as we aren't too hung up on the "original intent" of the Framers, let alone a close interpretation of the text of the Constitution.

Liberals are, at best, tentative when the subject comes up. Barack Obama cited the preface of the Declaration of Independence approvingly in his second inaugural address, but immediately drew back from embracing it as expressing a rational or timeless truth: "*[H]istory* tells us that while these truths *may* be self-evident, they have never been self-executing . . ." (emphasis added).

An especially revealing example of the aversion liberals have to embracing the principles of the Declaration is Justice Elena Kagan, who in the course of her confirmation hearings for the Supreme Court in 2010 declined to state whether she agreed with the ideas of the Declaration, especially the central idea of natural rights antecedent to all government:

SENATOR TOM COBURN: I'm not asking about your judicial— I'm asking you, Elena Kagan, do you personally believe there is a fundamental right in this area. Do you agree with Blackstone that the natural right of resistance and self-preservation, the right of having and using arms for self-preservation and defense? He didn't say that was a Constitutional right. He said that's a natural right. And what I'm asking you is do you agree with him?

KAGAN: Senator Coburn, to be honest with you, I don't have a view of what are natural rights, independent of the Constitution, and my job as a justice will be to enforce and defend the Constitution and other laws of the United States.

COBURN: So you wouldn't embrace what the Declaration of Independence says, that we have certain inalienable and God-given rights that aren't given in the Constitution, that are ours, ours alone, and that the government doesn't give those to us.

KAGAN: Senator Coburn, I believe that the Constitution is an extraordinary document, and I'm not saying I do not believe that there are rights preexisting the Constitution and the laws, but my job as a justice is to enforce the Constitution and the laws.

COBURN: I understand that. I'm not talking about as a justice, I'm talking about Elena Kagan. What do you believe? Are there inalienable rights for us? Do you believe that?

KAGAN: Senator Coburn, I think that the question of what I believe as to what people's rights are outside the Constitution and the laws—that you should not want me to act in any way on the basis of such a belief.[6]

What Thomas Jefferson called "an expression of the American mind" is now more a dusty relic for a mind that has moved on. As historian Pauline Maier put it in *American Scripture*, her widely regarded 1997 book on the Declaration, "in the twentieth century it became necessary to explain away the Declaration of Independence as Jefferson understood it."[7] There are myriad reasons for this reinterpretive necessity, but all can be reduced to a common cause—the need to get over the American Founding because of its philosophical and constitutional constraints on visionary politics.

The character and nature of the American Founding has always been—and always will be—hotly contested. In one sense American political argument can be understood as a series of endless sequels between the Federalists and anti-Federalists in the 1780s. And it should be prominently noted that it is not just modern liberals who are ambivalent about the American Founding and who disdain the Declaration of Independence. Russell Kirk's view of the Declaration is at times indistinguishable from Woodrow Wilson's highly critical and dismissive view. When he didn't criticize the Declaration, Kirk tended to ignore it. His most famous book, *The Conservative Mind: From Burke to Eliot*, omits the Declaration, barely mentions Jefferson, briskly dismisses Hamilton, and skips James Madison entirely. His chief founding-era heroes are John Adams and Fisher Ames—worthy men, but hardly the central figures in the story of the American Founding. The Constitution gets many favorable mentions, but little explication. This first cut of the conservative mind for mid-twentieth-century America is a distinctly *European* conservatism, that is to say, largely a cultural and literary conservatism. (Kirk's later book, *The Roots of American Order*, makes up for this strange lacuna; it can be seen as either a companion to *The Conservative Mind* or perhaps a revisionist work. There are charitable explanations for these antipodes of Kirk, which I'll pass over for the time being.)

Kirk was hardly an outlier in his insouciance about American political life. His literary and cultural sensibilities defined conservatism in America such as it existed before World War II—a conservatism that was apolitical or antipolitical. Albert Jay Nock, the casual tutor to the young William F. Buckley Jr., was correct in his statement that most politicians are rogues or knaves (though he thought *all* politicians were), and there is much to his view that the insatiable modern State is our enemy. Nock's remedy was for liberty-minded individualists to constitute a biblical "remnant," eschewing much effort at constructing serious intellectual defenses of limited government, constitutional reform, mass persuasion, or political action of any kind. Nock's slim biography of Thomas Jefferson, for example, doesn't discuss the Declaration of Independence at all, which is rather like a biography of Shakespeare that omitted any mention of his sonnets.

Nock's self-isolation from public affairs finds its analogue in the Protestant evangelicals who largely withdrew from the American political stage in the aftermath of the Scopes era, Roman Catholics who identified more with an international order, and a business community that, never very political to begin with, merely wanted relief from the boot of the New Deal. There was very little serious intellectual resistance to the constitutional deformations of both the Progressive Era and the New Deal. Here one is inclined to embrace the original title Russell Kirk proposed for his big book: *The Conservatives' Rout.*

Let us then take stock. Before World War II, Progressives rejected the American Founding; two generations of revisionist historians were happy to discredit it as a fraud against true democracy and right thinking; an exuberant tide of radical leftists expected the whole democratic capitalist order to collapse in due course anyway; and social science was lost in a miasma of behaviorism that promised, but failed, to deliver endless progress. The triumph of American arms in World War II left liberals in particular with a palpable buoyancy, despite the new specter of the Cold War. Who needed to look back to those outmoded figures from the age of powdered wigs? As for conservatism: there was no "conservative movement"—either intellectual or political—commensurate with the Progressive movement. There was no robust defense of the original understanding of the American political tradition. The so-called consensus school of mid-century "vital center" liberalism (of which Arthur Schlesinger Jr. was the dean) held a monopoly on the field and reinterpreted the American political story as a prelude to their own self-appointed wisdom and greatness. (I'll wade through that aspect of this story in chapter 4.)

The tale of the rise of the postwar conservative movement has been well told many times.[8] But the question of whether a distinctly American conservative tradition exists remains out of focus and is worthy of a closer look.

The next chapter will explore more fully the deeper philosophical roots of what Strauss called "the crisis of the West." To bring this chapter to a close it will suffice to plant a few thoughts about the importance of the American Founding *as a philosophical event*, and hence the centrality of the Declaration of Independence.

Strauss didn't write much that was directly about America. But the few occasions when he did refer to America typically involved an endorsement of the Declaration of Independence as Jefferson—and Lincoln—understood it. Strauss's most famous book, *Natural Right and History*, begins by invoking the preface to the Declaration and asking, "Does this nation in its maturity still cherish the faith in which it was conceived and raised? Does it still hold those 'truths to be self-evident'?" German historicism and relativism, the intellectual milieu in which he had trained in prewar Germany, was gaining ground in his adopted home nation of America, causing Strauss to wonder: "It would not be the first time that a nation, defeated on the battlefield and, as it were, annihilated as a political being, has deprived its conquerors of the most sublime fruit of victory by imposing on them the yoke of its own thought."[9]

Less often recalled is the conclusion of a review Strauss wrote in 1942 of *German Philosophy and Politics*, John Dewey's revised book on German philosophy, in which Dewey attempts to defend his "experimental" pragmatism against any confusion with German nihilism (that is, that they are both a species of "non-foundationalism"). Strauss states:

> No one will deny "that philosophical absolutism may be practically as dangerous as matter of fact political absolutism." But is it not also true that the "frankly experimental" "method . . . of success" has proved very dangerous in the hands of unscrupulous men, and that the belief in an "absolute" inspired the words "that all men are created equal, that they are endowed by their Creator with certain unalienable rights"?[10]

Here Strauss clearly indicates that the philosophy of the Declaration is a better intellectual redoubt against totalitarianism than Dewey's pragmatism.[11]

Strauss is known chiefly for his work on classical political philosophy, his focus on esoteric writing, and his interest in the "theological-political problem," none of which would seem to bear closely on current American politics. Many of Strauss's students followed these pathways. But a large number directed their focus to American politics and in particular the American Founding as a moment deserving respect as a serious expression of timeless political philosophy. While a number of important mid-century and contemporary figures deserve credit for "taking the American Founding seriously," the students of Strauss who took up the Founding formed a critical mass that challenged political science and changed historiography, so much so that the most prominent contemporary historian of the American Founding, Gordon Wood, took to the pages of the *New York Review of Books* on the occasion of the bicentennial of the Constitution in 1987 to complain about the "fundamentalists" of what he called "the Leo Strauss bicentennial."

Perhaps the most remarkable fact about the scholarship of the bicentennial celebrations is the extent to which that scholarship has been colored by the students and followers of Leo Strauss. . . . "Straussians" are everywhere in government and academia, in both high and low places, in conferences, in symposiums, in books and journals. More than any other single group the Straussians are attempting to set the agenda for public debate over the Constitution. . . . [N]early as important as governmental patronage has been their long and untiring philosophical interest in what they invariably call the "Founding," the principles embodied in America's nation-building at the end of the eighteenth century.

While Wood disparaged their philosophical orientation, he couldn't avoid noting the underlying sense of why they were rebelling against the mainstream of academic political science:

For a generation or more, while government departments in universities throughout the nation were being taken over by behaviorists and policy analysts and becoming departments of political science, tiny groups of scholars kept alive an old-fashioned concern for political philosophy and classic political texts. Among these minorities the most cohesive and determined were certainly the Straussians.[12]

Strauss-influenced thinkers remain a distinct minority in academia, but always punch above their weight class. To the annoyance and resentment of other faculty, they tend to be among the most popular professors on their campuses, and political science departments where they are a strong presence tend to have higher student enrollments than in conventional departments elsewhere. Strauss students are derided as a "cult," a sure sign of a liberal fearful of losing an argument. Even when dismissed by the likes of Wood (who is not a liberal) and attacked by the left, their influence is undeniable.

Their impact on conservatism has been profound, though it should be pointed out that not all the Strauss-influenced thinkers were conservative or even Republican. Allan Bloom endorsed Bill Clinton shortly before his death in 1992, for example. Strauss's students waged many epic feuds among themselves, some of which are likely to persist, and even formed distinct camps that somehow took on a geographical nomenclature ("East Coast" versus "West Coast")—though Mark Lilla suggests the two wings should be characterized with the terms "Wagnerian" versus "Sousa." Some of these feuds can seem as esoteric as Strauss's esotericism itself and some had regrettable personal dimensions, but some cut to the heart of questions on the minds of decent citizens everywhere.

During the George W. Bush years, Strauss was mistakenly identified as the fountainhead of neoconservatism, but in fact he deserves to be regarded for his deep influence on a full spectrum of conservatism in two ways. First, by inspiring a deep regard for the principles of the American Founding, he helped to launch what might be called a distinctly *American* conservatism, notably divergent from the rote traditionalist, religious, or European-accented conservatism of Kirk and the early *National Review*. Second, by emphasizing a rational and philosophical defense of the American Founding and the Constitution, he helped reinvigorate the case for constitutional originalism in jurisprudence.

This influence in turn has compelled liberals to adjust their position. After two generations of dismissing the Founders and their thought as outmoded if not corrupt and disreputable, many liberals today find themselves grudgingly bowing to the American Founding, even if in heavily tortured and often insincere ways. Count that as a win. The point is, this still-widening circle of thinkers has been as influential on political science and law as the Mont Pelerin Society (Milton Friedman, Friedrich Hayek,

George Stigler, Ronald Coase, and so on) was in political economy. It may be harder to make out the impact of Strauss because the issues are more diffuse and abstract than monetary policy or the conflict between open markets and central planning, whose outcome can be partially judged by empirical measures, but it is no less profound and long-lasting.

Arriving at this point required an intellectual revolution that was as jarring as the political revolution that started in 1776. America may be separated from the world by two large oceans, but it is not isolated from the currents of modern thought that have been threatening the West for two centuries.

CHAPTER 3

Starting Over

Something Has Gone Wrong ...

Nazism and Communism are an expensive education.
PETER DRUCKER, 1949

Why was progressivism not prepared for Hitler?
ARTHUR SCHLESINGER JR., 1949

*I began therefore to wonder whether the self-destruction of
reason was not the inevitable outcome of modern rationalism
as distinguished from pre-modern rationalism.*
LEO STRAUSS, 1962

In 1936 MGM Studios halted an expensive production of a film adaptation of Sinclair Lewis's best-selling novel *It Can't Happen Here*, which portrayed a fascist takeover of the United States. Although Huey Long was the novel's chief inspiration, there was concern the film would not do well in the German market, and indeed both Italy and Germany issued statements approving MGM's decision. An indignant Lewis complained, "I wrote *It Can't Happen Here*, but I begin to think it certainly can."[1]

A totalitarian takeover of America has long been a staple of pop culture, persisting right up to the present with another offering in 2015 of a counterfactual Nazi victory over America through an adaptation of Philip K. Dick's novel *The Man in the High Castle*, which was streamed on Amazon. Maybe this fascination with a fanciful tyranny in the land of the free is another expression of American exceptionalism, but this confidence in the resilience of American liberty distracts from a basic question: How did it happen *over there*? And should we be confident that totalitarianism will always stay *over there*?

Although firsthand memory of the Third Reich is now rapidly receding, these questions continue to fascinate historians and political scientists. The structural weaknesses of Weimar Germany's constitution and political institutions are well known, as is the pusillanimity of Paul von Hindenburg, Franz von Papen, and other German leaders who capitulated too easily to Hitler's swift and relentless drive for total power. The nature of German culture and latent anti-Semitism remain topics of fierce controversy. Daniel Jonah Goldhagen's *Hitler's Willing Executioners* (1997) issued a broad indictment of the German population as a whole that touched off a new chapter in the bitter debate about the collective guilt of Germans and German culture. But it did not explain how this collective hatred came about. Was it somehow all Nietzsche's and Wagner's fault?

These questions arose early in the Nazi regime. In "Hitler and His Choice," a controversial 1935 essay on Hitler's rise, Churchill wondered:

> But the astounding thing is that the great German people, educated, scientific, philosophical, romantic, the people of the Christmas tree, the people of Goethe and Schiller, of Bach and Beethoven, Heine, Leibnitz, Kant and a hundred other great names, have not only not resented this horrible blood-bath, but have endorsed it and acclaimed its author with the honors not only of a sovereign but almost of a God. Here is the fright-

ful fact before which what is left of European civilization must bow its head in shame, and what is to more practical purpose, in fear.[2]

The question was made more acute by the fact that fascism had limited appeal and made little headway in most of Germany's neighboring countries, despite German attempts to spread its doctrine.[3] The proposition that Nazism arose somehow from the depths of German philosophy and culture—indeed from German romanticism and *idealism*—presents grave challenges to Western civilization as a whole, regardless of the tenure of Hitler's specific regime. But you would look nearly in vain for an extensive treatment of this broad problem in American political science in the late 1930s and early 1940s. In one of his most famous dialectical engagements, Leo Strauss wrote that "A social science that cannot speak of tyranny with the same confidence with which medicine speaks, for example, of cancer, cannot understand social phenomena as what they are. It is therefore not scientific. Present-day social science finds itself in this condition."[4] This perfectly describes much of the academic political science assessments of the rise of fascism in the 1930s.

There were a few noble exceptions. Karl Loewenstein of Yale wrote extensively about fascism and Communism in the mid-1930s, noting that the missionary zeal of both posed a serious threat to the world order.[5] Most striking was Robert C. Brooks, a professor at Swarthmore College and president of the American Political Science Association in 1940, who was known chiefly for his research on garden-variety political corruption in the United States. Brooks chided the field in his presidential address at the annual meeting in December 1940 for avoiding "contemporary, controversial political affairs." He meant the situation in Europe, which called for breaking with the precedent of scholarly detachment, Brooks thought, because there could be no claim to justice by the Nazi regime. The overthrow of Hitler "should be the one great desideratum of democratic world politics." Brooks added a stinging criticism of the sentiment for appeasement that was still very much present in the United States at this late date: "If political scientists cannot scotch so obviously ruinous a policy, one may well despair for the future of our profession. What is far worse, one would have to despair of the future of free government."[6] Thank God for Churchill, Brooks added more than once in his address.

Brooks was right to express a note of despair for the future of his academic discipline. The contemporaneous voices that raised the alarm about the nature and consequences of totalitarianism came mostly from outside the ranks of political science. One thinks of Reinhold Niebuhr calling the moment a "crisis" for theology, or the erratic Walter Lippmann's sudden anxiety over the totalitarian potential of centralized power ("collectivism") in his 1937 book *The Good Society*. But even Lippmann had to shake off a default to wishful thinking, such as describing one of Hitler's 1933 speeches as "statesmanlike" and the "authentic voice of a civilized people" that was "evidence of good faith." Sounding like a dean of multicultural diversity on an American campus today, Lippmann argued that "to deny today that Germany can speak as a civilized power because uncivilized things are being done in Germany is in itself a deep form of intolerance."[7] The Nazi defector Hermann Rauschning's bestselling *Revolution of Nihilism: Warning to the West* attempted to convey that what was happening in Germany was a radical moral and spiritual disfigurement and not a transitory detour into dictatorship. (Rauschning's credibility was undermined by doubts about the authenticity of some of his subsequent work, especially *Hitler Speaks*; in any case, *Revolution of Nihilism* never defined or analyzed nihilism in a serious way.)

But in general, most of the flood of books and academic articles about Hitler's Nazi regime and the rise of fascism in Europe in the late 1930s partook of the current enthusiasms for historicism, evolutionism, behaviorism, and positivism that reigned supreme over the interment of political philosophy. Hitler's rapid and ruthless centralization of power, entailing the abolition of Germany's previously robust federal structure, was analyzed with the clinical detachment of a biologist looking at bacteria in a petri dish under a microscope. In some cases the phenomena of fascism and Communism were treated as reciprocal symptoms for the weaknesses of democracy. The diffuseness of fascism as an ideology, in stark contrast with Soviet Communism, reinforced the tendency to analyze it institutionally rather than ideologically or philosophically. Eric Voegelin wrote about debates over the changing political scene in Germany: "At that time there was the great debate among jurists about whether the Weimar constitution, which indeed was never abolished but only changed, was in fact still the constitution of the Hitler Reich or whether a revolution had occurred. Wonderful discussion among jurists. In the meantime, people were killed."[8]

Examples abound. One book at the time said that "the dictatorship of fascism is charismatic, nationalistic, and permanent." In "The Nazis Reform the Reich" (1936), Albert Lepawsky of the University of Chicago wrote:

> This process of the internal balance of power may be fruitfully examined in Nazi Germany today. What has the National Socialist government set out to do, what has it accomplished, and which way is it tending in this matter of the shifts in power in national, state, regional, and local government and administration? . . .
>
> The Nazis profess to be welding a true German Folk out of the confusion of social and economic groupings, but their job seems to be also one of fashioning an integrated state structure. Indeed, the class consciousness which the Nazis abhor may re-

main, and the Nazis themselves may pass it on. Nevertheless, they certainly will have made some contribution to the historic process of reforming the German Reich.[9]

Roger Wells of Bryn Mawr College, writing in 1935 about Hitler rolling up the previously robust local governments in Germany, concluded: "There is some justification, therefore, for the National Socialist contention that the *Deutsche Gemeindeordnung* does not destroy local self-government, but, on the contrary, aims to build it anew upon more secure foundations so that it may once again recover and bloom as in the nineteenth century."[10]

Or take Arnold J. Zurcher of New York University, writing about Hitler's popular referenda in 1935:

Although the ultimate form of the National Socialist political system in Germany is not yet clear, certain institutions are emerging which bid fair to make more than a passing claim to perdurance in that system. . . . Even after discounting intangible official pressure, of which there undoubtedly was a great deal, and downright coercion and intimidation at the polls, of which there was probably very little, the electoral record remains an amazing one, both as respects participation in the balloting and the endorsement given the cabinet's policy.[11]

The 1936 book *Fascism and National Socialism*, by Michael Florinsky, was an open apologia for Mussolini's regime, comparing it favorably to Franklin Delano Roosevelt's New Deal. A number of books and articles criticized fascism for failing to represent a true alternative to industrial capitalism, which was assumed to be on its last legs, even in the United States. Voegelin recalled in his memoirs the conversation he had while applying for a visa to leave Austria for America following the *Anschluss*: "In waiting for the visa, I had dealings with the American vice-consul in

Zurich, a very nice Harvard boy who had grave suspicions about me. He explained that, since I was neither a Communist nor a Catholic nor a Jew, I therefore had no reason whatsoever not to be in favor of National Socialism and to be a National Socialist myself." It was ironically not an entirely risible suggestion. Not normally given to demonstrative poses, Voegelin expressed disgust with the disposition of the West: "In the wake of the Austrian occupation by Hitler, I even for a moment contemplated joining the National Socialists, because those rotten swine who called themselves democrats—meaning the Western democracies—certainly deserved to be conquered and destroyed if they were capable of such criminal idiocy."[12] Voegelin escaped from Austria barely a step ahead of the Gestapo, which had him on a list of academics whose passports they planned to confiscate.

Was there a way out of this maw? If leading intellectuals and the mainstream of academic political science in America followed the appeasing politicians and wishful thinkers in averting their gaze from the abyss opening in Europe (and the Soviet Union), then the sustained attention and direct thinking about causes and remedies would have to come from somewhere else. Ironically the beginnings of a revival came from inside Nazi Germany itself. In other words, the revival of America came with a German accent, directed against German thought. "Only in America!," as Yogi Berra might have said.

———

To the extent that the Nazi regime could be said to have aimed at some kind of perfectionist vision, it was not, as they might say in faculty clubs today, inclusive. Hitler's murderous hatred for Jews and other non-Aryan peoples is credited with the exile of many of the world's leading physicists, who went on to develop the atomic bomb in the United States. But it also prompted the exile of a significant number of philosophers, social scientists, and other assorted thinkers who have been setting off explosions on the American intellectual scene ever since. Between 1933 and 1945 about one thousand European intellectuals were relocated to England and the United States, mostly to academic jobs.

One of the main heroes of this story was Alvin Johnson, who convinced the Rockefeller Foundation in the spring of 1933 to back the ad hoc Emergency Committee in Aid of Displaced German Scholars. According to one understated chronicle of this effort, Johnson and his circle "sensed that Hitler was not simply interested in the restoration of the old conservative order."[13]

While the displaced Germans scattered to universities throughout the United States, a critical mass gathered at the New School for Social Research in New York (in part because Ivy League and other leading universities were still hostile to Jews in the 1930s), where Johnson was the director. Johnson self-consciously thought of the New School as a "university in exile" for leading German thinkers, many of whom he had gotten to know well over the previous decade as editor of the *Encyclopedia of the Social Sciences*. In all, 173 German scholars ended up at the New School during the 1930s and 1940s. The notable figures among them included Hannah Arendt, Hans Jonas, Alfred Schütz, Karl Löwith, Adolph Lowe, Hans Speier, Max Wertheimer, Kurt Riezler, Arnold Brecht, and Leo Strauss.

The New School was an ideal place for unconventional thinking. Few of the émigré intellectuals were conservative in any contemporary sense of the term. In fact, most were social democrats or openly socialist in their outlook. Many were baffled by, if not critical of, America. One history of the New School circle records: "The course of fascism in Europe and *its unexplained failure to infect their new home* was the pressing topic of their work as individuals and of their General Seminar [at the New School]. As social democrats, these scholars were deeply critical of the weaknesses inherent in liberal political systems" (emphasis added).[14] A quick reading of Tocqueville would have clued in these otherwise brilliant thinkers as to why fascism was unlikely to find fertile soil in the United States in the 1930s, but Tocqueville was mostly ignored and little read in those days.

These political theorists and social scientists were understandably obsessed with diagnosing the causes of the German disaster. The weaknesses of the Weimar Republic constitution and the contingent accidents and mistakes that contributed to Hitler's accession to power were easy enough to mark out. On the surface, Strauss was not alone in thinking the explanation was straightforward:

> The weakness of the Weimar Republic made certain its speedy destruction. It did not make certain the victory of National Socialism. The victory of National Socialism became necessary in Germany for the same reason that the victory of Communism had become necessary in Russia: the man with the strongest will or single-mindedness, the greatest ruthlessness, daring, and power over his following, and the best judgment about the strength of the various forces in the immediately relevant political field was the leader of the revolution.[15]

But beyond the structural weakness of German political culture and the will to power of an evil man lay a more serious question that transcended the German catastrophe: was democracy fundamentally inadequate to the challenges of modernity? And if democracy was weak or inadequate, that raised doubts about the underlying philosophy of liberalism. If *the* central idea and legacy of Enlightenment rationalism was internally defective and somehow implicated in the rise of totalitarianism, it would require the most searching inquiries into what had gone wrong. More important, if the crisis of the West was rooted in the defects of Western rationalism itself, then the crisis would persist beyond the physical destruction of the Nazis or their successors in the Soviet Union.

Even before the rise of Nazism made these questions urgent,

a young Strauss was taking note of the compelling pessimism of Oswald Spengler's *Decline of the West*, along with the narrowing horizon of rationality wrought by the challenge of Nietzsche, the commanding positivism of Max Weber, all finally rounded off by the radical historicism of Martin Heidegger.

Nietzsche, Weber, Heidegger—a potent triple-play combination, though Heidegger looms largest. What to say about this dense, abstruse, and problematic thinker? Strauss attended Heidegger's lectures briefly at the University of Freiburg in the early 1920s, and was not alone among his generation in finding Heidegger's radical questioning of the Western philosophical inheritance to be entrancing and overpowering. Strauss confessed to "not understanding a word" of Heidegger's lectures, but recognized something in Heidegger's method of close reading of a classical text that revealed an openness to a radical questioning of the Western philosophical tradition. "I had never heard nor seen such a thing," Strauss wrote near the end of his life in 1970. "[S]uch a thorough and intensive interpretation of a philosophic text. . . . In comparison with Heidegger, [Max] Weber appeared to me as an orphan child in regard to precision, and probing, and competence. . . . Gradually the breadth of the revolution of thought which Heidegger was preparing dawned on me and my generation. . . . The most stupid thing I could do would be to close my eyes or to reject his work."[16]

Strauss wrote that he "ceased to take any interest" in Heidegger for about two decades, and while, narrowly speaking, this is true, in a larger sense Strauss's entire intellectual enterprise could be regarded as a confrontation with Heidegger's thought.[17] "What I could not stomach was his moral teaching," Strauss continued in his 1970 recollection; "for despite his disclaimer he had such a teaching. The key term is 'resoluteness,' without any indication as to what are the proper objects of resoluteness. There is a straight line which leads from Heidegger's resoluteness to his siding with the so-called Nazis in 1933."

While Strauss was repelled by Heidegger's thought, he nonetheless found much to admire and emulate in Heidegger's method and orientation toward the importance of classical Greek philosophy. The central common message of both Heidegger and Strauss was that philosophy needed to start over from the beginning and reopen fundamental questions, but the two men began with entirely opposite dispositions and directions.

Heidegger thought Western man had forgotten the meaning of "being" itself from the very beginning, starting with Plato and Aristotle. In other words, a wrong turn happened at the very beginning of the Western philosophical tradition. He suggested pre-Socratic thought offered the opening to recovering a sense of fundamental *dasein*—rendered typically in English as "being in the world"—because Heidegger thought consciousness could not escape its historical setting. Whether it is possible to detach Heidegger's philosophy from his Nazism remains a subject of heated controversy (as does the depth and character of his Nazi sympathies), but the controversy avoids the fundamental problem or challenge of Heidegger: by removing any ground for morality or ethics, Heidegger's almost mystical disposition toward *being in the present and only in the present* made "decisionism" or "resoluteness" his sole principle of action in the world. Toward what cause one ought to be "resolute" about Heidegger could offer no guidance.[18] His philosophy is, however, an invitation to extremism, or at the very least offers no ground of resistance to extremism, because the extremist is always by definition the most *resolute* person in the room.

The impenetrable paradox of Heidegger's existentialism is that he was trying to make out an escape from nihilism—a way for humans to avoid becoming the deplorable and soulless "last men" of Nietzsche's nightmare vision. He hoped to provide some basis for transcending the soullessness of radical individualism, for some kind of fulfillment of the longing in most human souls for a cause or purpose larger than their own selves. Heidegger supposedly offered an avenue to what passes in popular thought as "authenticity," but *it did not actually repudiate Nietzsche's nihilism*. In other words, it might be said that Heidegger sought a solution to nihilism by doubling down on nihilism, or at least by radicalizing the idea, *contra* Hegel, that a rational account of human history is impossible.

The problem becomes more confusing when we pivot to Strauss, who also appears to favor *resoluteness* as the necessary response to the crisis of the West. In other words, on the surface Strauss's position looks similar to, if not identical with, Heidegger's. In "Liberal Education and Responsibility," Strauss wrote: "[W]isdom requires unhesitating loyalty to a decent constitution and even to the cause of constitutionalism."[19] (This contrasts sharply with Heidegger's argument that the United States and the Soviet Union were metaphysically identical, and that constitutionalism was, at best, a "half-measure."[20]) A useful parallel can be found in C. S. Lewis, a thinker very similar to Strauss in many ways, who wrote in his short treatise of moral philosophy *The Abolition of Man* that "A dogmatic belief in objective value is necessary to the very idea of a rule which is not tyranny or an obedience which is not slavery."[21] *Dogmatism* and *loyalty* are traits of "commitment" or "resoluteness," and not plainly or self-evidently rooted in reason, even if they claim to be based on "objective" value.

We can see another striking example in Strauss's 1941 lecture about the nature of German nihilism, which explained that part of what was taking place was an understandable youthful rebellion against old ideas (a diagnosis that applied with equal force to the student New Left movement of the 1960s) along with a rejection of Communism:

Only one answer was given which was adequate and which would have impressed the young nihilists if they had heard it. It was not however given by a German and it was given in the

year 1940 only. Those young men who refused to believe that
the period following the jump into liberty, following the communist world revolution, would be the finest hour of mankind
in general and of Germany in particular, would have been impressed as much as we were, by what Winston Churchill said
after the defeat in Flanders about Britain's finest hour. For one
of their greatest teachers [Spengler] had taught them to see in
Cannae the greatest moment in the life of that glory which was
ancient Rome.[22]

Where then do we find the ground for a distinction between Heidegger and Strauss?

The difference can be grasped in several ways. If Heidegger
thought Western man suffered from a "forgetfulness of being,"
Strauss thought Western man suffered from a forgetfulness of *politics* as it was understood by the same classical philosophers that
Heidegger appealed to. In addition, Strauss thought the wrong
turn in philosophy occurred much earlier than Heidegger—starting most plainly with Niccolò Machiavelli, although certain problematic antecedents such as Thomas Aquinas also caught his attention. Whereas Heidegger wanted to return to the beginning
to recover an understanding of *dasein*, Strauss thought modern
man should start over again with the classics to recover practical
wisdom—*phronesis*—which was the cornerstone of just political
action. Another way of stating the distinction is to say that Strauss
sought to recover Aristotle's *virtue* in place of Heidegger's *resoluteness*—a recovery that requires reopening questions of human
nature and human excellence.

Strauss is often thought of for reopening and deepening the
distinction between ancients and moderns, but he should be
credited more for starting a quarrel about how to understand
the ancients alone. Another way of understanding the difference
between *dasein* and *phronesis* is just this: Socratic philosophy, as

Strauss understood it, starts with asking "What is . . ." Heidegger thought this question is impossible, and should be abandoned. Strauss's Socratic philosophy asks what is eternal, especially what is eternal in human nature. Heidegger says that nothing is eternal, and that it is nonsense to speak of human nature.

There is fierce controversy about whether Strauss thought a return to some form of classical political philosophy was possible, and numerous quotations on both sides of the question can be marshaled in service of either side of the argument. "We cannot expect that a fresh understanding of classical political philosophy will supply us with recipes for today's use," Strauss wrote in one of his later books.[23] Taken alone, this statement would seem to settle the issue. But the broader context of this statement reveals the likelihood that Strauss is here emulating Socratic paradox or irony. Strauss is known especially for his critiques of historicism in philosophy and positivism in social science, and the preface to the statement quoted above suggests exactly the opposite:

> He [the honest social scientist] is compelled to wonder whether not present-day social science but classical political philosophy is the true science of political things. This suggestion is dismissed out of hand because a return to an earlier position is believed to be impossible. But one must realize that this belief is a dogmatic assumption whose hidden basis is the belief in progress or in the rationality of the historical process.

But Nietzsche, Heidegger, and their successors had concluded that there is no rationality to the "historical process," meaning "progress" itself is unintelligible. Which would seem to leave honest social scientists no other avenue than to look back as Strauss suggests.

An additional complication is the long-held distinction between philosophically superior theoretical wisdom (*sophia*) and practical wisdom (*phronesis*), which leads to no end of confusion about Strauss and often bitter controversy among his students and followers. The acquisition of full or complete wisdom, Plato taught, is impossible; philosophy rightly understood is the *quest for wisdom*. Because Strauss took seriously Socratic ignorance— "I know that I know nothing"—he was cautious about asserting conclusions, knowing that the fundamental questions were easier to ask than to answer. "Philosophy finds that the problems are always more evident than the solutions," Strauss wrote; "All solutions are questionable."[24] Human wisdom will always be imperfect wisdom, and human political life as such will always be imperfect. Hence the need for moderation, as Aristotle understood it, depending ultimately on *phronesis*. One possible implication, however, is that practical wisdom may be more exacting or difficult than theoretical wisdom, and therefore superior to theoretical wisdom. To restate the issue: is Strauss trying to rehabilitate philosophy or statesmanship?

At the very least it can be said that Strauss wanted to return to the ancient questions about human life, with a genuine openness to the possible superiority of classical understandings of human nature over modern liberal understandings of human nature. A final complication is the role of religion, of the conflict between reason and revelation, in shaping the Western mind and Western political thought, making impossible a straightforward return to classical political thought. This bundle of issues became a central focus of Harry Jaffa and several others of Strauss's students and protégés.

Strauss began this kind of questioning and openness to classical thought before the Nazi menace became acute. In a little-known essay written in 1932, when he was still in Germany, Strauss observed that the intellectual climate of the time left it in a paradoxical position: "while the present is as *compelled to question as any age, it is less capable of questioning than any age.*" Political philosophy

had become, at best, merely the *history* of political philosophy—
a catalogue not just of defective answers, but wrong answers. It
is not just that the answers were wrong; by now the questions
made no sense, and as such they were being asked less and less.
The radical historicism and positivism that had marked out moral
questions as subjective "value judgments" had closed off the serious questioning of *the* right way of life. As Strauss summarized it,
"Because man is essentially historical, there are no eternal principles, no ideal of life." The premises of this intellectual outlook
were so firmly entrenched that Strauss could not make out an
answer. "Should it be answerable," Strauss argued, "this would be
possible only by *calling historical consciousness into question*. But is
this not a fantastic undertaking? *How* may historical consciousness be called into question?"[25] Strauss would spend the rest of his
scholarly career pursuing this radical challenge, in the course of
which his leading students would take up the banner he rescued
from the dust.

———

And what of America? Was there a credible answer to be found
somewhere in the recesses of American thought? Neither Strauss
nor the other European émigré thinkers could find much of a response from American thought at the time. Tocqueville was not
alone in thinking America did not produce great philosophers or
philosophic inquiry. "The Americans have no philosophic school
of their own, and they worry very little about all those that divide Europe; they hardly know their names."[26] Tocqueville may
be criticized for underestimating the philosophical depth of the
American story, but it was certainly true that by the middle third
of the twentieth century most of America's leading philosophers
and intellectuals found little in the American tradition to celebrate or draw from as an answer to the political conundrums fac-
ing the world.

Heidegger was unknown in America prior to World War II, and Nietzsche's reach was limited chiefly to the fringes. In his 1915 book on German philosophy, John Dewey dismissed Nietzsche as "but a superficial and transitory wave of opinion." Most of the leading currents of Continental philosophy that crossed the Atlantic were domesticated, such as Pragmatism, which can be regarded as an Americanized version of Hegelian historicism crossed with Darwinian evolution, which was much simpler to grasp than European phenomenology and its progeny. (Or perhaps American pragmatism is best described as the philosophical equivalent of Keynesianism: a convenient doctrine to justify what politicians want to do.) Most of the leading thinkers of Progressivism had given up on the American political tradition—an important fact that will be traced out in the next chapter.

Imagine you were a student interested in the graduate study of political science around this time. Where would you look for a different course? Harry Jaffa wrote later of this period (he began graduate study at Yale in 1939) that "A course in political philosophy was like a tour of a wax work museum. The figures may have been brilliant, but they were all dead. Hence there was literally no reason, other than the unburied presences, to study political philosophy." The powerful undertow of contemporary philosophy brought down and confused even thinkers who were seemingly in the best position to yearn for better answers. "As far as I can recollect," Jaffa added, "acceptance on faith of the fact-value distinction was never even discussed at Yale while I was a graduate student there."[27]

The extent of the problem can be seen with a digression to the poignant story of one of the more prominent exiled scholars recruited to the New School who has been largely forgotten today: Arnold Brecht. Brecht, trained in the law, had been a senior jurist in Germany, holding several high judicial posts in the province of Prussia after World War I and throughout the Weimar Republic. He was also a professor of law at the University of Marburg. Brecht was a dedicated constitutionalist and he recognized that the defects of Germany's constitutional structure contributed to the country's disastrous course in World War I. But the Weimar constitution adopted in 1920 weakened and fractured German politics further. Brecht wrote later in his autobiography that the battle for postwar democracy in Germany was lost before it began. A more carefully written constitution would have prevented Hitler's Nazi Party from acquiring power; its fatal defect was allowing antidemocratic parties to use its features to overwhelm democrats and destroy democracy. "The amazing thing indeed is not that the democratic constitution in Germany collapsed thirteen years later, but that it did not do so much sooner."[28]

In 1921 the first Weimar chancellor, Constantin Fehrenbach, sent Brecht to Munich to take the measure of local political agitators who were impeding the implementation of terms of the Treaty of Versailles. One of them was Hitler. "I did not know the name," Brecht recalled; "it had been mentioned occasionally in reports on riots in Munich. But who was Hitler at that time? The man we visited was rather anonymous, still a little man, a rioter and mob orator. . . . I cannot even remember what Hitler himself said. In any case it did not impress me. I cannot claim to have recognized his future significance."[29]

It would be a different story by February of 1933, when Brecht became one of the last German officials to attempt to stand up to Hitler. Following what Brecht called the "irresponsible thoughtlessness" that led to Hindenburg's appointment of Hitler as chancellor, and the subsequent "nationalistic inebriation," Brecht, then a senior delegate from Prussia, confronted Hitler on the occasion of Hitler's first appearance in the Reichsrat (the upper chamber of the German legislature, analogous to the U.S. Senate). In a polite but firm speech, Brecht reminded Hitler of his duty to the German constitution, "to use your strength for the benefit of the *entire* people, to uphold the *Constitution* and the laws of the Reich, to fulfill your duties conscientiously, and to conduct your office '*impartially and with justice toward everyone.*'" Hitler, furious, stood up when Brecht finished and left the chamber without looking at Brecht or acknowledging his remarks. "This was the last free speech in the Reichsrat," Brecht noted.[30] He was arrested shortly afterward by the Gestapo, but released and placed under surveillance. He obtained an exit visa and became one of the earliest exiles to the New School in November 1933.

Why this digression into a forgotten figure from the German tragedy? I have two significant reasons. First, Brecht serves as an object lesson in the difficulty of breaking free of the deeply ingrained presuppositions of twentieth-century political and social thought. Despite Brecht's profound experience and fundamental decency, his attempts to sort out the theoretical ground for a moral understanding of politics could not escape the confusion and nihilism that by then were bred so deeply in the Western mind.

Brecht understood the depths of the problem clearly and stated them directly. He labored long on a treatise, *Political Theory: The Foundations of Twentieth-Century Political Thought*, that appeared in 1959. He understood precisely that the descent of social science into a value-free methodology was the cause of the problem. Yet not even the rise of Nazism seemed to cause second thoughts among the mainstream thinkers of the time, let alone a skepticism of the moral dead end of relativism. As Brecht wrote,

> Five years after Hitler's ascendency to power in Germany, the senior of the American philosophers, John Dewey, still wrote: "Approach to human problems in terms of moral blame and moral approbation, of wickedness or righteousness, is probably the greatest single obstacle now existing to development of competent methods in the field of social subject-matter."
> . . . Albert Einstein, creator of relativism in physics, but deeply

religious and he, too, a refugee from National Socialism, wrote in 1940, "If someone approves, as a goal, the extirpation of the human race from the earth, one cannot refute such a viewpoint on rational grounds."[31]

Brecht concluded that "[Political science's] inability morally to condemn Bolshevism, Fascism, or National Socialism in unconditional terms was to become the tragedy of twentieth-century political science, a tragedy as deep as any that had ever occurred before in the history of science."[32]

Yet Brecht was unable to reacquire fully a foundation for making an "unconditional" condemnation of totalitarianism. While Brecht argued against what he scorned as "value-relativism," he could not break from Max Weber's view that "ultimate values," while real, were *scientifically* indemonstrable. But since scientific objectivity is *the* canon of modern inquiry, it ipso facto relegates moral questions to second-class intellectual citizenship. You can see how this works in just about any social science journal article today, in which the empirical analysis typically concludes with a nod toward "normative" questions, after which most authors fall mute.

In other words, while truth exists, moral truth cannot be known. Brecht thought the standard critique of moral relativism depended on misrepresenting social science to embrace nihilism, to suppose no values were true. Brecht's position, faithful to Weber, assumes that a true hierarchy of values can be known, but not *scientifically* known, which is the same as saying objectively known.

Early in his book Brecht wrote:

This [Scientific Method] does not enable us to state, in *absolute terms*, whether the purpose pursued by us or by others is good or bad, right or wrong, just or unjust, nor which of several conflicting purposes is more valuable than the other. . . . In particular, Scientific Method cannot state in absolute terms which of several conflicting ultimate purposes is better than others except in relation to some presupposed goal or idea.[33]

But see if this works:

> No scientific relativist would condemn words like cruelty, civilization, prostitution, or, for that matter, crime or slums, wherever they are used within a clear frame of reference as descriptive in accordance with known standards, *as long as these standards are not themselves at issue.* Whenever the latter is the case, then indeed, according to Scientific Value Relativism, is it scientifically not correct to continue using one's own standards as though their absolute validity had been proven.[34]

At least two objections come readily to mind. This kind of scientism closes off any serious engagement with the perspectives of classical and even Enlightenment philosophy. Do not look to Aristotle or Plato for any practical wisdom about the ordering of human life. The variability of human circumstances and the contestable problems of justice make the search for answers *the* problem of humanity, which is why civilization could be said to be one continuous revisionist argument. But *hard* to know does not mean the same as *impossible* to know.

My second reason for discussing Brecht is that this disposition to be confident in the future of scientific progress might have seemed coherent and compelling in the late nineteenth and early twentieth centuries, when unlimited material and moral progress were assumed to stretch ahead as far as the mind could imagine, and major war seemed a thing of the past. World War I shattered this easy optimism, and the subsequent mass events of mid-century and after made the self-willed moral atrophy of science an irrelevance at best and possibly a pernicious danger over the long term.

How exactly would this scientific disposition enable an unconditional condemnation of an ideology (fascism, Communism, radical Islam) that proceeds precisely from making an issue of "known standards"?[35] If "ultimate values" are not demonstrable, how is one to choose between them *when they are at issue*? Even a scale of utility, the easiest social science calculation to make, falls short in the face of ideologies that find holding slaves, or lynching blacks, or murdering Jews or infidels to have a high utility function.[36] Can anyone be satisfied with the scientistic conclusion that we cannot say that "Nazism is evil" is a *fact*?

In other words, value-free social science and historicism cut off recourse to an older mode of moral-political reasoning just when it was most needed. Weber's figurative "iron cage" of sterile scientific bureaucracy became a literal iron cage under the Nazis. Political philosophy was at a dead end, if not in fact fully dead. The triumph of Enlightenment rationality—and therefore liberalism itself—had barely lasted a century.

In one of his more shocking pronouncements, Strauss said in his 1941 lecture on German nihilism that Hitler was forgettable and Nazism itself relatively unimportant: "Hitler? The less said about him the better. He will soon be forgotten. He is merely the rather contemptible tool of 'History': the midwife who assists at the birth of the new epoch. . . . The Nazis are as unsubstantial as clouds."[37] Strauss was surely mistaken in thinking Hitler and Nazism to be ephemeral, given how persistent the imagery of Hitler persists in popular culture and vulgar political discourse. But that is to miss the larger point: nihilism had prepared the abyss well before Hitler opportunistically plunged headlong into it. More importantly, nihilism would survive Hitler's destruction, because, Strauss perceived, it was more indestructible than Nazism.

The second reason for this digression about Brecht is that he was Harry Jaffa's first teacher in the study of political philosophy at the New School in 1940, even before Leo Strauss. Jaffa came to the New School and Brecht (and therefore ultimately Strauss) through a circuitous route. Jaffa started as an undergraduate at Yale University in 1936. "In my freshman year at Yale I had five courses; three of them were subjects that I had studied in high school, but in each case the high school course was better than the Yale course," Jaffa recalled later.[38] But he liked both English and Government and decided early on that whichever field he chose as a major at Yale, he would study the other in graduate school. He settled on English as an undergraduate major, became "infatuated" with the poetry and criticism of T. S. Eliot, and conducted independent study under the direction of Eugene O'Neill Jr. At the time Jaffa entertained the ambition of writing a history of Elizabethan drama. Had he chosen Government as an undergraduate major instead, he might well have gone on to become a preeminent literary critic instead of a political philosopher, though it is less certain that he would have become an eminent contrarian in that field, because there was no figure in literary criticism analogous to Strauss to inspire his direction. (It is not a coincidence that the contemporary study of English literature has been corrupted by historicism every bit as much as political philosophy, nor is it happpenstance that Jaffa went on to produce original and provocative analyses of Shakespeare, Dostoyevsky, Camus, Mark Twain, and other classics of literature.[39])

After finishing his undergraduate coursework, Jaffa enrolled in Yale's graduate program in Government in 1939, but he stayed in the program for only a year. His Yale adviser—Harvey Mansfield Sr., father of the Harvey Mansfield well known at Harvard today—had discouraged him from pursuing a Ph.D. because, as a Jew, Jaffa would not be able to find university employment. But, more important, Jaffa found the content of the graduate curriculum wanting. "I made a good decision in going to Yale when I did, but I made an equally good decision in leaving Yale when I did," Jaffa told Ed Erler in a 2003 interview. "I had spent a year as a graduate student in Government, but I was completely disillusioned with the course there. And I could have stayed and got my Ph.D. at Yale ["in a mindless stupor" Jaffa put it in another recollection] if I had wanted to but I just saw that there was nothing there that I wanted to learn. . . . As far as the Socratic tradition was concerned, Yale was a land of dead souls."[40]

Instead, Jaffa decided to pursue employment with the federal civil service in Washington. In those days, the civil service exam was very difficult, and to prepare for it Jaffa decided to enroll in a two-semester course in public administration with Arnold Brecht at the New School. Ironically, Brecht's course on public administration, a subject Jaffa had found "infinitely boring" at Yale, was more about political theory than management. "[Brecht] was a great gentleman, a great scholar, and a fine teacher," Jaffa wrote of him later, "and I learned more political theory in his first class than I had learned in the year long theory course I had taken [at Yale]. . . . Later I had a wonderful course with Brecht on the End of the Weimar Republic."[41]

Having passed the civil service exam in 1941, Jaffa spent the next three years in Washington, D.C., during which he several times failed the eye exam for active military duty, but also got married. He decided to return to the New School in 1944 to pursue a Ph.D. after all. Brecht secured a scholarship for him. "I thought at first only of Brecht, with whom I had established a good relationship," Jaffa recalled. "But nothing had prepared me for Leo Strauss."

Jaffa knew nothing of Strauss and, with no special forethought, signed up for a course on political theory with Strauss in the fall of 1944. "Saul on the road to Damascus was not more stunned, nor more transformed than I, by my encounter with Strauss," Jaffa recalled. "It was some time before I realized . . . that he was reversing the assumptions underlying my Yale education, which were the assumptions of what we would later come to call 'Historicism,' which meant that the thought of any person is ultimately determined by the age in which he lives and by the assumptions of the society in which he lives."[42] The historicist assumptions of our era, Jaffa thought, are buried so deeply that the thinker himself is unaware of them—just like the prisoners of the cave in *The Republic*.

The difference between Brecht and Strauss displays the margin between good and great, between proficient and profound. Brecht rightly noted the self-contradictory nature of supposedly value-free social science, namely, that it cannot escape making value judgments. But only with great difficulty, tentativeness, and qualification could Brecht embrace "value judgments" himself. He was unable to break free of the long shadow of Weber. Brecht was a good man and a serious thinker, but Strauss was a *radical* thinker, willing to question everything from the ground up, including the accepted premises of modern science.

Jaffa never looked back: "Over the next seven years (five in New York and two in Chicago), I attended some nineteen of his courses."[43] Jaffa became one of Strauss's earliest graduate students, and when the University of Chicago lured Strauss from the New School in 1949, Strauss brought Jaffa along with him.

While Jaffa was finishing and revising his dissertation, he attended the series of Strauss lectures that became *Natural Right and History*. Strauss did not in these early lectures mention the Declaration of Independence, but he included a prominent reference to it in the opening of the book when it came out a few years later. Although Jaffa was working on what would become his first book, *Thomism and Aristotelianism*, he had had his first chance encounter in 1946 with the Lincoln-Douglas debates (a story to be told more fully in the next chapter), and was having extensive private conversations with Strauss about America and American politics. In his last memoir Jaffa recalled one in particular:

> When he first came to this country, in the 1930s, he said he found (whether rightly or not) that, in polite society, the word "atheist" might not be pronounced. According to his account, it was what the "N" word has become today. When he discovered this,

he told me, he realized that he had "come home." The "coming home" of Leo Strauss was no different than the Americanization of the European immigrants celebrated by Lincoln.[44]

While Strauss was influencing Jaffa, Jaffa was having a reciprocal influence on Strauss; he noted not only Strauss's direct invocation of the Declaration of Independence in *Natural Right and History* but also his indirect reference to Lincoln—the use, without quotation marks, of Lincoln's famous opening phrase at Gettysburg about "the nation dedicated to this proposition." "In speaking of the nation's dedication to a proposition, and of the faith in which it was conceived and raised," Jaffa observed, "he speaks with Lincoln's voice as if it were his own."

Strauss's famous book was a frontal challenge to the idea that History had replaced Nature as the ground of being and political morality. While Strauss concentrated his work chiefly on classical authors, Jaffa soon turned his attention almost wholly to the American Founding, seeing, by way of Lincoln, the depths of the founders' thought that our current age was discarding or trivializing, and its connection to the rational tradition of classical political philosophy. It did not happen all at once, and the enterprise was not conducted by Jaffa alone. Soon a number of other important thinkers would come to study with Strauss at Chicago and work on parallel paths: Walter Berns, Herbert Storing, Joseph Cropsey, Robert Goldwin, Martin Diamond, and Allan Bloom, among others. While Jaffa would later feud with many of these figures, he noted that he "profited greatly from conversations" with Diamond, Bloom, Goldwin, and Cropsey during his years at Chicago.

Cropsey had been a childhood friend of Jaffa; they went through bar mitzvah classes together in Brooklyn. Cropsey's route to becoming one of Strauss's closest collaborators was more circuitous and curious than Jaffa's, and it explains why Cropsey was the one figure from the larger circle of Strauss students who wrote cogently and deeply on political economy. Cropsey had been a doctoral student in economics at Columbia and, after returning from infantry service in World War II, he joined the economics faculty at City University of New York (CUNY). Cropsey arranged for Jaffa to teach three sections of introductory economics at CUNY; Jaffa reciprocated by prodding a reluctant Cropsey to ask the woman who would become his wife to go out for a first date. Jaffa also convinced Cropsey to come listen to Strauss at the New School. "I saw him regularly in those days and plied him assiduously with tales of the miracles I had witnessed in the seminars of Leo Strauss," Jaffa wrote on the occasion of Cropsey's death in 2012. "I tried several times—unsuccessfully—to get him to accompany me to one of Strauss's classes. Then one night— miraculously—he accompanied me to one of those classes. The result was instantaneous."[45]

Several years would pass before Cropsey followed Strauss and Jaffa to Chicago. He first had to get Columbia University to accept his dissertation on Adam Smith's *Theory of Moral Sentiments*, which offered a qualified defense of capitalism on moral grounds, rather than the utilitarian grounds of *The Wealth of Nations*, a topic and approach that would be impossible in most economics departments today. It was an uphill struggle in the early 1950s, with "vicious infighting" at Columbia over Cropsey's departure from convention, because his final product, *Polity and Economy*, was a work of political philosophy more than political economy, and indeed, once his Ph.D. was in hand, he "jumped ship" wholly for the world of political philosophy at Chicago.[46] Jaffa's influence can be seen in the background here, too; Cropsey's introduction includes a passage about the importance of Lincoln and the Gettysburg Address that reads as though it came straight from the pages of Jaffa's yet-to-be-published *Crisis of the House Divided*.

Cropsey is the author of one of the more typically difficult and enigmatic "Straussian" formulations: "It follows that the United

States is the microcosm of modernity, repeating in its regime, on the level of popular consciousness, the major noetic events of the modern world."[47] One way of reading this, in or out of context, is as an affirmation of the supreme philosophical importance of American ideas and principles. While acknowledging that our "popular consciousness" can be prone to corruptions of numerous kinds (Cropsey took special note of the influence of Freudianism, very popular at mid-century when he was forming his views), implicit is a premise of nobility that runs against the horde of the detractors, both domestic and foreign, who find American thought insubstantial or contemptible.

Cropsey, Jaffa, and others from this Straussian circle that started to form up in the late 1940s and early 1950s understood that any intellectual enterprise setting out to reconsider America's philosophic principles and the Founding itself would have to grapple with the central idea of "the proposition"—what is meant by "all men are created equal"? Just as in the 1850s and again in the 1950s, this question remains at the heart of political dispute in America today.

Strauss and Jaffa talked of "the crisis of the West." Strauss wrote in 1963 that "The crisis of the West consists in the West's having become uncertain of its purpose."[48] For Jaffa the crisis of the West was more profound than uncertainty or confusion; to the contrary, it consists in the dogmatic certainty by which the leading institutions of the West, from the universities on down, are actively repudiating the great traditions of Western liberalism. Jaffa summarized the decay of modern liberalism in one sentence: born ultimately of nihilism, contemporary liberalism means "every man his own tyrant." The Heideggerian nihilism and postmodernism that has percolated through popular culture and moral sentiments has led us to the point where "the subjective intensity of one's convictions matters more than their objective validity," and where the object of political activity is to create a world "in which there is no external obstacle to the will." The rejection of human nature now rampant in our intellectual elites means that "whether you want to belong to the human race is now a matter of personal preference."

This gets right to the heart of this book: the tyrant of the "liberated self" cannot be a patriot, because the "self," as the greatest cause any individual is taught to think of, cannot conceive of a cause or purpose or meaning beyond himself. At some point, the self-centeredness of radical individual autonomy makes fellowship—and fellow citizenship—impossible. "Patriotism is civic friendship," Jaffa argued; "Patriotism is the link between justice and friendship in its purest or transpolitical form. . . . Those who see each other as utterly alien cannot be fellow citizens."[49] I would go further, and say that a person who does not respect the country in the end will not respect himself. This may be one reason why so many America-hating leftists are such unpleasant and unhappy people.

The dogmatic liberalism of our time is the enemy of patriotism. Hence for Jaffa, Berns, and others from this circle, political philosophy is not merely a matter of theory informing practice, but literally a means of saving souls. Jaffa wrote: "I believe that the enterprise of western civilization is consummated each time a soul is saved from the dark night of fanatical obscurantism. It is consummated whenever one soul is released from the pessimism that truth is unobtainable, or not worth the trouble to obtain it."[50]

CHAPTER 4

Statesmanship and the Renegade Revival

*We cannot exert our understanding without from
time to time understanding something of importance.*

LEO STRAUSS

Chapter 2 opened with a short discussion of Lincoln's eulogy for Henry Clay on the ground of patriotism. That same speech is a useful portal into the question of whether *statesmanship* is an intelligible idea. What is a statesman? Sophisticated opinion, and certainly academic political science, today regards the idea as without rigorous or objective content, and as therefore meaningless or unfit for serious study. Cynics point to the illustrious Speaker of the House Thomas Reed, who quipped that "A statesman is a politician who is safely dead."

Lincoln, who called Henry Clay his "beau ideal of a statesman," would beg to differ, but he does bring up the difficulties with the concept in his celebration of Clay's greatness:

It is probably true he owed his pre-eminence to no one quality, but to a fortunate combination of several. He was surpassingly eloquent; but many eloquent men fail utterly; and they are not, as a class, generally successful. His judgment was excellent; but many men of good judgment, live and die unnoticed. His will was indomitable; but this quality often secures to its owner nothing better than a character for useless obstinacy. These then were Mr. Clay's leading qualities. No one of them is very uncommon; but all taken together are rarely combined in a single individual; and this is probably the reason why such men as Henry Clay are so rare in the world. . . .

That his views and measures were always the wisest, needs not to be affirmed; nor should it be, on this occasion, where so many, thinking differently, join in doing honor to his memory. A free people, in times of peace and quiet—when pressed by no common danger—naturally divide into parties. At such times, the man who is of neither party, is not—cannot be, of any consequence. Mr. Clay, therefore, was of a party. Taking a prominent part, as he did, in all the great political questions of his country for the last half century, *the wisdom of his course on many, is doubted and denied by a large portion of his countrymen.*[1] (Emphasis added.)

Here Lincoln points out that, above and beyond the rarity of the qualities of soul comprising the statesman, the partisanship natural to political life is a barrier to recognizing statesmanship. As we disagree about what constitutes "the common good," we'll naturally fall into disputes over every political leader with a serious account of the common good and a record of choices on how to get there. In other words, we tend to bestow the exalted title of "statesman" on political figures who agree with us. Thus the question of statesmanship is indissolubly connected to the problem of justice. The rarity of the personal qualities that make for a statesman is problem enough, but given the disagreement about justice it is no wonder that the idea of statesmanship is held in low repute. This is also why many people, including many conservatives, denounce Lincoln and Churchill.

Jaffa wrote in *Crisis of the House Divided*: "Free government would be an absurdity did it require citizens all like Abraham Lincoln; yet it would be an impossibility if it could not from time to time find leaders with something of his understanding."[2] The need for such statesmanship is becoming acute to the point of crisis today. How can we find such people? The first step is to recover the outlook of statesmanship from the decay of a mode of political thought that exists on both the left and the right that holds that the problems of political life can be reduced to or solved by resolute ideology—"principles"—alone. But mere skill in politics is not sufficient without a vital and deep connection to the philosophical ground of the principles of republican government. "Enlightened statesmen will not always be at the helm," Madison warns us in *The Federalist*, but unless we study Madison closely and deeply, statesmen will never again be at the helm.

Add in one more complication—Enoch Powell's axiom that "all political lives end in failure." Even the giant political figures of history typically lauded as "statesmen" cannot escape a large measure of disappointment, if not tragedy. The case of Lincoln's assassination followed by the bitter divisions of the Reconstruction Era is too obvious to need retelling. Other examples worth pondering include Winston Churchill (voted out of office at the moment of his greatest triumph, but leaving Europe divided into a new confrontation), Ronald Reagan (leaving a large structural budget deficit after having promised a balanced budget), Woodrow Wilson (his idealism shredded at the Versailles peace conference), and Charles de Gaulle (despite his towering presence in French politics, he was nonetheless judged a failure at the end of his career). Countless older and classical examples, stretching back to Cyrus the Great (or at least to Xenophon's fictionalized account of Cyrus), can be added to the inventory. Does this melancholy fact highlight the inherent limitations of individual human beings or of our institutions? Popular opinion sways between these alternatives, with enthusiasm for the idea that the "right man" can fix our problems counterbalanced with the view that "the system" needs to be changed before anything can be done. That political life, like individual human life itself, has inherent limitations seems to be rejected as a working hypothesis.

The gulf between academic political science and the real world of politics is at its greatest at just this point. Consider a simple comparison: While the president has a Council of Economic Advisers (CEA), whose members are almost invariably drawn from academia, there is no Council of Political Advisers. Most presidents have chief political advisers, but they tend to be practitioners of the art of winning elections—Karl Rove or David Axelrod—and are seldom academics. Most government agencies have a position of chief economist, again usually someone drawn from academia. The White House CEA and chief economists in agencies have considerable influence on policy design; academic political scientists, not so much.

The distance between academic political science and the real world of political life is a source of recurring embarrassment and handwringing in the discipline.[3] It's especially notable whenever the American Political Science Association holds its large annual convention in Washington, D.C., and the center of the world's political activity . . . yawns. Ezra Klein wrote about this in the *Washington Post* in 2010:

> There were no political luminaries in attendance at the American Political Science Association's convention last week, however. The fact that the country's brightest political scholars had all gathered at the Marriott Wardman Park barely seemed to register on the rest of the town. Worse, you got the feeling that the political scientists knew it. One of the conference's highlights, according to its Web site, was a panel titled "Is Political Science Relevant?"[4]

Can you imagine a conference of the American Economic Association offering a panel entitled, "Is Economics Relevant?" (Though I might pay money for an AEA panel on the topic "Why Did None of Us Foresee the Housing Bubble and Collapse?") In 2009, Joseph Nye of the Harvard Kennedy School observed:

> Scholars are paying less attention to questions about how their work relates to the policy world, and in many departments a focus on policy can hurt one's career. Advancement comes faster for those who develop mathematical models, new methodologies or theories expressed in jargon that is unintelligible to policymakers.[5]

There's something perverse about an academic discipline that decides to address its lack of relevance by deliberately rewarding further irrelevance. And while positivism, regression-model obsession, and rational choice theory still dominate academic political science today, it is amusing to see the recurring spasms from the left against the straitjacket of this horizon-shrinking methodology. Contemporary academic political science is constantly in the throes of a crisis of confidence, a crisis to which it occasionally cops to publicly, while academic history has practically ceased trying to speak to the general public about large or meaningful subjects. Every few years sees a prominent social scientist lament the defects of the "fact-value distinction," along with fresh complaints of "who took the 'politics' out of political science?" And there was, for a brief time, a self-described "raucous rebellion in political science" that called for "perestroika" in the discipline, missing the irony that the original "perestroika" (or "restructuring") of the Soviet Union was a colossal failure.[6]

The origin of this sorry state lies ironically with the confidence in the belief held several decades ago that the era of scientific politics was at hand, which meant that scientific administration was possible, an enthusiasm that flowered in the Progressive Era. Progressive political scientists and historians held that the principles of the American Founding were either obsolete (pay no attention to the preface of the Declaration of Independence or the separation of powers, Woodrow Wilson said), or were fraudulently antidemocratic (Charles Beard, J. Allen Smith, and Vernon Parrington, for starters). Indeed, the purpose of Progressive Era political science and historical revisionism was to get over the American Founding—to say good-bye to all that.

This project was highly successful. Two generations of students and interested general readers were told that the American Founding was fraudulent or that the requirements of twentieth-century democracy made the Founding obsolete. With the partial exception of Walter Lippmann, there was little serious intellectual resistance of any prominence during the decades in which this view was regnant. John Dewey, to take the most representative example of an eminent Progressive thinker, had no serious critic disputing his formal philosophy of Pragmatism.

While the concept of scientific administration was mostly theoretical for Woodrow Wilson and the Progressives, by mid-century advances in social science methodology—especially the behavioral revolution—gave political scientists confidence that they could now deliver on the Progressive promise. Modern political science aims willy-nilly to replace the statesman with the bureaucrat, and substitute science (supposedly) for ambition.

Science is not concerned with morals, but there is something odd about an inquiry into an essentially moral domain that averts its gaze. Mid-century political thought had little use for the American Founding; readings of the *Federalist Papers* and Tocqueville became perfunctory when the works didn't disappear from curricula altogether. There are almost no major articles about the Founding, or the *Federalist Papers*, in the *American Political Science Review* from 1920 to the 1950s. Dewey had replaced

James Madison as the preeminent guide for understanding democratic government. Lincoln was a more curious but instructive case. His towering memory was distorted in ways that denied or transformed his core philosophy in a modern "progressive" direction. Theodore Roosevelt and Woodrow Wilson honored Lincoln while carefully separating Lincoln from his thought—a project that continues today with Lincoln's liberal admirers. It's a body-snatching operation.

Science is reductive as well as amoral, and, since politics involves institutions of power, political science entered what might be called the "Age of Lasswell," after Harold Lasswell, who was the eminence at the University of Chicago at the same time Strauss was building out his project of reviving classical political philosophy. Lasswell simplified politics to the process of deciding who gets what, when, and how. Hence academic political science at that time went whole hog for positivism and narrow empiricism, with a side dish of the Freudianism that was then very popular.

But the lassitude of Lasswell had a problem: positivist empirical methodology was unable to recognize, let alone reckon seriously with, the moral character and willfulness of modern tyranny. The study of political philosophy in those days, Jaffa observed, was like a tour of a waxworks museum—none of the figures or their ideas were alive in the present. The distinguished political scientist Aaron Wildavsky reflected on his graduate education around this time, writing that "in 1955 the Yale University political science department was fast becoming a hotbed of vile and amoral behaviorism, not to say an emporium of hyperfactualism and vulgar empiricism. . . . [H]istory was out of style and political theory [was] a subject fit only for unscientific dilettantes."[7]

The project of reviving political philosophy thus represented a counterrevolution in political science analogous to the counterrevolution in political economy that was being waged at the same time by such figures as Milton Friedman, Friedrich Hayek, and the Mont Pelerin Society. (Is it merely a coincidence that many of these figures also came from the University of Chicago?) The story of the counterrevolution in political science is harder to tell because there is no "curve" you can draw on a napkin analogous to the Laffer Curve, no blackboard equations you can match up to a quantitative indicator like the consumer price index or GDP growth. And it has been by no means as successful as the economic counterrevolution. While behaviorism has faded from the scene, academic political science today is still dominated by behaviorism's quantitative cousin, regression modeling.

It also bears mentioning that political *philosophy* and political *theory* are not the same thing, though the two are still confused or conjoined today, and reviving the older tradition of political philosophy directly challenged the self-confidence in mainstream political science and political thought. At the core of the challenge to conventional liberal thinking on politics is the view that positivism and historicism both close off direct contact with the central questions of political life, and cannot give serious, meaningful answers. Strauss liked to compare social science to Nero, fiddling while Rome burns, but, in a contribution to *Essays on the Scientific Study of Politics*, he added that "It is excused by two facts: it does not know that it fiddles, and it does not know that Rome burns."[8]

Walter Berns wrote a long essay for the same volume, offering his own critique of social science technique, in which the result is "the sacrifice of political relevance on the altar of methodology."[9] One of Jaffa's typical formulations runs: "It sometimes seems as if the highest goal of 'mainstream political science' is to be able to predict the outcome of the Emperor Nero's chariot races, while viewing his despotism in the tolerant light of 'value free' methodology."[10] Edward Banfield, another student of Strauss who went on to a controversial career at Harvard, wrote: "It is a dangerous delusion to think that the policy scientist can supplant successfully the politician or statesman. Social problems are at bottom political; they arise from differences of opinion and interest and, except in trivial instances, are difficulties to be coped with (ignored, got around, put up with, exorcised by the arts of rhetoric, etc.) rather than puzzles to be solved."[11]

You can understand why such men were not always warmly received in political science department meetings, especially when the curriculum was being discussed.

Beyond the critique of social science methodology and philosophical historicism, the counterrevolutionaries put the politics back in political science by taking the idea of statesmanship seriously. The argument against the political philosophers and other traditionalists was that, while their criticisms of "value-free" relativism had merit, the alternative was an "absolutism" that was defective in theory and practice. Statesmanship, as Strauss and his students conceive it, presents the way out of the stale antinomy of "relativism" versus "absolutism," but this is a subtle point that takes a while to grasp. The question of the statesman is the point of contact between political philosophy and the human soul. As Angelo Codevilla, a Jaffa student, puts it: "Politics, if practiced as anything but an art of the soul, is bound to fail."[12]

The statesman in the real world can't be bound by a narrow absolutism. The classical point of contact with this problem is Aristotle's enigmatic remark in the *Nicomachean Ethics* that natural right is changeable. Does this mean that human nature changes, or that circumstances will admit variable judgments? As Strauss put it in *Natural Right and History*, "justice and natural right reside, as it were, in concrete decisions rather than in general rules."[13] In other words, the Straussian project is an attempt to overcome the defects of absolutism through the moral latitude of the statesman without surrendering the objective moral basis of human life. Ultimately this cannot be done without a view to the good of the human soul, with an idea of human excellence and happiness that is not just an idiosyncratic individual exercise of the will.

Human freedom and willfulness will always impose hard limits on any politics that is not despotic. Modern political science finds itself degraded by two extremes that deny that there are inherent limits to politics. The first is radical utopian ideologies that believe perfect justice is possible, but always decay into justifications for totalitarian power. The second is the positivism that believes— or at least once believed—that political problems can be sorted out by the progressive application of the scientific method. The large schemes of the former, especially Communism, have been discredited in history, though the impulse lives on in numerous subdivisions, such as environmentalism, feminism, and the whole domain of today's "social justice warriors." And while almost no one speaks any longer about social science methodology with the perfectionist confidence of Dewey, it remains the reigning orthodoxy by default, in large part because the older focus of political thought with the moral character of citizens and the capacities of statesmen has atrophied. Nearly every quantitative social science journal article today concludes with an admission that the finding at hand is narrow or specific, and that "further research is needed," as though a subsequent string of multiple regressions will somehow unearth the key to solving a complex social problem. Richard Weaver was on to this problem in *Ideas Have Consequences*: "The theory of empiricism is plausible because it assumes that accuracy about small matters prepares the way for valid judgment about larger ones. What happens, however, is that the judgments are never made."[14]

At its best, political science today is strongest at institutional analysis, though even this concedes a premise and obscures a paradox by avoiding a simple question: Why do we laud as statesmen the founders and writers of the Constitution who warned that an "enlightened statesman will not always be at the helm"? More particularly, despite the durability of the Constitution—now the oldest written constitution in the world—why did the initial success of the Constitution depend on the stature and character of a single individual, George Washington? Why, without him, might the presidency itself have been omitted from the Constitution, as it was from the Articles of Confederation?

The seemingly unrepeatable example of Washington is too often taken as proof of the radical contingency of political life, or dismissed as so much myth or patrimonialism. Safer to stick to studying "democratic values" and institutions, whose rule-based nature lends some consistency, rather than plumb the depths of human character at the core of any notion of statesmanship. Allan Bloom described the problem succinctly in *The Closing of the American Mind*:

> But the unity, grandeur and attendant folklore of the founding heritage was attacked from so many directions in the last half-century that it gradually disappeared from daily life and from textbooks. It all began to seem like Washington and the cherry tree—not the sort of thing to teach children seriously.[15]

Never mind children. What about graduate students? In contrast to the main currents of political science and history, thinkers like Jaffa and Berns thought statesmanship could be understood and studied philosophically. Jaffa argued that "political science, properly so-called, would have at its heart the study of the speeches and deeds of statesmen." Walter Berns felt the same way. In my last conversation with Berns, he said he hoped I would continue working in the vein of my Reagan and Churchill books because "the proper method for the study of politics is *biography!*"

In this approach Berns and Jaffa were following the lead of their great teacher Strauss, whose famous classroom eulogy of

Winston Churchill in 1965 praised in particular Churchill's *Marl-borough*. Strauss called it "the greatest historical work written in our century, an inexhaustible mine of political wisdom and understanding, which should be required reading for every student of political science." I'm sure Strauss knew that *Marlborough* was required or recommended reading precisely nowhere in political science curricula, because it is neither a philosophical nor an empirical work. But if "history is philosophy teaching by example"— an axiom often attributed to Thucydides—it becomes clear why great teachers like Jaffa, Berns, and others who emerged from Strauss's classroom would emphasize the careful study of statesmen like Lincoln and Churchill.

It is not an accident, to shoplift the old Marxist idiom, that this circle of political scientists would focus so intently on Churchill. From *Marlborough* it is possible to make out the central problem of politics for Strauss and his disciples: *prudence*—the central trait of statesmanship. The prudence of the statesman may be described as the combination of attachment to principle along with a profound understanding of the circumstances. The gulf between principle and practice is expressed in one of Strauss's most enigmatic formulations, which appears at the very center of his most famous work, *Natural Right and History*: "There is a universally valid hierarchy of ends, but there are no universally valid rules of action."[16]

In writing about war—the highest subdivision of statesmanship—Churchill's *Marlborough* gives a sensible description of prudence in action: "Circumstances alone decide whether a correct conventional maneuver is right or wrong. The circumstances include all the factors which are at work at the time." But while prudence can be described, it cannot be taught—at least not in any scientific or schematic way. "That is why critics can write so cogently," Churchill continued, "and yet successful performers are so rare." He might well have said "political scientists" instead of "critics."

"[G]enius," Churchill continued, "though it may be armed, cannot be acquired, either by reading or by experience. In default of genius nations have to make war as best they can, and since that quality is much rarer than the largest and purest diamonds, most wars are mainly tales of muddle."[17] So political life is in general a muddle, though usually for lower stakes than war. And even statesmanlike genius is no guarantee of success, as Marlborough's own eventual downfall attests.

Therefore the first principle of the study of statesmanly genius is that it is impossible to reduce it to rote formulas, still less to sustain it with the windy clichés of "leadership." The study of statesmanship partakes of the essence of Socratic philosophy, which begins with the irony of ignorance: I know that I know nothing. The first step in learning the essence of statesmanship is knowing that it can't be learned in the ordinary way—if it can be learned at all. Thus "the study of the speeches and deeds of statesmen" will be more illuminating than the study of institutions or behavior alone. Statesmen will be as rare as real philosophers, and for the same reason. (In addition to rejecting predominant liberal and leftist approaches to understanding politics, this perspective also departs from popular and influential conservative approaches, such as public choice theory, where institutional design explains everything. I would say public choice theory is correct about 90 percent of the time: but what of the other 10 percent of the time, which may be 90 percent more important, as in the case of war?)

A second paradox for students of politics lies in the example of Churchill—that the need for statesmanship is greater precisely under the modern conditions that make it ever more difficult to attain. Churchill's *Marlborough* contains a subtext about the attenuation of human excellence—and therefore statesmanship—

in democratic culture. Churchill is often regarded as a Victorian romantic, but he had no illusions about the British aristocracy of the seventeenth and eighteenth centuries that was the setting for *Marlborough*: it was corrupt and venal, full of "weaknesses, vices, and favouritism." He was a convinced liberal democrat on principle, and celebrated that democracy was more just and equal than the aristocratic society it replaced. But he was also troubled by what was lost with the passing of that older society, writing early in *Marlborough*: "It is strange indeed that such a system should have produced for many generations a succession of greater captains and abler statesmen than all our widely extended education, competitive examinations, and democratic systems have put forth."[18]

Churchill later gave fuller voice to this puzzlement in two essays from 1924 and 1931, "Shall We All Commit Suicide?" and "Mass Effects in Modern Life," in which he wrote that the democratic age was not producing the character of men equal to the challenges of advancing science—science that threatened our doom. Earlier in his career as a young member of parliament, at a time when there was widespread optimism that the age of general European warfare was gone forever, and when Churchill *opposed* higher spending for the British military, he foresaw the likelihood of both the scale and nature of modern warfare. In a 1901 speech in the House of Commons, Churchill warned that "[T]he resources of science and civilization sweep away everything that might mitigate their fury, a European war can only end in the ruin of the vanquished and the scarcely less fatal commercial dislocation and exhaustion of the conquerers. *Democracy is more vindictive than Cabinets. The wars of peoples will be more terrible than those of kings*" (emphasis added).[19]

By 1924, looking back on the apocalypse of the Great War and foreseeing the growth of our destructive capacity ahead (including, at that very early time, the concept of nuclear weapons), Churchill worried:

> Mankind has never been in this position before. Without having improved appreciably in virtue or enjoying wiser guidance, it has got into its hands for the first time the tools by which it can unfailingly accomplish its own extermination. . . . They would do well to pause and ponder their new responsibilities. . . . Let it not be thought for a moment that the danger of another explosion in Europe has passed.[20]

The worry that science and technology was outstripping human wisdom and capacities was not new or unique to Churchill, but adding to his anxiety were the aforementioned defects of mass democracy. In "Mass Effects in Modern Times" he concludes that "Modern conditions do not lend themselves to the production of the heroic or super-dominant type."[21]

Churchill wrote these gloomy essays—just two of several examples of his pessimism *before* Hitler arrived on the scene—during his decade-long work on the *Marlborough* project. The age of great captains and statesmen like Marlborough was gone forever, he thought. Not just individuals, but democratic institutions might not be fully equal to the challenge of modern conditions. In a 1930 lecture at Oxford on "Parliamentary Government and the Economic Problem"—note the date: just as the Great Depression was deepening its grip—Churchill doubted the ability of democratic assemblies to respond competently to economic crises, and he flirted with the idea of economic authoritarianism. (Jaffa thought this Churchill's worst essay, and in any case Churchill later repudiated this position.) Yet the example of his own heroic statesmanship over the next decade stands as the rebuttal of his pessimism. Jaffa noted the irony of Churchill's self-refutation of his own gloomy prognostication: "Can there be another Winston Churchill? In 1939, Winston Churchill did not think so. But, as so often in life, he was mistaken. Let us take comfort in that."[22]

The final cause of Churchill's great words and deeds went beyond principle, circumstance, ambition, and chance. Jaffa thought Churchill's "attachment to the cause of human freedom had metaphysical no less than moral roots." If statesmanship—and the crucial art of prudence—can be taught at all, it has to begin with contemplation of the metaphysical roots of human freedom. This requires a political science of an entirely different disposition, one that is concerned first and foremost with the condition of the human soul rather than the structure of government institutions or the foundations of law. This kind of political science is necessarily more capacious—the kind of capaciousness displayed in Churchill's account of Marlborough.[23]

At the end of the day, the excellence of the teacher cannot be separated from the excellence of the subject matter. While there are "self-evident truths" of politics, they are not evident to every self walking down the street. The art of teaching about politics is nearly as difficult as politics itself. Just as genuine statesmen are rare, very few teachers are capable of the capacious kind of political science described here. There are many excellent professors, thinkers, and writers in the ordinary sense—and then there are the few figures that stand clearly higher. It is not a coincidence that the teachers graced with the ability to convey effectively the capaciousness of political life in its true depths tend to attract the best and most serious students. In turn, the students of these great teachers frequently are marked out for significant and distinctive careers, often away from academia—an additional bit of evidence that there is something substantively different about studying politics with such teachers.

CHAPTER 5

The Vital Center Cannot Hold

*The great vogue of revisionism in the historical
profession suggests, in my judgment, ominous weaknesses
in the contemporary attitude toward history.*

ARTHUR SCHLESINGER JR., 1949

*For consistency, in any narrow sense, is seldom
if ever the path of wise statesmanship.*

HARRY V. JAFFA, 1959

Mid-century liberalism—the intellectual milieu in which Jaffa, Berns, and the rest of Strauss's students came of age—was an odd combination of high confidence and inner confusion. The high self-regard of liberals in the immediate postwar years is entirely understandable. It was a function of both the nation's triumph of arms in World War II and the triumph in politics of the New Deal coalition. The importance of Harry Truman's come-from-behind victory in 1948 cannot be overstated, as it showed the resiliency of "vital center" liberalism to withstand simultaneous challenges from both the left (Henry Wallace) and the reactionary right (Strom Thurmond) as well as a Republican Party still not ready for prime time. The startling result of that stunning election upset inspired one of the classic books in political science, Samuel Lubell's *The Future of American Politics*, which ratified the presumption that liberalism would dominate under the bright sun of the Democratic Party. History and social science alike testified to the supremacy of liberalism. Even the election of Dwight Eisenhower in 1952 did not fundamentally change this outlook, because Eisenhower governed from within the new parameters of the New Deal, just as, forty years later, Bill Clinton would govern largely from within the parameters of the Reagan Revolution.

Underneath, liberalism was wrestling with some related dilemmas and contradictions. The first was what to do about Progressivism; the second, what to do about both the challenge of radical Marxism in ideological thought and the practical geopolitical challenge from the Communist Soviet Union. Except for intellectual historians, no one today bothers much to read either the leading authors of the Progressive Era—such as Charles Beard, J. Allen Smith, Vernon Parrington, John Burgess, or Herbert Croly—nor their mid-century successors, the "consensus liberals"—such as Louis Hartz, Richard Hofstadter, Lionel Trilling, Daniel Boorstin, and Arthur Schlesinger Jr.—whose active project was to restart liberalism in light of the bitter experience of the Western world that culminated in World War II. The "remarkable monographic uprising of the 1950s," as Hofstadter called it, was partly a repudiation of Progressivism, though this repudiation or revision was half-hearted and incomplete.[1] "Why was progressivism not prepared for Hitler?," Schlesinger asked in 1949; "Progress had betrayed the progressives."[2] The trouble was, liberals were divided about how to rebuild.

The leading consensus school figures were graceful writers but often shallow thinkers. They were generally correct about the American liberal tradition, but specifically wrong about some important aspects of that tradition. Their motives were mixed. One impulse was the typical generational rivalry in academia, more pronounced in history than in other fields, that worked to overturn the interpretations of the previous generation (as indeed "consensus liberalism" was repudiated by most historians who came of age in the 1960s and 1970s). Their decent motive was to lead American liberalism away from the kind of fierce ideological class conflict that fueled revolutionary and totalitarian ideologies. These liberals were not willfully blind to class conflicts between the Haves and Have Nots, but, as we shall see, their work led to a strange deformation of our understanding of the greatest Have Nots in American history—slaves. Even though the consensus liberal account was superseded by the next generation, certain of its traits live on in American political thought and political science. It is worth noting that the cadre of thinkers who would form the critical mass of conservative criticism considered themselves at that time to be fellow liberals. Most—Jaffa, Berns, other students of Leo Strauss, and Strauss himself were Democrats. Most voted for Truman and Adlai Stevenson. Walter Berns would later recall driving Strauss to the local precinct to cast his 1952 vote for Stevenson.

The story of the Progressive revolution in American political thought has been well told, but surprisingly is still not well known, an especially odd circumstance given the revival of the term "progressive" on the left today. The central idea of Progressivism was that we needed to get over, and get beyond, the American Founding. The Progressive historians, especially Beard, Smith, and Parrington, all regarded the Founding as an antidemocratic fraud, while the philosophers and political scientists, such as John Dewey, Frank Goodnow, John Burgess, and especially Woodrow Wilson, rejected the political philosophy of the Founding. (I'll have more to say about the important theoretical and practical aspects of this in chapter 9.) The Founders' Constitution was a nuisance to the Progressives, as it remains for contemporary liberalism. The Constitution is to modern liberal politics what the gold standard is to modern liberal economics—a barbarous relic that somehow retains enough value and clout with the terminally retrograde that it can't be ignored or got rid of entirely.

In particular, Progressives thought the Lockean philosophy at the heart of the Founding was wholly obsolete. (A later generation of left-leaning thinkers attempted to read Locke out of the Founding entirely, as we shall see.) The natural rights of the Declaration? Fuggedaboutit, said Oliver Wendell Holmes Jr. "All my life," Holmes wrote in a letter to Harold Laski in 1916, "I have sneered at the natural rights of man—and at times I have thought that the bills of rights in Constitutions were overworked."[3] In a 1929 letter to Frederick Pollock, Holmes goes further: "I see no reason for attributing to man a significance different in kind from that which belongs to a baboon or to a grain of sand."[4] By 1927 he had given free rein to his positivism in his infamous opinion in *Buck v. Bell*.

Perhaps the best example of how the historicism of German philosophy had permeated American thought is found in the later Progressive Era historian Carl Becker. In his justly regarded 1922 book *The Declaration of Independence*, Becker wrote in conclusion that "To ask whether the natural rights philosophy of the Declaration of Independence is true or false is essentially a meaningless question."[5] Meaningless, because History and Progress had replaced nature as the ground of political thought. The faith of the founders, Becker concluded, "could not survive the harsh realities of the modern world."

Yet Becker also provides the portal to the problems of mid-century liberalism, as Jaffa was to observe much later. When the "harsh realities of the modern world" took horrific shape over the next two decades, a confused Becker backtracked. He published a new edition of *The Declaration of Independence* in the fall of 1941, in the shadow of the European (and soon to be American) war, and struck a very different note in a new introduction:

[It] may be thought that just now, when political freedom, already lost in many countries, is everywhere threatened, the readers of books would be more than ordinarily interested in the political principles of the Declaration of Independence. Certainly recent events throughout the world have aroused an unwonted attention to the immemorial problem of human liberty.

Suddenly, the principles of liberty, taken for granted as simple and solved by Woodrow Wilson and other Progressives, had returned as an "immemorial problem" in need of foundations. To continue with Becker:

The incredible cynicism and brutality of Adolf Hitler's ambitions, made every day more real by the servile and remorseless activities of his bleak-faced, humorless Nazi supporters, have forced men everywhere to re-appraise the validity of half-forgotten ideas, and enabled them once more to entertain convictions as to the substance of things not evident to the senses.[6]

The ideas Becker identified as "half-forgotten" were only so because of a self-willed forgetfulness.[7]

But what recovered memory did consensus liberalism offer? Like the Progressives, mid-century liberals mostly rejected Marxism but couldn't quite make up their minds about how to think about class conflict in American history and how it related to the principles of the Founders. Consensus liberalism can be understood as the thesis that the American political tradition, like turtles in the apocryphal story of a question put to Bertrand Russell, is liberalism all the way down, with an emphasis on continuity and a de-emphasis of class conflict. As such, consensus liberalism was following a central thread of Tocqueville, namely that America never had a class-based revolution because it never had a feudal phase. (Not coincidentally, Tocqueville, perhaps the original theorist of "liberal" America, began to make a comeback around this time.)

Some of the consensus liberals, such as Louis Hartz and Richard Hofstadter, were unable to shake their Progressive forebears entirely and thought the liberal tradition was a problem or defect to overcome, and subsequent leftist historians and theorists have done just that. Hartz, sounding like a wingman for Dewey, lamented that America was in thrall to an "irrational" and confining Lockean individualism that ought to be overcome or "transcended" so that enlightened social experimentation could proceed. The founding philosophy of natural right, Hartz argued, was "a primitive starting point for political thought." Only in America, Hartz sneered, could something as retrograde as Friedrich Hayek's economic philosophy find any popularity: "What they used to say about England, that it was the home of dead German philosophies, would have to be altered in this case to apply to America: it is the home of dead English philosophies [Adam Smith and Locke] retained by Austrian professors."[8] Hartz thought the problem with the Progressives was that they couldn't break free of the liberal tradition. "The Progressives failed because, being children of the American absolutism, they could not get outside of it," Hartz wrote; "Here lies the real intellectual tragedy of the time."[9]

Richard Hofstadter had an even harder time breaking with the Progressives, even though he was critical of their historiography. While he rejected the rigid Progressive scheme of conflict between democrats and aristocrats, he could not shake class conflict entirely. If anything, Hofstadter conceived of himself as being to the left of the Progressives. He admitted in one of his later books that his idea of consensus liberalism "had its sources in the Marxism of the 1930s" and, in his most famous book, *The American Political Tradition*, he found it regrettable that "the issues of the 20th century are still debated in the language of Jefferson's time," because Jefferson's thought and language were thoroughly obsolete. Hofstadter couldn't be any clearer than in the conclusion of his chapter about the Founding Fathers:

> But no man who is as well abreast of modern science as the Fathers were of eighteenth-century science believes any longer in *unchanging human nature*. Modern humanistic thinkers who seek for a means by which society may transcend eternal conflict and rigid adherence to property rights as its integrating principles *can expect no answer* in the philosophy of balanced government as it was set down by the Constitution-makers of 1787.[10] (Emphasis added.)

While Hofstadter couldn't help regrowing his Beard and Hartz was trapped in a Locke-box, Schlesinger took precisely the opposite view. Progressivism was a dead end precisely because it rejected the American liberal tradition. "[T]he progressive," Schlesinger observed, "has cut himself off from the useable traditions of American radical democracy." Schlesinger, at least, wanted liberals to take back and embrace the American political tradition, including, inter alia, the Founders' more conservative view of human nature. Progressives, he charged, had "a soft and shallow conception of human nature," and their penchant for perfectionism or utopianism "has turned it into, if not an accomplice of totalitarianism, at least an accessory before the fact." He added that "ignorance is never any bar to certitude in the progressive dreamworld."[11]

Taking back an American political tradition that the Progressives had derailed or denigrated was a fine idea, but Schlesinger and the other consensus thinkers did so at the cost of oversimplifying American political thought.[12] In any case, the consensus liberal de-emphasis of fundamental ideological conflict made it inevitable that it would mishandle the elephant in the room, namely, the greatest and most obvious conflict in the American story—the Civil War. It is impossible to make the war simply disappear, though the Progressives tried by virtually ignoring it. Their consensus successors downplayed its significance by denying the Civil War held any special significance for American political thought. Hartz went so far as to suggest that the Civil War didn't really represent a departure from the American liberal consensus. He barely treats it in *The Liberal Tradition in America*, and when he does it is dismissed quickly as a bizarre exception, explained as a self-contradictory emulation of the French Revolution. Daniel Boorstin, in his famous work from that period, *The Genius of American Politics*, likewise expressed the thought that the Civil War was "unproductive of political theory"—in other words, with little significance for American political thought—because there was no fundamental difference of principle between North and South. The implication was that, contrary to Lincoln in his famous Springfield speech, the American house wasn't really divided, and was at little risk of falling down. (The very title of Boorstin's chapter that labors for thirty-three pages to make this point reveals its defect: "The Civil War and the Spirit of Compromise." Compromise?)[13] Hofstadter denied the Civil War had any notable moral or theoretical significance with the acerbic comment: "I can best put my own dissent by suggesting a cartoon: a Reb and a Yank meet in 1865 to survey the physical and moral devastation of the war. 'Well,' says one to the other consolingly, 'at least we escaped the ultimate folly of producing political theorists.'"[14]

This facile framework led Harry Jaffa to quip that "history is much too important to leave to the historians" because the tendency to depreciate political ideas and downplay the depths of the issues involved around the Civil War reinforced historicism and relativism, and spawned ongoing confusion about the principles and practice of self-government. In fact, Hofstadter's dismissive comment above was written specifically in response to Jaffa, who had contested Hartz in a public forum in 1962. Jaffa had noticed how the confluence of historicism, value-free social science, and the conflict-diminishing tendency of "consensus liberalism" had infected our understanding of the causes and nature of the Civil War and distorted our understanding of Lincoln. Hartz, he thought, was egregiously shallow on all counts.[15] This was not a matter of mere historical inaccuracy; the causes of these misperceptions were plaguing political thought and affecting political issues in the mid-twentieth century and today. "The Civil War," Jaffa argued repeatedly, "is the most characteristic phenomenon in American politics, not because it represents a statistical frequency, but because it represents the innermost character of that politics."[16]

Jaffa came to develop his now-famous line of argument slowly, as the result of serendipity. In 1946, while Jaffa was still early in his Ph.D. studies at the New School, he wandered one Saturday afternoon into one of the many used bookstores that used to line Fourth Avenue in New York and happened across an 1895 edition of the Lincoln-Douglas debates. He was immediately captivated and read through the book until the store proprietor kicked him out at closing time. Not having the money to buy the book—$5 was a steep price for an impecunious graduate student in 1946, the equivalent of $60 today adjusted for inflation—he returned to the store the next day, and the day after that, to keep reading, because the tiny New School library apparently did not have a copy. Chance? Jaffa says the epiphany inspired by stumbling across the debates "is irrefutable proof of the role of divine providence in human affairs." (Eventually he scraped together the $5 to buy the book.)[17]

It helped that Jaffa was studying Plato's *Republic* with Strauss at that point. What Jaffa noticed, as he would explain more than a decade later, was that "the issue between Lincoln and Douglas was in substance, and very nearly in form, identical with the issue between Socrates and Thrasymachus in Book I of the *Republic*, namely, whether justice is merely the interest of the stronger. In the crisis of the 1850s, Douglas's position that the status of slavery should be decided by "popular sovereignty" meant that justice was no more than the interest of the majority. Despite what might be said on behalf of Douglas—and Jaffa concedes that Douglas had a potent practical case for trying to muddle through the sectional division—he thought accepting this "degradation of democratic dogma" would be catastrophic, because it "transforms democracy into 'permissive egalitarianism.'" Jaffa was prescient here, since today most claims for "equal rights" are not based on nature or mutual consent but rather on willful self-assertion, identical to the willful self-assertion of the rightness of owning slaves. The argument today for "democratic socialism," made popular recently by Bernie Sanders, is identical in form to Douglas's argument in favor of majoritarian popular sovereignty for deciding the slavery question, as "democratic" socialism deems it acceptable to abridge the property rights of a class of people by majority rule. "Lincoln," by contrast, "insisted that the case for popular government depended upon a standard of right and wrong independent of mere opinion and one which was not justified merely by the counting of heads."[18]

The dimensions of the theoretical limitations of majority rule were not fully clear to Jaffa right away, and Jaffa's own views went through distinct phases of development over time. While he encountered the Lincoln-Douglas debates in 1946 and began teaching a course based on the debates in 1950, his first article on the subject didn't appear until 1957, in a most unlikely journal: the first issue of the *Anchor Review*, which featured excerpts from Vladimir Nabokov's *Lolita* in the same issue. (Jaffa's critics might well suggest a scandalous parallel.) At the time Jaffa was still working on his dissertation, which became his first book, *Thomism and Ar-*

istotelianism, in 1952. This rich treatment of the conflict between the biblical and philosophical understandings of virtue and morality, which contains along the way its own lacerating critique of modern social science, deserves separate treatment. Alasdair MacIntyre called it "an unduly neglected minor modern classic."[19]

As he worked through the Lincoln-Douglas debates as a form of Socratic dialogue, Jaffa noticed that the spirit of consensus liberalism could be observed in contemporary historical writing about the Civil War, whose parallel revisionism held that the Civil War involved no fundamental issues. In particular Jaffa singled out James G. Randall and Avery Craven, two of the most prominent Civil War historians of his time, though Allan Nevins also shared this outlook. What previous historians had seen as an "irrepressible conflict" sown by the contradiction of the Founding itself—the toleration of slavery in a regime dedicated to freedom—had given way to a revisionist conclusion that it was a "needless" war brought on by a "blundering generation" (phrases that appear in Randall and Craven). Randall went so far as to say that "One of the most colossal misconceptions" was the "theory" that "fundamental motives produce war." Instead, Randall concluded, it was "fanaticism" and "irresponsible leadership" that caused the "stumble" into a ghastly war. Craven's argument was similar.

In addition to blurring the political ideas and principles behind the friction between North and South, this line of analysis also casts a dark shadow on Lincoln. While Randall and other revisionists didn't blame Lincoln alone for the coming of the war, the absence of "fundamental causes" opens Lincoln to the charge of being motivated primarily by personal ambition, transforming the Great Emancipator into the "Great Self-Promoter," heedless of the carnage his ambition cost the nation. Indeed this attitude toward Lincoln persists today and is especially popular with libertarians. At the very least, this outlook would diminish regard for Lincoln as a great statesman for the ages.

Jaffa was not the first to notice and call to account the defects of Civil War revisionism. Schlesinger wrote a scathing attack on Civil War revisionism for an unlikely venue, *Partisan Review*, in 1949. He slammed the "sentimentalism" that thinks "history teaches us that evil will be 'outmoded' by progress and that politics does not impose on us the necessity for decision and struggle.... To reject the moral actuality of the Civil War is to foreclose the possibility of an adequate account of its causes. More than that, it is to misconceive and grotesquely to sentimentalize the nature of history." If the revisionists lacked clarity about the moral conflict at the heart of the slavery controversy—Randall had called it merely "a very ancient labor system"—was there reason to have confidence in their judgments about other issues and times of historical importance (like the Cold War subsequently)? Schlesinger wondered:

> Are we to suppose that some future historian will echo Professor [Allan] Nevins' version of the "failure" of the eighteen-fifties and write: "The primary task of statesmanship in the nineteen-thirties was to furnish a workable adjustment between the United States and Germany, while offering strong inducements to the German people to abandon the police state and equal persuasions to the Americans to help the Nazis rather than scold them"? Will some future historian adapt Professor Randall's formula and write that the word "appeaser" was used "opprobriously" as if it were a "base" thing for an American to work with his Nazi fellow?[20]

But if Schlesinger was clear about the grave defects of the same kind of revisionism that would come to infect contemporaneous thinking about the Cold War a decade later, like his fellow consensus liberals he didn't go further to grapple with the more difficult aspects of the problem of squaring America's liberal tradition with the ruction caused by its most illiberal practice. Historians might be forgiven for being neither equipped nor inclined to probe deeply into the theoretical and abstract issues glossed over by revisionist consensus liberalism. Hartz, for example, responded weakly to Jaffa's critique of *The Liberal Tradition in America* with the understated acknowledgment that "Professor Jaffa is correct, I think, in stressing the deep ethical significance of the Civil War. There can be no doubt that the issue of slavery, like the issue of the Indian on a smaller scale, has posed a peculiar problem for the American liberal tradition."[21] But in his reply Hartz could do no better than to say that a comparative approach (that is, comparing U.S. history to European history) requires that the Civil War, and political conflict in America generally, be subsumed to a general liberal narrative, without evincing the slightest awareness or curiosity about the inner difficulties of liberalism. "The absence of a feudal inheritance," Jaffa argued to Hartz, actually *intensified* conflict in American politics "by reason of the immediacy of the demands of equality. . . . Hartz does not examine the genuine difficulties which inhere in the attempt to create a society dedicated to the proposition that all men are created equal."[22] Certainly today it is indisputable that political agitation about equality in America is more intense than in Europe. In later years Jaffa would complain that Hartz ignored him, but Jaffa did not appreciate that, behind his flowing prose, Hartz was simply incapable of engaging political ideas in a serious way. (Jaffa would later notice this at least in the case of Hofstadter, who, Jaffa wrote, lacked not only scholarly accuracy but also the "philosophical competence" to treat Lincoln adequately.)

But even allowing for the limited purview of historians, one should expect leading historians to avoid simplistically wrongheaded judgments like that of Daniel Boorstin on the Declara-

tion of Independence. While acknowledging that some Southern thinkers such as George Fitzhugh rejected the Declaration,
Boorstin thought it was not incompatible with Southern political
thought:

> Some southerners, for example, Chief Justice Taney in the Dred
> Scott decision, even argued that their position had been well
> stated in the Declaration. They adduced historical proof (*in my
> mind convincing*) that the authors of the sacred document had
> intended that Negroes be excluded from their professions of
> "equality."[23] (Emphasis added.)

No one who had carefully read Lincoln's Cooper Union address—
or his many replies to Taney's dreadful opinion in *Dred Scott*—
could think so, though in fairness to Boorstin this view had a lot
of company over the decades. The so-called "Social Darwinist"
William Graham Sumner wrote in the 1870s:

> But no man ever yet asserted that "all men are equal," meaning
> what he said. Although he said, "all men," he had in mind some
> limitation of the group he was talking about. Thus, if you asked
> Thomas Jefferson, when he was writing the first paragraph
> of the Declaration of Independence, whether in "all men" he
> meant to include negroes, he would have said that he was not
> talking about negroes. Ask anybody who says it now whether
> he means to include foreigners—Russian Jews, Hungarians,
> Italians—and he will draw his line somewhere. . . . Now, if we
> draw the line at all, the dogma is ruined.[24]

Apparently Sumner never read Lincoln's speeches on this point
either—not to mention any of Jefferson's many writings expressing exactly the contrary—and in any case it is ironic to see mid-
twentieth-century liberals aligning themselves with the thought
of a figure they (especially Hofstadter) otherwise reviled. It's dou-

bly ironic, since Sumner unwittingly ends with the same point Lincoln made about Douglas and the "wreck-mangled ruin" (Lincoln's phrase) that Douglas made of the Declaration by drawing a line against any racial or ethnic group.

Failing to take the Declaration seriously was of a piece with failing to take Lincoln seriously, which is usually done by sentimentalizing him or separating him from his thought. This was especially true of Progressive Era figures, including Theodore Roosevelt, Woodrow Wilson, and Herbert Croly, who all lionized Lincoln as a figure of nationalist power and purpose while omitting what that purpose was or what the anchoring principles behind it were.[25] Jaffa observed that "in some respects the vast accretion of Lincolniana has shrouded rather than disclosed the figure of the man within." Jaffa noticed that, while earlier historians held the Lincoln-Douglas debates in high regard, by the mid-twentieth century historians ignored or denigrated the debates. Lord Charnwood, in his 1917 biography of Lincoln—still in many ways the best political biography of Lincoln—judged that Lincoln in those debates "performed what, apart from results, was a work of intellectual merit beyond the compass of any American statesman since Hamilton."[26] But the self-professed revisionists soon came to declare that the debates had no serious content or meaning beyond mere partisan campaign rhetoric. Like Schlesinger, Jaffa trained his sights on the most prominent names among Civil War–era historians at that time, including Avery Craven and Allan Nevins, but held special scorn for James G. Randall, whose multivolume 1945 political biography *Lincoln the President* was thought to be the preeminent current work.

Randall was among those historians whose very fluid and readable prose effectively disguised the fact that he didn't have much to say. In *Crisis of the House Divided*, Jaffa quotes a long passage from Randall that in isolation is an embarrassment for its verbose insubstantiality. Randall conducted a "reanalysis" of the Lincoln-

Douglas debates, in which he concluded that Lincoln and Douglas had no fundamental differences between them but only "*seemed to differ*" (Randall's italics), which was the predicate for his eventual conclusion that the Civil War was a "needless war." Randall did not, however, follow the consequent logic of his argument, which would have cast Lincoln in a most unfavorable light as a person who exploited sectional friction merely to fulfill his selfish ambition, heedless of dividing the nation and plunging it into catastrophe. One wonders about the cognitive dissonance of approaches to Lincoln that celebrate his greatness while undermining the thought behind his political life.

Randall's contradictions live on in the work of his preeminent student, David Herbert Donald, whose much-heralded 1995 biography of Lincoln was purportedly "written from Lincoln's point of view," while missing or distorting Lincoln's actual point of view almost entirely. Like Randall, Donald thinks "Lincoln and Douglas naturally exaggerated their differences," none more so than on the meaning and importance of the Declaration of Independence:

> [T]he controversy over whether the framers of the Declaration of Independence intended to include blacks in announcing that all men are created equal dealt with an interesting, if ultimately unresolvable, historiographical problem, but it was not easy to see just what it had to do with the choice of a senator for Illinois in 1858. And the heated arguments [why "heated" if it was so inconsequential?] over the capacity and the future of the Negro race, with related controversies over social and political equality of the races, while showing fundamental philosophical differences between the two candidates, did not deal with any issue or legislation that was, or was likely to be, under consideration by the Congress of the United States.[27]

One might let this studied obtuseness pass had not Donald proclaimed that he was writing a biography "from Lincoln's point of view," never mind that there were many state laws at issue then, including in Illinois, based on racial distinctions that singled out blacks for discriminatory treatment because of their presumed inequality with whites. By failing to take the Declaration seriously, Donald fails to take Lincoln seriously. But Donald's final insult to Lincoln as Lincoln understood himself comes in this summary:

> One way to formulate that difference was to see Douglas as the advocate of majority rule and Lincoln as the defender of minority rights.[28]

Calhoun was the defender of "minority rights"; Lincoln was a defender of *natural* rights, which was the ultimate principle that qualifies majority rule, but which receives not a single mention in Donald's copious work, probably because the idea was so out of fashion or foreign to him. Donald overlooks, for example, Lincoln's defense of the practical necessity of majority rule rightly understood in Lincoln's First Inaugural Address. If you're going to make out Lincoln as a pre-twentieth-century "pragmatist"—the actual interpretive theme of Donald's biography—best to leave this inconvenience behind. (You can tell there is trouble ahead when Donald says in the preface that "My interpretation of Lincoln's political philosophy and religious views has been much influenced by the ideas of John Rawls.")

The question of Lincoln's understanding of equality, its relation to the problem of majority, and why it remains relevant to today requires a separate treatment in the next chapter. For my present purpose, it is useful to focus on one aspect of the bad historiography of Lincoln, namely, that once you downgrade Lincoln's ideas and principles, it follows as night follows day that Lincoln the statesman disappears from view—*but so does Douglas*. It wasn't just Lincoln whom revisionist history diminished; Douglas was swept away, too. From a literary point of view, on the surface the most remarkable aspect of Jaffa's *Crisis of the House Divided* is its extended treatment of the case in favor of Douglas's statecraft, which thereby sets the scene to understand more deeply Jaffa's case opposing the charge made in common against both Lincoln and Douglas—that they were *inconsistent*, if not in fact hypocritical or duplicitous. In other words, mere politicians.

Randall and Donald are superficially correct that Lincoln and Douglas did not differ on some key points, particularly in that Douglas privately shared Lincoln's goal of preserving the Union and placing slavery on a course of ultimate extinction, without, however, publicly acknowledging the latter aim. Douglas's sensible view was that the problem of slavery was not susceptible to a political solution, because, just as there is no such thing as being "a little bit pregnant," there was no middle ground between pro- and antislavery principles that could form a basis of compromise. Douglas's doctrine of "popular sovereignty"—allowing the people of the territories to vote slavery "up or down" and "not caring" himself what the result was—was based on his view or hope that the people of the new Western territories would reject slavery, while the South would feel itself secure. His was a plausible strategy of muddling through even though there are good reasons for doubting Douglas's calculations of the future, but it was marred by the required sacrifice of moral principle involved, which Lincoln thought fatal to republican government over time if not checked.

In this respect, the clash between Lincoln and Douglas finds some parallels with Churchill's reflections on the Munich crisis of 1938. (Indeed, Jaffa cites Churchill's essay "Consistency in Politics" as part of his context for understanding Douglas's strategy; I am merely following Jaffa's lead as I think he'd want his students to do.) Douglas's doctrine of popular sovereignty wasn't exactly an appeasement of the slave interest, but neither was a deliberate policy of muddling through self-evidently imprudent. As Churchill reflected about the "principles of morals and action" that should be learned from the Munich disaster, he admitted that there is a case for muddling through:

> Those who are prone by temperament and character to seek sharp and clear-cut solutions of difficult and obscure problems, who are ready to fight whenever some challenge comes from a foreign Power, have not always been right. On the other hand, those whose inclination is to bow their heads, to seek patiently and faithfully for peaceful compromise, are not always wrong. On the contrary, in the majority of instances they may be right, not only morally but from a practical standpoint.[29]

Churchill's ultimate case against the appeasement of Munich was not the ex post facto judgment of the adverse result, but that the principle of *honor*—in that case honoring a commitment to join allied France in defending Czechoslovakia against German aggression—would have resulted prospectively in the correct decision. The rough parallel in the case of Lincoln against Douglas is Lincoln's view that the principles of the Declaration needed to be honored or else they would ultimately be lost, and the cause of self-government along with them.

But this did not mean that a direct crusade for the abolition of slavery was the best course of action. Lincoln understood, as single-minded abolitionists often disappointed or frustrated with Lincoln did not, that *securing* a right is not as easy as *declaring* a right. Perhaps the single most meaningful passage in Lincoln's eulogy to Henry Clay is this observation of Clay's statesmanlike bearing:

> He ever was on principle and in feeling, opposed to slavery. . . .
> He did not perceive, that on a question of human right, the negroes were to be excepted from the human race. And yet Mr.

Clay was the owner of slaves. Cast into life where slavery was already widely spread and deeply seated, he did not perceive, as I think no wise man has perceived, how it could be at *once* eradicated, without producing a greater evil, even to the cause of human liberty itself. His feeling and his judgment, therefore, ever led him to oppose both extremes of opinion on the subject.[30]

This describes perfectly Lincoln's outlook on the problem as well. (Incidentally, it is later in the same paragraph of this 1852 speech that Lincoln takes note of Southern attacks on the Declaration of Independence, adding "So far as I have learned, the first American, of any note, to do or attempt this, was the late John C. Calhoun.")

Thus in Jaffa's treatment of the Lincoln-Douglas debates we see an acute example of matching ends and means amid difficult circumstances, and a demonstration of why the idea of statesmanship as an intelligible mode of political thought is so controversial. Jaffa's treatment of Douglas is more generous and sympathetic than a pro-Douglas biographer might produce, and indeed was more favorable to Douglas than Allan Nevins, for example. At the same time, Jaffa's vindication of Lincoln emphasizes Lincoln's prudence, which so many historians miss—his detractors deliberately so. Ultimately Jaffa's evaluation of the two combatants comes down to explaining the ground for making distinctions between the surface moderation of both men. In this respect, *Crisis of the House Divided* is more than a study in the issues of the Lincoln-Douglas debates, but is a profound reflection on statesmanship.

No one expressed the smug and cynical view of Lincoln, and less comprehension of the idea of statesmanship, than Richard Hofstadter, whom Jaffa made a special target of withering scorn. Jaffa judged Hofstadter's famous essay "Abraham Lincoln and the Self-Made Myth" in *The American Political Tradition* to be an "intensely supercilious work" that conveys contempt for politics with its judgment that Lincoln "was thoroughly and completely a politician" and an "opportunist," which in context is not a compliment.[31] The theme of honor in political life and political thought turns out to be central to this disputation.

Hofstadter sets out a problem common to many treatments of Lincoln, namely, that while he may have been a great president, his prepresidential career is less exemplary, if not dubious. But can the two distinct phases of Lincoln's career be so neatly separated? Hofstadter simply repeats Douglas's charge that Lincoln was a "trimmer," someone who says one thing before one audience and a different or opposite thing before another—the most typical practice of nearly all practicing politicians and the source of public disrespect of the political class. But the charge carries extra weight if the politician is presenting himself as engaging matters of the highest moral principle. "Trimming" on the issue of equality and slavery is more problematic than hedging about ethanol subsidies in Iowa. In regard to Lincoln expressing opposition to full social and political equality for Negroes before some southern Illinois audiences where racial prejudice ran especially strong while speaking more broadly about equality in northern Illinois, Hofstadter says, "It is impossible to avoid the conclusion that so far as the Negro was concerned, Lincoln could not escape the moral insensitivity that is characteristic of the average white American."

Any would-be politician or statesman today can learn important lessons from a close look at Jaffa's quarrel with Hofstadter on this point. Jaffa begins his disputation of Hofstadter by defending the honor of politics, without which human sociality is ultimately unredeemable:

> That Lincoln was a professional politician and vote getter may be freely granted, but the case for democracy, we believe, rests upon the possibility that this occupation may be an honorable

one. . . . Hofstadter would have us believe that the evidence of the pre-presidential Lincoln, at least, is not evidence to suggest the possibility of reconciling the demands of the vocation of democratic politics with the demands for honor.[32]

The case for Lincoln's course rests on understanding why he was confronting exactly the same difficulty as the Founders did at the time of the Constitution:

> But if [the Founders] had attempted to secure *all* the rights of *all* men they would have ended in *no* rights secured for *any* men. The truth of the proposition, or the sincerity of their intentions, was in no wise impugned by the moderation of their actions.[33]

Likewise, for Lincoln to have contested for greater social equality for as-yet unfreed slaves amid a general climate of racial hostility would have meant splitting the nascent Republican Party and ensuring that his own political career would be very short.

Strangely, Hofstadter seems to perceive this ground of understanding Lincoln perfectly well, in a passage that Jaffa nowhere acknowledges:

> As a practical politician he was naturally very much concerned about those public sentiments which no statesman can safely disregard. It was impossible, he had learned, safely to disregard either the feeling that slavery is a moral wrong or the feeling—held by an even larger portion of the public—that Negroes must not be given political and social equality.[34]

Yet Hofstadter somehow can't make out whether Lincoln might have trimmed his rhetoric in service of any consistent purpose or understanding of how to maneuver under these circumstances:

It is not easy to decide whether the true Lincoln is the one who spoke in Chicago or the one who spoke in Charleston. Possibly the man devoutly believed each of the utterances at the time he delivered it; possibly his mind too was a house divided against itself. In any case it is easy to see in all this the behavior of a professional politician looking for votes.[35]

Hofstadter adds to his criticism of Lincoln with his memorable—and accurate!—description of the Emancipation Proclamation as having "all the moral grandeur of a bill of lading." After noting the essential temporizing of this strictly war measure, Hofstadter concludes that "Perhaps the largest reasonable indictment of [Lincoln] is simply that in such matters he was a follower and not a leader of public opinion."

The glaring anomaly of the barrenness of the Emancipation Proclamation ought to be a large clue about Lincoln's prudence, which is especially apparent in a close reading of Lincoln's overall handling of this delicate problem both before and after he became president. But if you begin with the theme that Lincoln was a mere grasping politician, a person of expediency, then indeed you will have trouble perceiving the "true" Lincoln. Hofstadter neither acknowledges Lincoln's lengthy answers to Douglas's charge, nor evinces any interest in examining Lincoln's statements closely. Here we see that the historian's tendency not to take political ideas seriously is matched by a tendency not to treat political rhetoric seriously.

The first thing that a careful listener or reader might note in Lincoln's "trimmed" speeches is his equivocations about social and political equality. In denying Douglas's demagogic (but very effective) charge that he intended full social and political equality for slaves, Lincoln allowed that "Certainly the negro is not our equal in color—perhaps in many other respects." Here "equal" can mean *same* as much as it might mean equal in a social sense.

"Only the prejudice of his audiences would find a judgment of Negro inferiority in such an assertion," Jaffa notes. "Perhaps" is another word Lincoln chose carefully. About the equal right not to be ruled without consent, "in the right to put into his mouth the bread that his own hands have earned, he is the equal of every other man, white or black," Lincoln said repeatedly. "The contrast," Jaffa argues, "between the ambiguity of what Lincoln says about Negro inequality and the unambiguousness of what he says about Negro equality is striking."[36]

Jaffa goes further to note that Lincoln's verb tense sequence was revealing to the careful listener. While he often said some variation of "I am not now nor have ever been in favor of full equality for the Negro," he didn't say what he *would be* in the future. The silences of political thinkers and statesmen are often as important as their pronouncements. In *A New Birth of Freedom* Jaffa compares Lincoln's careful handling of the implications of equality amid widespread public racial animus to Macaulay's analysis of the British Toleration Act of 1689, which was in substance a halting and wholly inadequate protection of religious liberty for a similar reason—public prejudice against Catholics and other nonconformist Protestant sects. As Thomas Macaulay put it:

> That the provisions which have been recapitulated are cumbrous, puerile, inconsistent with each other, inconsistent with the true theory of religious liberty, must be acknowledged. All that can be said in their defense is this; that *they removed a vast mass of evil without shocking a vast mass of prejudice.* (Emphasis added.)[37]

The rough parallel is obvious: ending first the spread of slavery, and then slavery itself, would "remove a vast mass of evil without shocking a vast mass of prejudice." But of course Lincoln understood that political contests involve shaping and changing public opinion by maneuvering within the existing confines of public opinion.

Just as Lincoln thought the rise of the idea of slavery as a positive good was the result of the "debauching of the public mind," so too did he understand the importance of planting and defending axioms of right in the public mind to germinate over time. Lincoln noted that their debates were being widely reprinted in newspapers around the country; it would be odd to suppose that he was deliberately inconsistent in his replies to Douglas's "trimming" charge. But a more subtle clue is perhaps a short, unexplained reference Lincoln made in the Charleston debate of September 18, 1958. There, in a highly effective and often sarcastic attack on Douglas, Lincoln denied any intention of pursuing full equality for Negroes, saying that "I have never seen to my knowledge a man, woman, or child who was in favor of producing a perfect equality, social and political, between negroes and white men." But then he added this detail in the next sentence: "I recollect but one distinguished instance that I ever heard of so frequently as to be entirely satisfied of its correctness—and that is the case of Judge Douglas' old friend Colonel Richard M. Johnson." The transcripts of the debate record "laughter" after this remark, likely for Lincoln turning the tables on Douglas by drawing in Douglas's "old friend" on the side of a more expansive understanding of equality. It was not the only turn of phrase that brought laughter and cheers from the audience. Jaffa says, "Lincoln was using this hilarity both to conceal and to reveal some serious thoughts."[38]

Who was Colonel Johnson, and how well known was his personal story to the public that Lincoln addressed? Johnson had been a military commander, a congressman, a senator, and was President Martin Van Buren's vice president from 1837 to 1841. He had two children with a slave, Sally Chinn, whom he inherited from his father. Unlike the nature of Thomas Jefferson's supposed connubial relations with Sally Hemings, this relationship was no mere indulgence of appetites. Johnson provided for his children's education and wrote a heart-wrenching letter expressing his grief when one of his daughters died. Because Kentucky law prohibited him from marrying Chinn or leaving his estate to Chinn or his mixed-race children after his death, Johnson simply deeded part of his estate to them before his passing. Here, then, was an actual example of someone practicing racial equality. Lincoln did not draw out the significance of this example; he merely mentioned it, planting it as a stumbling block to Douglas's overt racism. Lincoln also needled Douglas and other racists for needing laws against interracial marriage, and pledged to defend laws against interracial marriage to save Douglas and his friends from the temptation of it, to roars of laughter from the audience.

Ascending from careful rhetoric to the practice of statesmanship, Jaffa comments:

> For consistency, in any narrow sense, is seldom if ever the path of wise statesmanship. . . . Mere verbal consistency is no criterion of genuine consistency in politics. . . . Different words may advance the same cause in different circumstances, and sometimes words of contrary bearing must be used at the same time to advance that cause given the circumstances. A statesman has only a limited control of the conditions within which he must act. If, within the limits of his control, he acts inconsistently with the ends of true policy, he is justly to be blamed.[39]

One might pause here and reflect on the recent case of gay marriage in the United States, where both Hillary Clinton and Barack Obama, until as late as 2012, followed the majority of public opinion in publicly opposing gay marriage, even though it was widely believed that they privately supported it. That Obama in particular was lying (Jon Stewart's term in 2009) could be seen by the refusal of his Justice Department to defend the Clinton-era Defense of

Marriage Act, or the conspicuous absence of any public argument from either Clinton or Obama in favor of traditional marriages. The end of their policy was clearly inconsistent with their public pronouncements. It will be curious to see whether historians of later eras evaluate Obama's and Clinton's prevarications on the issue in the same way Hofstadter and others treated Lincoln.

Jaffa continues:

> The problem of applying the moral judgment of history to a statesman requires, therefore, a fourfold criterion: first, is the goal a worthy one; second, does the statesman judge wisely as to what is and what is not within his power; third, are the means selected apt to produce the intended results; and fourth, in "inconsistently" denying any intention to do those things which he could not in any case do, does he say or do anything to hinder future statesmen from more perfectly attaining his goal when altered conditions bring more of that goal within the range of possibility?[40]

It is not too hard to make out Lincoln's deliberate course from the earliest moments of his return to politics in the early 1850s as the slavery controversy reached critical mass. Jaffa argued that "Negroes have voting rights and serve on juries today owing in large measure to the fact that Lincoln in the 1850s disavowed any intention to make them voters or jurors." This is hard for the contemporary mind to grasp, just as paradox of all kinds often eludes comprehension. And so modern historians and intellectually lazy political observers champion Lincoln's brief remark that "I claim not to have controlled events, but confess plainly that events have controlled me" to make him out as little more than an improvising "pragmatist," and therefore a prototype for Franklin Delano Roosevelt and Bill Clinton. (Seriously.)

It is no exaggeration to say that *Crisis of the House Divided*

changed the course of subsequent Lincoln scholarship in several
ways. First, it routed the revisionism and sentimentalization of
Lincoln, such that even liberal writers who wish to contest Jaffa's
interpretation have to treat Lincoln more seriously as a thinker,
and therefore wrestle directly with Jaffa's underlying philosophical
approach. (In this regard, David Herbert Donald's flaccid biography of Lincoln is an anomaly.) The number of titles that depart
from the gauzy revisionist mode of the Progressive and consensus liberalism era are too numerous to mention. Several historians and political scientists have taken up the Lincoln-Douglas
debates and closely related aspects of Lincoln along similar lines
as Jaffa, especially Allen Guelzo, Joseph Fornieri, William Lee
Miller, William C. Harris, and David Zarefsky. But the most im-
pressive example is John Burt's 2013 book, *Lincoln's Tragic Pragmatism: Lincoln, Douglas, and Moral Conflict*. Although Burt uses
the regrettable "P" word (pragmatism) in his title, his presentation
of what he calls "pragmatism" bears a strong resemblance to what
Jaffa means by statesmanship. More significant is Burt's emphasis
on the unavoidable tragedy of the defects and limitations of liberal democracy that made the Civil War inevitable—a theme not
uncongenial to Jaffa's literary side going back to his undergraduate
days. Jaffa more than once compared Lincoln to one of Shakespeare's tragic heroes. (It is probably not a coincidence that Burt is
a professor of English rather than an academic historian or political scientist.) Above all, Burt singles out Jaffa as the unavoidable
landmark from which he has to take his bearing:

> The ultimate model for this book, however, and its ultimate
> antagonist, is Harry Jaffa's great book *Crisis of the House Divided*
> (1959) and its sequel, *A New Birth of Freedom* (2000). Like Jaffa,
> in this book I seek to engage in historically situated philosophy
> without assuming that philosophical truths are completely the
> prisoners of their own age.[41]

In contrast to Jaffa, Burt argues for making Kant and Rawls the true philosophical lodestars for understanding Lincoln, though Rawls's apolitical liberalism is a very poor fit. Some people just can't shake Rawls even for a moment. I heard at the time that Jaffa appreciated Burt's book, but was too old and infirm to write a review or reply. A response might have noted that Burt doesn't really succeed in effectively disputing Jaffa's central claims about Douglas, and essentially agrees with Jaffa's understanding of the reciprocal relation of equality and consent. Most significantly, Burt agrees with Jaffa's contention that Lincoln believed, and aimed for, genuine racial equality in the fullness of time.[42]

While forcing liberals in particular to treat Lincoln's ideas—and by extension the American Founding—more seriously, Jaffa also called a halt to the liberal Brinks Job of making Lincoln an honorary Democrat. The Progressives severed Lincoln from his ideas, which made it possible for Franklin Delano Roosevelt to say "I think it is time for us Democrats to claim Lincoln as one of our own." New York Governor Mario Cuomo edited a collection of Lincoln's writings and speeches in the late 1980s, writing in his introduction that "I've always admired Lincoln because he's reassuring to politicians like me," by which he meant liberal politicians. Tony Kushner, the left-leaning playwright who wrote the very good screenplay for Steven Spielberg's movie *Lincoln* asserted that, if Lincoln were alive today, he'd be a Democrat. And no list of liberal Lincoln larcenists would be complete without mention of Barack Obama, who began his presidential campaign in homage to Lincoln on the steps of the state capitol in Springfield, Illinois. Like other liberals, Obama's Lincoln is divorced from Lincoln's understanding of the American Founding, though Obama is more artful and subtle than most.[43]

This attempted assimilation will persist so long as conservatives and Republicans cede Lincoln so easily, as they are often wont to do. Right now every aspiring Republican identifies the party's soul with Ronald Reagan, which makes perfect sense not only because he's more recent but also because many of the hot-button issues from Reagan's presidency are still front and center today. As worthy as the example of Reagan is, the Party of Lincoln would be well advised to pay closer attention to the principles of Lincoln. It is astonishing how seldom Republican candidates mention that the GOP is the Party of Lincoln or bother to employ even a crude approximation of the theme offered by an accolade to the Great Emancipator, which would allow candidates to talk about how we might achieve emancipation from dysfunctional or oppressive government today.

While the GOP identifies imperfectly with Lincoln, it is significant that Jaffa's work caused Lincoln to be embraced by conservatives after decades of neglect and in some cases hostility. Much hatred of Lincoln on the right remains, especially among old Confederate die-hards, but also among libertarians such as Lew Rockwell, who has long charged that Lincoln "fastened the federal leviathan on the body of the old republic."[44] The idea that secession on behalf of slavery could be a defensible example of limited government strikes most ordinary citizens as plainly bizarre, but that's perhaps emblematic of why libertarianism attracts so few adherents. These kinds of attacks are as predictable as they are unoriginal, though the irony of attributing the Civil War to economic conflicts (specifically tariffs), which aligns libertarian Lincoln critics with Marxist explanations, goes largely unnoticed.

More curious was the neglect or dismissal of Lincoln among more traditional conservatives. As mentioned previously, Russell Kirk ignores him in *The Conservative Mind*, though not in later works. *National Review* was mostly hostile to Lincoln in its first decade, a quirk—though not the only quirk of the magazine's early years—of its idiosyncratic senior staff and their main targets of interest in its first decade. Jaffa was the first person to defend Lincoln in the pages of *National Review*, appearing for the first time in 1965 to dispute Frank Meyer, the legendary "fusion-ist" writer who had attacked Lincoln for undermining both the Constitution and federalism.

That first appearance in *National Review* began a long friend-ship and association between Jaffa and William F. Buckley Jr., whose quiet generosity extended to paying travel expenses for Jaffa and his wife to attend his son's graduation from Yale after, as Jaffa explained after Buckley's death, he had "scraped the bar-rel" to enable his son to attend Yale in the first place. But it also marked the first skirmish between Jaffa and other prominent con-servatives, which I will analyze in the following chapters. Of more immediate note, recent conservatives have come to embrace Lin-coln accurately and without reservation. A string of conservative writers, such as Andrew Ferguson and Richard Brookhiser, have produced pro-Lincoln books that take account of Jaffa. Ferguson spoke of "the strange bravery" of the author of *Crisis of the House Divided*. Brookhiser wrote at Jaffa's death that "Harry was a hand-ful," but he meant that as a compliment.[45]

Maybe the most significant recent Lincoln title is from the cur-rent editor of *National Review*: Rich Lowry's *Lincoln Unbound: How an Ambitious Young Railsplitter Saved the American Dream— And How We Can Do It Again*. The book answers the challenge of how today's Republicans can become the Party of Lincoln once again. Jaffa received only a single passing reference in Lowry's book, but his spirit is amply abundant throughout.

Just as Jaffa's serendipitous discovery of the Lincoln-Douglas debates led to a moment of lifetime inspiration, so too a num-ber of students and general readers have stumbled across *Crisis of the House Divided* and found it profoundly transformative. Allen Guelzo, whose own contributions to the literature about Lincoln are of the highest quality, says *Crisis* is "incontestably the great-est Lincoln book of the [twentieth] century." Thomas Pangle, an-other target of Jaffa's criticism, said *Crisis* was "the single most

influential volume of Strauss-inspired 'American politics' literature." Harvey Mansfield Jr. called it simply "the best book ever
written on Abraham Lincoln."⁴⁶

But, as mentioned previously, the sequel to *Crisis* that Jaffa
promised upon its publication in 1959—*A New Birth of Freedom*, which would extend his analysis of Lincoln as a philosophic
statesman through the Gettysburg Address—was forty years in
coming. The popular account is that Jaffa became obsessed with
picking fights with his friends, who became former friends in
most cases. There is an element of truth to this perception. His
students would often unsuccessfully attempt to dissuade him from
aiming gratuitous personal insults at some of his targets and wince
at the rancor he instigated. Mansfield, an occasional Jaffa target,
charitably ascribed this aspect of Jaffa to "an excess of fighting
spirit," of which, as the author of *Manliness*, Mansfield couldn't
wholly disapprove. (And unlike Berns, Jaffa and Mansfield did
largely reconcile before Jaffa's passing.)

The long delay in the appearance of *A New Birth of Freedom*
and some of the fights Jaffa started with his friends were connected to a big problem that Jaffa recognized he needed to solve:
how to get the idea of *equality* right. It could be said that the
greatest phrase in American political thought is "all men are created equal," which is likewise the most problematic and mischievous phrase in American political thought. In an age of destructive runaway egalitarianism, already quite evident to Jaffa in the
1950s, understanding the nature and limits of equality is the most
crucial intellectual and political task of our time.

Jaffa acknowledged this difficulty in one of his essays from the
late 1950s, where he observed that "the Declaration of Independence, while it propounded a purpose, propounded a problem as
well." Sorting out that problem took him forty years, and by his
own admission he didn't finish to his satisfaction. There is still a
lot of work to be done.

CHAPTER 6

Equality as a Principle and a Problem

*... the Declaration of Independence, while it
propounded a purpose, propounded a problem as well.*

HARRY JAFFA, 1961

The *Federalist Papers* are rightly regarded as the "owner's manual" to the Constitution. Although I never
thought to ask Harry Jaffa whether he had a favorite single passage
or number from *The Federalist*, I have a hunch he'd have pointed
to this sentence by James Madison in *Federalist 55*: "Had every
Athenian citizen been a Socrates, every Athenian assembly would
still have been a mob." Jaffa was fond of quoting a remark Leo
Strauss liked to make in class that "Socrates had more in common
with any intelligent American than with any stupid Athenian."
For Strauss, the difference between intelligence and stupidity was
more important than any difference between an ancient Athenian
and a modern American," Jaffa explains.[1] The intelligent middle-
class American represented the achievement of a certain thresh-
old of enlightened political literacy and civic virtue—a "universal
aristocracy," Strauss theorized. In other words, Americans at their
best were not a mob. But how is such a level of civic virtue to be
maintained?

Both Madison and Strauss raise the question of wisdom in political life, and how to square the circular problem of democratic
rule and individual rights, or how to mark out the nature and limits of majority rule and the limits of equality—the problem at the
center of Lincoln's dispute with Douglas. Although the forms of
majority rule carry on as before, increasingly Americans are governed without their consent on vital questions, by either bureaucratic or judicial usurpation of legislative power.

Jaffa summarizes the essential problem of political life in any
regime that aspires to be just in his typically compact way:

> The dilemma of political life consists above all in this: how to
> obtain an appropriate recognition of wisdom among the un-
> wise, among those whose very unwisdom creates the need for
> wisdom in political affairs. The difficulty is not so much that
> the unwise always reject the claims of wisdom; on the contrary,
> they have sometimes been too prone to give power to those
> who advance those claims. The difficulty stems from the fact
> that it is pretenders to wisdom, who unscrupulously exploit the
> need for wisdom of the unwise.[2]

Berns has his own version of this challenge:

> The political problem, more visible at some times than at oth-
> ers, is how to get consent to wise decisions or wise leadership.
> In a democracy this means how to educate, how to form the
> characters of citizens so that they will give their consent to wise
> leadership and withhold it from fools, bigots, and demagogues.[3]

This statement of the problem immediately brings to mind
some of the best-known axioms from *The Federalist*, starting with
the observation from number 51 that if men were angels—meaning wise and just—no government would be necessary, or that if
angels governed men, no controls on government would be neces-

sary. Likewise, one thinks also of Madison's reminder in *Federalist* 10 that "enlightened statesmen will not always be at the helm."

This leads to the first major objection to Jaffa's treatment of Lincoln, and to the problem of securing political wisdom through statesmanship. Since Jaffa himself admits that the supply of Lincolns is limited, the question might be put thus: Is there an alternative to Lincoln? In a democratic regime does not the virtue of the statesman presuppose or require the virtue of the people to some large extent? How to untangle this reciprocal necessity?

Beyond this paradox lies a more urgent contemporary problem that connects to the Lincoln question, and this is the problem of *equality*. Equality is the scourge of our time, the founding principle for every conceivable grievance and demand for redress. The effacement of the distinction between natural rights and positive rights has opened the door to the endless expansion of "rights," with the ultimate object of creating a "right" to other people's property and, increasingly, even the "right" to control other people's speech. While rights expand, duties disappear. Tocqueville, about whom Jaffa had little to say, just as Tocqueville omits any mention of the Declaration of Independence or natural rights, warned of this. Tocqueville predicted that the passion for equality would become a "delirium," in which equality would trump liberty. "But for equality they have an ardent, insatiable, eternal, invincible passion; they want equality in freedom, and, if they cannot get it, they still want it in slavery."[4]

In other words, the principle of equality in the American Founding was unable to remain within the boundaries of the Founders, and has become the basis for an endless welfare state. And Progressives enlist Lincoln on behalf of this project. That this is a faithful reading neither of the Founding nor of Lincoln has become lost in the battle of the books and rejected as an obsolete opinion of the past. It is almost futile to point out that James Madison explained in *Federalist* 10 that the *first* object of government is "the protection of different and *unequal* faculties of acquiring property," which would inevitably result in "different degrees and kinds of property" (emphasis added). In other words, a regime of equal *rights* would have to recognize and protect unequal *results*, which became the axis of today's divide between equality of opportunity and equality of result. When the left complains today that the Constitution is "undemocratic," what they mean is that it contains obstacles to majoritarian pursuit of redistribution and endless equality.

Lincoln would seem to have been well within Madison's compass in his scorching reply to the *Dred Scott* decision, where he said that the "all men are created equal" clause of the Declaration did not mean to declare that people are equal *in all respects*, but just in their natural rights—rights that are today denigrated as "negative liberties" against government power. So far so good—but Lincoln went on to say that the Declaration's equality principle was intended for "future use," by being "a standard maxim for free society, constantly looked to, constantly labored for, and even though never perfectly attained, constantly approximated, and thereby constantly spreading and deepening its influence."[5] This can be read as an expansive understanding of equality, and liberals zoom in on the Gettysburg Address as *the* moment when Lincoln clarified or even *refounded* the nation on egalitarian lines. Garry Wills argues that Lincoln at Gettysburg proclaimed a "new constitution . . . substituted for the one they brought there with them. . . . Because of [the Gettysburg Address], we live in a different America."[6]

This view finds equal (pun intended) recognition on the right—in fact, Wills borrowed his interpretation from conservatives, as we shall see. Conservative political scientist George Carey writes: "It certainly is not unreasonable to associate Lincoln's words and thoughts with the egalitarianism that characterizes the modern, centralized welfare state." But it is also perfectly reasonable to argue the opposite, as Carey generously acknowledges in a footnote I can't resist citing: "For a fine effort along these lines, particularly to 'unlink' Lincoln from the Progressives, see Steven Hayward, 'Whose Lincoln?' *Reason* 23 (May 1991). Hayward may well be right in arguing that Lincoln's language and concerns place him well outside the Progressive camp."[7] Carey doesn't think so, though John Murley of the Rochester Institute of Technology, in reviewing the matter, concludes that "Hayward is indeed correct."[8]

The article to which Carey, Murley, and several other authors refer was a cover feature in the unlikely venue of *Reason* magazine in 1991 that commented on the way Lincoln and equality were portrayed in director Ken Burns's wildly popular documentary film *The Civil War*, which aired on PBS. I was surprised to see what I regarded as a mere act of journalism take on such a long half-life, but perhaps this indicates a failure of Lincoln defenders to advance his case more broadly. In his Civil War film Burns says that America is "constantly trying to enlarge the definition and deepen the meaning of 'all men are created equal,'" and that "we have not fulfilled the promises that we made at the end of the war." One of the "talking heads" featured in the film was historian Barbara Fields, who said that the war "established a standard that will not mean anything until we have finished the work. . . . If some citizens live in houses and others live on the street, the Civil War is still going on. It's still to be fought, and . . . it can still be lost." Over to you, Black Lives Matter.

That Lincoln's own views, the expansiveness of his *Dred Scott* remarks notwithstanding, do not make him out as a prototype Great Society liberal is an easy proposition to establish. One thinks of his letter to the Workingmen's Democratic-Republican Association, in which he wrote, "That some should be rich, shows that others may become rich, and hence is just encouragement to industry and enterprize. Let not him who is houseless pull down the house of another; but let him labor diligently and build one for himself, thus by example assuring that his own shall be safe from violence when built."[9] Closer to home, Lincoln conditioned a request for charity from his own ne'er-do-well stepbrother John D. Johnston with the offer of matching one-for-one every dollar Johnston earned for a year. But Johnston refused to work and received nothing. Lincoln clearly recognized that unqualified charity would corrupt the character of the recipient, and he would unquestionably be aghast at a modern welfare state that makes charitable aid an "entitlement."

But even if we bust Progressives for attempted Grand Theft Lincoln, that still leaves undisturbed the general argument about the meaning of "all men are created equal" in the Declaration. The loot is still in the vault. Is the contemporary liberal version so easily contained? Leave aside for the moment the cognitive dissonance of the left, which can't decide whether the Founders were contemptible hypocrites for saying "all men are created equal," or whether the nation today is hypocritical for not living up to those terms. The great thing about being a liberal is never having to worry about consistency or the philosophical provenance of your views. One result of the Civil War is that the term "equal" made it into the text of the Constitution by way of the Fourteenth Amendment, which became in time *the* entire Constitution for many liberals, and a source of endless possibility. Back in his law school lecturer phase, Barack Obama perfectly expressed the left's position on the constitutional meaning of equality when he lamented that the Supreme Court of the Earl Warren era didn't go far enough in expanding the principle of equality: "The Supreme Court never ventured into the issues of redistribution of wealth and sort of more basic issues of political and economic justice in this society. . . . It didn't break free from the essential constraints that were placed by the Founding Fathers in the Constitution."[10] What are the alternatives?

One reason there might be a need for an alternative to Lincoln or a Lincolnian understanding of equality is that Jaffa might be wrong about Lincoln, or Lincoln might be wrong about how to understand the principle of equality in the Founding, which amounts to the same thing. The first witness for the prosecution, and Jaffa's main adversary on the right much more than Walter Berns, was Willmoore Kendall, one of the great political scientists of the conservative revival of the 1950s. Like Jaffa, he was concerned above all else with the principles of the American Founding and the practice of majority rule. He developed a line of argument that sought for the stability of America in the virtue of the people more so than in the virtue of the statesman. But he didn't stop there. Like Jaffa, he knew that a serious answer to these problems required thinking about the most profound depths of democratic philosophy.

It is worth pausing a moment here for a few words about Kendall's extraordinary intellect, character, and career before proceeding to his arguments. He was William F. Buckley Jr.'s mentor and principal teacher at Yale in the late 1940s, and suggested some of the more provocative and memorable passages in Buckley's debut book *God and Man at Yale*, later becoming an early senior editor of *National Review*. Buckley later made him a character in one of his Blackford Oakes spy novels, and he was the basis for a character in a Saul Bellow short story. Kendall was strongly influenced by Strauss, at one point calling Strauss "*the* great teacher of political philosophy, not of our time alone, but of any time since Machiavelli"—an extravagant claim that perhaps only Jaffa publicly shared.[11] In a letter to Strauss in 1960 Kendall proclaimed that "I come back to a profession in which you and your students have so changed the standards of excellence that I find myself writing with the lot of you—I almost said the whole damn lot of you— peering constantly over my shoulder."[12]

Kendall holds the distinction, or perhaps we should say the

honor, of provoking Yale University to get rid of him in the early 1960s by buying out his tenure contract for a confidential figure rumored to be five years' salary (in part because he was so popular with students). He liked to provoke students and colleagues with seemingly outlandish positions—especially the argument that Athens rightly executed Socrates—that were grounded in some fundamental inquiries into the defects of liberal theory. Jaffa especially liked Kendall's Socrates provocation, writing that Socrates "would have chuckled to himself that the people of Athens would have executed Kendall a lot sooner than they did him, had they been given the chance." Leo Paul de Alvarez, one of Kendall's colleagues at the University of Dallas, recalled that Kendall "always tuned in to Walter Cronkite to find out what the Liberal line was for the day, and would end up shouting at the screen, 'And that's not the way it is, Walter!'"[13]

Buckley recalled the time in late 1949 when a Yale faculty meeting convened to deplore the Smith Act, by which members of the Communist Party were being convicted for subversion, where Kendall dropped a brick on his colleagues:

> When it was Willmoore Kendall's turn to comment, he said, "You know, there's an old colored gentleman who looks after my Fellow's suite. He said to me this morning, 'Professor, is it true there's people who want to overthrow the government by force and violence?' I said, 'Yes, that's true Jamieson.' He said, 'Well, Professor, why don't we just run them out of town?' I think Jamieson has a more sophisticated understanding of democratic theory than any of you gentlemen."[14]

You can see why Kendall was not popular with the Yale faculty.

But he also didn't get along with many conservatives. Buckley observed that Kendall was seldom on speaking terms with more than one colleague at a time at *National Review*, and he resigned from the magazine in a huff in 1963, barely communicating with Buckley again afterward. In this respect he was the perfect analogue for Jaffa, and but for his untimely death in 1967 at age fifty-eight, Kendall and Jaffa might have carried on an epic disputation, while yet agreeing with each other on many issues apart from the mainstream of popular conservative thought. Kendall, for example, joined Jaffa in regarding the Civil Rights Act of 1964 and the Voting Rights Act of 1965 as *conservative* political triumphs, against the views of many conservatives who objected to the constitutional defects and erosion of federalism those laws contained. More so than Jaffa, he did not think much of Russell Kirk's brand of Burkean conservatism, which he found "hopelessly confusing." Kendall said that Kirk's writing addressed "the wrong topics in an inappropriate vocabulary. . . . Let us ask, Is [Kirk's] teaching *sound*, that is, a teaching that contemporary American conservatism would be well-advised to let the Benevolent Sage of Mecosta talk it into accepting? And let us at once give the only possible answer, which is No."[15] Here he found perfect alignment with Walter Berns, who wrote a harsh and sarcastic critique of Kirk's conservatism in the *Journal of Politics* in 1955.[16] Kendall, like Jaffa, thought we should seek for conservatism from American sources and traditions.

Kendall was capable of large changes of mind and inconsistencies, perhaps not surprising from someone who moved from the far left to the right. He was a Communist or at least a Trotskyite of some kind early in his life; like George Orwell and Arthur Koestler, his experience in the Spanish Civil War, where he worked as a journalist, opened his eyes to the innermost character of the Communist left. No less than Jaffa or Lincoln, Kendall had devoted a lot of thought to the problem of majority rule. He wrote on that very problem, which he called "the 'dark continent' of modern political theory," in his doctoral dissertation, which was published later as *John Locke and the Doctrine of Majority-Rule*.[17]

Kendall departs radically from the common view of Locke as a champion of the supremacy of individual natural rights, and sees Locke instead as vindicating virtually unlimited majority rule—or, to be more precise, he conceived of "virtually" limited majority rule, that is, majority rule undergirded by virtue. In large measure, Kendall sounds like the perfect Madisonian, emphasizing the constitutional mechanisms of deliberation that go into making any majority. But he was too profound a thinker, and too attuned to historical crises—the Civil War being one—to rest on an easy assumption of enlightened citizenry or wise outcomes. Kendall's skepticism of natural rights partially aligned him again with Berns, though Berns did not share Kendall's skeptical view of Locke or Locke's supposed unimportance for American thought.

Like Jaffa, Kendall was not willing to repair easily behind the usual main lines of defense against majority tyranny, such as the institutional designs of the Constitution (checks and balances and such) and the Bill of Rights. Worthy and practicable as all of these designs are, they are insufficient against the willfulness of human nature, which, according to one line of criticism, is made worse by a liberalism that celebrates acquisitiveness and, in recent times, unlimited self-definition ("every man his own tyrant" again). Like Jaffa, he feared that the defects in liberal theory would overwhelm the American republic in practice over time. Kendall's views on majority rule and natural rights changed toward the end of the 1950s. The evolution of his views can be seen in his slow-brewed confrontation with Jaffa.

Kendall published an enthusiastic review of Jaffa's *Crisis of the House Divided* in *National Review* in 1959, calling Jaffa's defense of Lincoln's understanding and application of the principles of equality, consent, and natural right in the Declaration of Independence to be "as nearly as possible irrefragable." Kendall understood that the book was no mere historical exploration, lavishly stating that "[U]nless the United States be as sick intellectually as some of us believe it to be, [*Crisis*] will provoke the most profound and far-reaching debate of our generation about American politics."

But a note of misgiving crept in at the end, and it concerned *the* central questions of our own time: What are the limits of equality? Can majorities be trusted with safeguarding individual rights, and to mark out the limits of equality? And can we be satisfied with leaving these issues to be settled by statesmen or would-be Lincolns? Lincoln may have been an anti-Caesar in 1860, but the example of Lincoln might lead us astray in the future. Kendall worried about a potentially "hair-raising" political future:

A future made up of an endless series of Abraham Lincolns, each persuaded that he is superior in wisdom and virtue to the Fathers, each prepared to insist that those who oppose this or that new application of the equality standard are denying the possibility of self-government, each ultimately willing to plunge America into Civil War rather than concede his point— and off at the end, of course, the cooperative commonwealth of men who will be so equal that no one will be able to tell them apart. . . .

[T]he Caesarism we all need to fear is the contemporary Liberal movement, dedicated like Lincoln to egalitarian reforms sanctioned by mandates emanating from national majorities—a movement which is Lincoln's legitimate offspring. In a word, it would seem that we had best learn to live up to the Framers before we seek to transcend them.[18]

Kendall's misgivings about Jaffa's interpretation of Lincoln and the American Founding, along with his own struggles with the problems of majority rule, seemed to grow over the next few years.

By degrees, Kendall decided that Lincoln should be thought of as a "derailer" of the good rather than a rail-splitter made good.

In 1970, three years after Kendall's death, *The Basic Symbols of the American Political Tradition* by Willmoore Kendall and George W. Carey appeared. Carey had been a collaborator with Kendall on several journal articles and based the book on a series of lectures Kendall had given in 1964 at Vanderbilt University. The thesis of this very readable and compelling book is that the principle of equality in the Declaration of Independence is *not* the central principle of American political thought, and that Lincoln at Gettysburg (a "new nation, . . . dedicated to the proposition that all men are created equal") was responsible for "derailing" the true American political tradition whose authentic roots are found in the lineage of the social compact. In other words, *Basic Symbols* contends the Declaration *is not* a "basic symbol" of the American political tradition. Kendall and Carey attempt to sever the Constitution and the Declaration as neatly as an obstetrician snips and discards an umbilical cord at birth. The American Revolution, by this account, is understood as the colonists vindicating their historic rights as Englishmen, and the Constitution is seen not as a new product of the Revolution but as belonging to a long lineage of compacts, starting with the Mayflower Compact. In other words, the Constitution should be thought of as a product of history more than reason, a continuity rather than a novelty. Above all, it should be understood very much as a *positivist* construction, rather than a product of any version of the natural law and natural right tradition.

But if the Declaration wasn't a basic symbol of the American Founding, what about the undeniable Lockean elements that can be discerned in so much political writing around the time of the Founding? The evidence on behalf of Locke's place in the American mind at the time of the Founding is so overwhelming that if Kendall's case were a lawsuit, every judge would grant a motion for summary dismissal.[19] Never mind the Declaration; the Lockean understanding of natural rights, social contract, and consent is found prominently in, for example, Jefferson's *Summary View of the Rights of British America,* and in the countless mentions of Locke in sermons from the pulpit in colonial churches.

But even before *Basic Symbols* appeared in 1970, Kendall had gone beyond his critique of Locke in *John Locke and the Doctrine of Majority-Rule.* He staked out the bold position that the undeniable presence of Locke was wholly deniable after all. And there is evidence that Jaffa provoked it. In a 1963 book, *The Conservative Affirmation*, Kendall throws out the Lockean baby, bathwater, bathtub, and entire plumbing system. He then attempts to pour concrete into the well to make sure the Lockean waters never flow again. In Kendall's scheme, Locke is *the* cause of modern liberal egalitarianism, and he wishes conservatives would forcefully reject Locke:

> The emphasis of Locke's political theory is, ultimately, egalitarian, since if the consent of *all* is necessary for the "compact," then each man's consent is as "good" as any other man's; so that *if* you marry Locke you are ultimately without grounds for resisting current egalitarian trends—which is exactly where most of our Conservative intellectuals have ended up. . . .
>
> . . . The Lockeans in America, in other words, are the Liberals; and the Conservatives, who disagree and must disagree with the Liberals on all crucial points, must learn to understand themselves as anti-Lockeans.[20]

There is no mention of Lincoln in this essay, which is one reason Jaffa may not have taken note of it. At the very least, he did not respond to it at the time.

It is tempting to explain Kendall's remarkable position as a function of his contrary nature and the exigency of trying to find a radical way of cutting off the source of oxygen for the runaway modern politics of egalitarianism and endless demands of rights.

But there is also the problem of the understanding of individual rights as it emerged from the Enlightenment that encouraged unapologetic selfishness and an individualism unconnected to any larger understanding of the good life or human excellence. This is the heart of Leo Strauss's controversial interpretation of Locke in *Natural Right and History*, a book Kendall praised highly many times. Strauss's account of Locke is not easily summarized, but key elements include the view that Locke implicitly followed Hobbes in legitimizing hedonism and a purely materialist understanding of human happiness. Though Strauss did not say so explicitly, the implication is that the Lockean foundation of the American republic is low and defective. Strauss concludes his analysis of Locke with the famous epithet: "Life is the joyless quest for joy." The American regime, as the cliché goes, is founded on "low but solid ground," but is becoming ever less solid as time passes because of the defects in Lockean liberalism.

This view of Locke and his relation to America presents a serious problem, for it deprives America of a solid ground for patriotism. Lockean America may be stable and tolerable, but it is less than admirable. It is prosperous and powerful, but is it excellent and good? By emphasizing rights without duties, it established a political order that does not create or require virtue. This understanding of America's philosophical core opens the way for the nihilism of our time and is strikingly similar to the New Left critique of American materialism in the 1960s.

Did Strauss think the defects he saw in Locke extended to America? This has been a major source of controversy within the Straussian community. A related question is whether the Founders read Locke in the same way Strauss read Locke. I once put this question directly to Thomas Pangle, who answered without hesitating, "Yes, I think they did." Yet the writers of the Founding era, while citing Locke, always disdained Hobbes, so this view is unpersuasive unless you think James Madison and other thinkers of the Founding era wrote as esoterically as Strauss supposes Locke to have written.[21]

In the fullness of time, as we shall see presently, Jaffa would come to challenge Strauss's view of Locke. But there is some evidence that Strauss may have agreed or at least sympathized with Kendall about Locke. In 1964, Strauss wrote to Kendall about Kendall's attack on Locke in *The Conservative Affirmation*:

> I fully agree with the main thesis of the essay. One notices the tactical disadvantages of a man who wishes to base conservatism on the Declaration of Independence and hence on Locke (cf. your book, 264, paragraph 1 end). From this point of view the *Federalist Papers*, based as they are on Montesquieu, are preferable, especially if one considers that they give the interpretation of *the* Constitution, and the D of I is not strictly speaking a constitutional document. (By this I do not wish to deny, of course, that the D of I carefully and soberly read is quite conservative.)[22]

In his typically enigmatic style, Strauss leaves himself some wiggle room here—by referring to the "tactical" disadvantages of the Declaration and how it can be read as conservative—to keep faith with Jaffa's interpretation of the conservative character of the Declaration. The passage Strauss refers to in the first parentheses is from Kendall's review of John Courtney Murray's 1960 book *We Hold These Truths*, where Kendall says that Murray's critique of Locke sidesteps the question of Locke's place in the Founding: "Are we to conclude, if the Framers of the Constitution wrought so well, that they were *not* under the spell of Locke's 'law of nature'? (If so, here certainly is a topic that wants another book.)"

It does not require a fanciful leap in logic to surmise that the other book Kendall had in mind would become his *Basic Symbols of the American Political Tradition*. It is curious that, unlike

John Burt, who said that Jaffa is his "major antagonist," Jaffa goes unmentioned in Kendall's work against Locke and Lincoln. Perhaps this was out of respect for, or fear of, Jaffa's supreme intellect and doggedness. (George Anastaplo of Loyola University once remarked that "anyone who has ever published on a subject of interest to Jaffa realizes upon seeing him take apart another's writing, 'There but for the grace of God—or, at least, the good will of Harry—go I!'") But Kendall may have shared his intention with Strauss of directly taking on Jaffa's thesis about Lincoln, Locke, and the Founding. There's a hint of this in another letter from Strauss to Kendall in 1964, where Strauss says, "I took cognizance with the greatest interest of what you told me about your plans re: Jaffa. I will keep them strictly secret."[23]

Catherine and Michael Zuckert do an excellent job of describing and analyzing Jaffa's posthumous clash with Kendall in their fine book *The Truth About Leo Strauss: Political Philosophy and American Democracy*, and it would be redundant of me to repeat their work here. (Though I should add that I once heard Jaffa say, quite characteristically, that the Zuckerts' account was "The most extended critique of my work that has ever appeared anywhere, and it is all very friendly and very nice, and mostly wrong!" He never fired back in print, however, instead calling their book "a remarkable example of connubial collaboration." Jaffa was fond of alliteration.) Readers interested in more details of the arguments outlined here should see the Zuckerts' book. I'll presently say more about the thesis that Kendall provoked Jaffa's "second sailing," but for the moment want to linger on a few overlooked aspects of Kendall's argument.

One thing that can be said in favor of Kendall's Lockephobia is that he anticipated the ur-text of the modern left, John Rawls's 1971 book *A Theory of Justice*, in which he remodels the liberal tradition, starting with Locke, in the service of justifying a redistributionist case. It is no exaggeration to say that Rawls has replaced

Marx as the most significant thinker for the modern left, though the postmodern theorists of pure power, such as Foucault, give Rawls a run for your money. With just a few notable exceptions, most Strauss-inspired scholars have ignored Rawls for the sensible reason that Rawls's political philosophy is so antipolitical that it is hard to take seriously. Allan Bloom was one exception, and his handling of Rawls was a combination of mockery and contempt: "Its ridiculousness quenches indignation. . . . Can one wonder that a generation has turned away from reason when this is the level of its most eminent representatives, when this is the sort of guidance it can get from them? Rawls speaks to men with the souls of tourists."[24] The durability of Rawls indicates that even if Kendall is wrong about Locke as a matter of historical accuracy, he and Strauss were not wrong about Lockean liberalism lacking an immune system against degeneration. It would have been immense fun to have seen Kendall manhandle Rawls.

But more curious is that the left can't make up its own mind about Locke. For every Louis Hartz, Daniel Boorstin, or John Rawls, there is a Garry Wills or Michael Sandel, with their own "derailment" narrative that tries to sever Locke from the Declaration of Independence (Wills's preposterous thesis), or follow Kendall in reading Locke out of the Founding entirely. The left grabbed with enthusiasm the mid-1970s work of Gordon Wood, who is no leftist, but whose *Creation of the American Republic, 1776–1787* expanded the historical literature that downplays Locke and ascribes the core of the American Founding to a "civic republican" tradition that de-emphasizes individual rights—a scheme that, in the hands of the left, seeks to remake republicanism into "the valet of liberalism," to borrow Charles Kesler's phrase.[25] Wood parallels Kendall in seeing a decisive break between the Declaration and the Constitution, the only difference being that Kendall approves of the break, while the left deplores the Constitution as a counterrevolution against the egalitarianism of the Declaration. It is the perverse twist of Garry Wills to read Locke out of the Declaration, thereby finding it to be a crypto-socialist document, and as such approving Lincoln's recovery of this non-Lockean Declaration in the Gettysburg Address.

However, Jaffa's initial interpretation of Lincoln and the Declaration is similar enough to Garry Wills, in that Jaffa's account of Lincoln in *Crisis of the House Divided* understands Lincoln as having completed or revised the Founding. In Jaffa's account, Lincoln went beyond both Locke and Jefferson to enlarge the depth and meaning of the Declaration. Here is one of Jaffa's problematic formulations:

> At this point we must obtrude some critical reflections concerning the adequacy of Lincoln's assertions with regard to the meaning of the signers of the Declaration. If we ask, first of all, if Lincoln's vindication of the consistency of the Fathers was altogether accurate from a historical standpoint, the answer, we believe, cannot be an unequivocal affirmative. . . .
>
> . . . While Lincoln most assuredly accepted the Declaration in its minimal, revolutionary meaning, he gave it a new dimension when he insisted that it provided a test not merely of legitimate government—i.e., of government that *may* command our allegiance because it is not despotic—but of *good and just* government—i.e., of a government which may be loved and revered because it augments "the happiness and value of life to all people of all colors everywhere."[26]

Although this account is not identical to Kendall's "derailment thesis" or Garry Wills's view that Lincoln essentially changed the Constitution and "refounded" the nation by elevating the Declaration, it clearly has defects. While Jaffa understandably spends his time and energy in *Crisis of the House Divided* showing how Lincoln argued against allowing a majority that would approve slavery amid a current of public opinion that was hostile to racial equality, he did not then think through how to confine the idea of equality from bursting the bounds of the Founding era—how to keep modern majorities from transforming equality into reckless egalitarianism, the age-old bane of democracy. You could say that Jaffa's work led to a "crisis of the Strauss divided"—a title Jaffa took for his final book in 2012.[27]

The problem of majoritarianism and its limits is connected to the problems of philosophical positivism, and at the time Jaffa was writing in the 1950s positivism was beginning its rampage through constitutional thought and especially constitutional law, though the worst predations of the Warren Court still lay ahead. Even before Kendall's "derailment" thesis made its full appearance in 1970, Jaffa was rethinking and extending his views on majority rule and the deeper meaning of the Declaration.

The dilemma of the Declaration, whether looked at in theory or from the point of view of the practical statesman, found its expression in the conflicts inside the mind of Jefferson. Jaffa liked to say in class, but never put down in print, that "the Civil War was Thomas Jefferson arguing with himself." It could just as easily be said that Jaffa began arguing with himself about the implications of his arguments. Jaffa's earliest work after *Crisis* acknowledged the practical difficulties of the Declaration, as in this 1961 essay:

It was not to be supposed, because of America's dedication to the political creed set forth in the preamble to the Declaration of Independence, that conflicts as to national purpose were thereby to be avoided. . . . In inviting men to aspire to what they could never wholly attain, it engendered frustrations which could not but embitter political life. Like the Gospel, in the name of peace it brought not peace but a sword. . . .

Sooner or later the experiment in popular government had to face the question of just how wrong the opinion of the governed might be and still continue to constitute the foundation for the just powers of government. *From this you will see that the Declaration of Independence, while it propounded a purpose, propounded a problem as well.*[28] (Emphasis added.)

A sign of the uniqueness of Jaffa's inquiry is the fact that this early essay appeared in an edited volume titled *Goals and Values in Agricultural Policy*, published by Iowa State University Press. (Perhaps Jaffa had transposed "farmers" for "framers" in his instructions to a department secretary.) Farmers looking for thoughts on parity pricing or subsidy policy must have been bewildered indeed.

Jaffa spent the next forty years exploring and explaining—and then re-explaining—his solution to this problem. In perhaps his most significant return to this question, a 1972 lecture on "What Is Equality? The Declaration of Independence Revisited," Jaffa noted that "we have reached a state of affairs where, as the demand for equality becomes ever more intense, its meaning becomes ever more indistinct, if not absolutely incoherent."[29] Thinking about the problem of Douglas's unqualified majoritarianism, and the destructive majoritarian egalitarianism of contemporary liberalism, led Jaffa to explore the reciprocal relationship between *equality* and *consent* in the Declaration. It is a rich and complicated argument, the most important part of which is this: majority rule is a practical substitute for unanimous consent over the first principles of equality and equal rights. A majority, James Madison argued in his essay on sovereignty, may only do those things that can be done rightfully by unanimous consent. A simple majority that seeks to abrogate the equal rights of others is illegitimate. (This is one reason why, in a separate famous essay, Jaffa argued that it is perfectly legitimate to outlaw the Communist Party, which, were it ever able to gain a majority through democratic elections, would end the very process by which it gained power in the course of assaulting individual rights.) This is one reason why Jaffa liked to draw attention especially to Thomas Jefferson's line in his first inaugural address in 1801—following the first time that ballots had replaced bullets, and a new government was installed by free election instead of violence and exile for the losers—that "though the will of the majority is in all cases to prevail, *that will to be rightful must be reasonable*; that the minority possess their equal rights, which equal law must protect, and to violate would be oppression" (emphasis added).[30]

Here one must keep in mind that the "self-evident" truths of the Declaration do not mean that they are obvious truths, or "self-evident" to every self who walks down the street. It is a proposition of internal logic.[31] Just because the principles of the Declaration are universal in nature does not mean that they are universally recognized or understood (this is a source of much confusion and superficial criticism, especially from conservatives). Likewise, "consent" is an abstract idea—though connected closely to "consensus"—that is much abused or oversimplified these days. It is typical to hear a person say "I didn't consent" to particular decisions or policies. (Paying taxes for the Vietnam War in the 1960s was a popular example.) Or consent is said to be expressed by or in each election. Sometimes it is said that you tacitly "consent" to a government merely by living under its laws and accepting its protection of your rights. All of these understandings have merit, but have the defect of suggesting that consent requires active affirmation at all times and can be withdrawn according to one's own will.

Consent is a more notional and substantive idea in Jaffa's scheme, and involves the theoretical unanimous agreement at a founding to form a body politic that agrees to be bound by the initial common consent of its members in perpetuity—or until that government becomes "destructive of these ends," in which case revolution is justified according to the very same principles of equality and consent. Jaffa argues that this occurred as a practical reality in the American Revolution by the fact that most dissenting Tories left the thirteen colonies and thereby were not part of the "one people" who declared independence. In this understanding, consent replaces wisdom as the ground of legitimate government.

There is much more to Jaffa's theory about the nature of majority rule, but this surface treatment is already difficult enough. As foundations for patriotism go, this is not exactly a platform for the masses. But, at the very least, it is entirely harmonious with James Madison. Though Jaffa does not say so, this intricate line of argument could be seen as a Thomistic commentary on *Federalist* 49, where Madison reflects that "a nation of philosophers is as little to be expected as the philosophical race of kings wished for by Plato." In other words, we can't expect supreme political wisdom among passionate and interested human beings. Madison also says that, since "all governments rest on opinion . . . the strength of opinion in each individual, and its practical influence on his conduct, depend much on the number which he supposes to have entertained the same opinion."

Jaffa thought that the American people and their democratic culture were *enlightened,* which is not the same thing as *wise* in the philosophical sense. Madison spoke of how "a reverence for the laws would be sufficiently inculcated by the voice of an enlightened reason. . . . The most rational government will not find it a superfluous advantage to have the prejudices of the community on its side." A prejudice in favor of the American Founding, and its key aspirational document, deserves the most serious and sophisticated defense. In this Jaffa was being faithful to one of Strauss's enigmatic remarks that "wisdom requires unhesitating loyalty to a decent constitution and even to the cause of constitutionalism."[32]

But Strauss's comment leaves open the possibility that the Constitution was a sufficient basis for patriotism and defense of the country against the wrecking ball of modern liberalism. But what informs our constitutionalism, if not the principles of the Declaration? Kendall and many others think the answer is virtue, which will be the result of *deliberation*, a more reliable means of enlightening the citizenry than the statesman or statesmanship. Kendall can also make a Madisonian case that the majority in America will be the repository of the sensibilities of freedom and justice, suitably guided and constrained by constitutional mechanisms. Historical memory—what today we wistfully call "civic education," I suppose—is a key element in Kendall's view of how to keep America grounded.

But Kendall understands that virtue is not to be assumed. In an enthusiastic essay about Richard Weaver, Kendall tacitly admits that the subject of virtue is largely missing from *The Federalist*:

> How are "we, the people" to keep "ourselves" virtuous? There is a "missing section" of *The Federalist*, in which *that* question, the question as to how "we the people" shall *order* "ourselves" so as to remain virtuous, and become ever more virtuous. Worse still: "we, the people" have been only too ready to conclude, from the fact that Publius left out the section in which he might have discussed the ordering of society, of "we, the people" *qua* "virtuous people," that no such section was needed, and, even the best of us, to focus our thinking on the range of problems to which Publius did address himself.[33]

The first observation to make about Kendall's emphasis on virtue is that it is not that much less philosophically exacting than Jaffa's deep theoretical teaching. As was so often the case with Kendall, he got carried away in thinking Richard Weaver's last book, *Visions of Order*, was *the* missing section of *The Federalist*. It is a worthy and sophisticated book, but it culminates with the instrumental argument that the preservation of American virtue depends on a self-chosen minority that assumes responsibility for perpetuating a healthy culture. In substance, this is not that distinct from Jaffa's focus on the necessity of statesmanship.

But Kendall's emphasis on virtue, which, as we shall see, was also a central concern for Walter Berns, exposed a further problem with Jaffa's understanding of the Declaration. The early Jaffa of *Crisis of the House Divided* accepted Strauss's view of Locke and therefore of the purely "low but solid" Lockean character of the Declaration's teaching about natural right. In his 1972 essay on the Declaration, Jaffa says that "The substitution of consent for wisdom has meant a lowering, in a certain way, of the ends of government."[34] Jaffa chiefly has in mind the role of religion or the classical idea of the completion of the soul through the best regime.

He also says in a 1970 American Political Science Association paper that "In the Declaration of Independence there is a certain presumption in favor of democracy, since all political power is originally in the hands of the people, whatever they afterward consent to have done with it. However, the Declaration contemplates nondemocratic forms, to which consent may reasonably be given."[35] Elsewhere Jaffa notes that had King George III not violated the natural rights of the colonists, the revolution would not have been justified; the Declaration leaves open the possibility that a monarchy or some other form of government that secures the natural rights of individuals can meet its criteria. "[The Declaration] does not specify the form of government to be established, other than that it must be nondespotic. . . . The people are not even obligated to set up popular governments."[36] This is what is known as the "no guidance" thesis—the idea that the Declaration does not necessarily entail the form of representative government of the Constitution.

Jaffa would rethink and substantially modify both of these views over the next thirty years, but not before he became embroiled in a series of strenuous fights with his fellow students of Strauss over these points, for these views were close to orthodoxy. One way of restating the issue more simply is to ask whether America is the best regime, or merely the best regime *possible*? By degrees Jaffa changed his mind, coming to discover what has been caricatured as "Lockistotle," in other words, that America should be understood as the *best regime* in the Aristotelian sense after all, "high and solid" rather than "low and solid."

Jaffa attempted to bridge the divide between ancients and moderns by incorporating the modification of the rise of Christianity, which severed for all time *religious* obligation from *political* obligation. This revolution in human consciousness entailed the necessity for freedom of conscience in religious matters, which came only very slowly. This is one reason Jaffa drew close parallels in his subsequent work between the significance of the British Toleration Act of 1689 and the struggle to end slavery.

In other words, Locke is what Aristotle would have been had Aristotle experienced the challenge of Christian revelation—the dominant political fact of Europe. As Jaffa explained succinctly in a letter to Catholic scholar Ernest Fortin: "[I]f Aristotle had in the 17th or 18th centuries been commissioned to write *the* political book for modern constitutions, he would have written something very closely approximating, if not entirely identical with, Locke's *Second Treatise.*"[37] As with Jaffa's teaching on equality, consent, and majority rule, there is a lot to this analysis, which he put together in a massive case in the long-awaited sequel to *Crisis* that finally appeared in 2000: *A New Birth of Freedom: Abraham Lincoln and the Coming of the Civil War.* Thomas G. West offers a good short summary of the mature Jaffa:

> The founders' doctrine of toleration eliminates salvation of the soul as an end of politics. Paradoxically, this elevates political life, by removing from it a leading source of its degradation—namely, persecution arising from the conviction of one's own sanctity. The founders' doctrine also elevates politics by

announcing a sacred cause, the cause of liberty, which elicits the noble virtues of statesmanship and citizenship. The social compact theory challenges men to live up to its moral demands, which require concern for others (respecting their rights) and self-restraint (the virtues of parents and citizens).[38]

One important change is that Jaffa no longer saw Lincoln as *modifying* the Declaration of Independence and the Founding; he was *defending* its original meaning. Lots of readers noticed and commented on the change, which Jaffa explained thus:

> That the Founding, which Lincoln inherited, was dominated by an Aristotelian Locke—or a Lockean Aristotle—has been a conspicuous theme of my writing since 1987. It has gone largely unnoticed because it contradicts the conventional wisdom of certain academic establishments. . . .
>
> My critics, friendly and unfriendly, may ask why it took me so long to see the purloined letter on the mantelpiece. The reason is that I took for granted that the account of the Hobbesian Locke in Leo Strauss's *Natural Right and History* represented the Locke that informed the American Founding. That rights were prior to duties, that duties were derived from rights, that civil society arose from a contract solely for mutual self-preservation, and that the goods of the soul were subordinated in all decisive respects to the goods of the body, were conclusions of Strauss's interpretation. Strauss himself never said this Locke was the founder's Locke, but the spell cast by his book led many of us to apply it to the founders.[39]

The date here—1987—is significant, because it coincided with the first unfurling of Jaffa's "second sailing," with the argument that the United States represented the best regime in the classical sense. Among other observations from the Founding Era that

Jaffa emphasized was a passage from George Washington's first inaugural address, which he thought sheds a bright light on how to think about "the pursuit of happiness" in the Declaration:

> [T]he foundation of our national policy will be laid in the pure and immutable principles of private morality; . . . since there is no truth more thoroughly established than that there exists in the economy and course of nature, an indissoluble union between virtue and happiness; between duty and advantage; between the genuine maxims of an honest and magnanimous policy and the solid rewards of public prosperity.[40]

Jaffa thought Washington had been wrongly dismissed as not being of the same theoretical caliber among the Founders as Madison, Hamilton, and Jefferson, but I'll leave that case for another day. There is no mistaking, however, that Jaffa made out the distinct echoes of Aristotle:

> It is sometimes said that the American Founding, as an expression of modern (notably Lockean) political philosophy, lowers the ends of human life in order to make them more easily attainable. For Americans, comfortable self-preservation, implemented by free-market economics and the scientific enhancement of man's productive powers, replaces eternal salvation or contemplation as the end of man. Whatever may be true of the thought of John Locke, this is not the way in which the American Founding understood itself. . . . It did not limit the ends of man. The ends of the regime, considered as ends of government, were lowered. But the ends both of reason and revelation served by the regime, in and through the limitations on government, were understood to enhance, not to diminish, the intrinsic possibility of human excellence.[41]

That year (1987) also saw the publication of Allan Bloom's *Closing of the American Mind*, which Jaffa severely criticized for slighting the goodness of the American Founding.[42] Jaffa may not have been entirely fair to Bloom, as Bloom lamented that the nation is slowly dissipating the "stored-up capital" that came down to us from the Declaration, Constitution, and our "painstakingly earned" history. (It is also worth pointing out that, like Strauss, Jaffa, and Berns, Bloom was a great admirer of Churchill.) But Bloom subscribed to—and even invoked the phrase—that America's foundations were "low but solid."

A defense of Bloom, like the defense of Kendall, rests on the larger current problem he was struggling valiantly against. I have long thought that Bloom mischaracterized or overstated the moral relativism of students. Most students are not pure or consistent moral relativists. The problem is actually worse: for all of the emphasis on "critical thinking skills" in universities, most students are simply unchallenged to develop moral reasoning. And so they tend to be a hot mess of contradictions and prejudices. Their relativism melts away under the slightest pressure, and they easily spout about the wrongness of racism, sexism, or genocide in Darfur. On such questions, most students express a moral surety approaching absolutism.

I find it useful to ask political science students if it is legitimate to vote in favor of ending democratic elections. The invariable answer is Yes, because democracy! Which means simple majority rule. What about voting by majority to enslave yourself? Usually, with some hesitation, the answer is the same. Then how about voting to enslave someone else? Here comes the first flicker of puzzlement.

Or you can ask whether it would be rightful to outlaw the Communist Party. Students are nothing if not steeped in the attitudes of free speech (or were, until quite recently), and typically default to the ACLU position of absolute freedom of expression.

It would be wrong to outlaw the Communist Party! Very well, then: does the class approve of Germany outlawing the Nazi Party or any expression of radical extremism? *That's different!* Those are *Nazis* you're talking about, and everyone *knows* they're evil racists!

Bloom was certainly right in calling out the "impoverishing certitudes" of the moral assumptions of today's intellectual culture, but his remedy was to demand that students have a more direct confrontation with nihilism—in other words, to challenge and shock the "easy-going" nihilism of youth with the real thing. A restatement of Bloom's position might be that, if the American Founding is "low," at least it is "solid," whereas there is nothing solid about the moral-cultural scene today. Was this just Bloom's indirect way of trying to engage young Americans where they are now in a desperate attempt, like Strauss, to draw them back to classical perspectives? A return to genuine openness, if it could be achieved in higher education today, might ultimately entail an openness to the same classical tradition Strauss was trying to revive more directly, an openness to things beyond mere self-interest. It's possible—though I was struck by the one and only time I ever met Bloom, when I put to him the question of whether he wasn't, at the end of the day, a closet Nietzschean nihilist. I was startled at how defensive and tentative he was in his (very long) reply. It had none of the bravado and flamboyance of his usual answers to questions and challenges.

The problem with a solid foundation that is low is that it may not prove to be solid over time. To extend the metaphor, a low foundation that is engulfed in a flood is difficult to shore up, and the foundation will be hopelessly cracked and eroded by the time the water pumps drain the flood. Even if Jaffa's complete argument about Locke and the classical character of America as the "best regime" is not fully accepted, his effort to establish the vital connection between the Declaration of Independence and the

Constitution has gained ground, and there are several examples of leading conservatives backing away from the older "low but solid" foundation understanding of the Founding.

One significant example is George Will, who based much of his 1983 book *Statecraft as Soulcraft: What Government Does* on the argument that America was "ill-founded." Jaffa was quick to hammer Will's book when it appeared. Almost twenty years after the book's appearance, Will repudiated its premise at an American Political Science Association panel:

> I am also guilty of *lèse-majesté* of criticizing the Founders, and I may as well begin my withdrawal from that position here. I said essentially that I thought America was "ill-founded." The Madisonian revolution in democratic theory was inadequate. . . . I said robustly and falsely that this meant that the Founding Fathers thought that their system was designed to work if no one was public spirited and had good motives. I think that is not fair to what they thought or to what indeed has transpired. . . . What I wrote twenty years ago was too facile in assuming that the Founders simply, in search of a new science of politics, said we should focus on the low but strong and steady passions of people, and act accordingly because they produce predictable forces—a kind of crude physics of politics. But they did not simply want to leave human nature unimproved by the workings of our constitutional institutions.[43]

This is a remarkable public repudiation of his previous position, and Will credited his change of mind more to the constitutional outlook of Harvey Mansfield Jr., along with his own closer study of Woodrow Wilson's violence toward our republican heritage, than to Jaffa's work.

But there are other signs of how Jaffa's argument about the

centrality of the Declaration has won the day. Consider this short statement of the relationship between the Declaration and the Constitution:

> [C]ontrary to what is implied by the internal organization of our universities, constitutional law and philosophy or political theory are not isolated from one another, and emphatically not in the United States. The law in question derives from a constitution that is related to the Declaration of Independence as effect is related to cause, and the Declaration, the cause, is a political statement of a philosophical teaching concerning the nature of man, Providence, and nature itself. In it we learn that nature's God endows all men with the rights of life, liberty, and the pursuit of happiness, and that government is instituted to secure these rights. That the Constitution was understood by its framers to have as its purpose the establishment of such a government there can be little doubt. Thus, if he is to do his job properly, the professor of constitutional law must be thoroughly familiar with the political philosophy that informs the Constitution.[44]

That sounds like something straight from the pen of Jaffa, but in fact these are the words of Walter Berns, written in 1986. But the Declaration doesn't tell us exactly how the Declaration should guide our understanding of the Constitution. Berns and many others understand key parts of the Declaration differently than Jaffa and his allies. Those differences led directly to the next level of refinement in how to think about America's foundation.

CHAPTER 7

How to Think about the Constitution

Two Views

*[H]ow one understands the Constitution will depend utterly
upon principles, not stated in the Constitution, that one brings
to bear upon its interpretation. And it will be those principles,
not the Constitution itself, that determine the nature of the Union.*

HARRY JAFFA, 2000

*The rule has not yet been formulated that will decide for the judge
when he must trust and when he must distrust the majority.
For, as a matter of fact, some judges are to be trusted and others not.*

WALTER BERNS, 1957

One day in the early 1970s, before they started feuding by letter and in print, Jaffa and Berns were walking down the street together in Claremont when Berns was visiting on a lecture tour, and Berns remarked that the opening of the Declaration of Independence was one of the best things ever written but the ending was one of the worst. "And the fight was on," one witness recalled.

The substantive difference between Jaffa and Berns might be reduced to which single term in the Declaration each man emphasized as the most important. For Jaffa, the key word is *equal* ("all men are created *equal*"); for Berns, it is *secure* ("to *secure* these rights, governments are instituted among Men"). It is tempting to paraphrase Lincoln's famous letter to Alexander Stephens about slavery, that "this is the only substantial difference between us."[1]

Berns's argument is simple and straightforward: natural rights aren't worth a darn thing without a government to secure them. A strong but decent government transforms *natural* rights into *civil* rights by a supreme act of positive law—in our case, the Constitution. This is the voice of Hobbes speaking, as modified and domesticated by Locke. The basic social compact involves individuals surrendering the enforcement of their natural rights (starting especially with the first one—the right of self-preservation) so that paradoxically they will be more secure. George Washington states the theory succinctly in his letter of transmittal for the draft Constitution on the last day of the Philadelphia convention in 1787:

> Individuals entering into society, must give up a share of liberty to preserve the rest. The magnitude of the sacrifice must depend as well on situation and circumstances, as on the object to be obtained. It is at all times difficult to draw with precision the line between those rights which must be surrendered, and those which may be reserved.[2]

This difference of emphasis might seem slight, but, for Berns and many others, it affects our understanding of the original intent of the Constitution, and therefore our jurisprudence. Berns and many other eminent thinkers—Robert Bork was the most prominent—believe it to be a mistake to try to apply natural rights and natural law ideas in jurisprudence, while Jaffa and several of his allies think it is essential. While Jaffa, following Lincoln, sees the Declaration as the solid center of gravity in American political thought, Berns and others think the Constitution, while informed by the Declaration, is a sturdier center of gravity for American political thought. As Thomas G. West summarizes the difference, Jaffa and his followers think America has a "Declarational" soul, while Berns and especially Harvey Mansfield Jr. think America has a "constitutional" soul.[3] (In fact the title of one of Mansfield's books is *America's Constitutional Soul.*) Berns, Mansfield, and other constitutionalists do not join Willmoore Kendall in rejecting the Declaration, Locke, or the principle of equality, but they think the Declaration has severe limits as a practical guide to political life, when it isn't in fact susceptible to misinterpretation by radical egalitarians. Berns and Mansfield worry, with good reason, that appeals to equality and natural rights can do more to harm than help the cause of limited constitutional government. As Mansfield wrote in 1993, "A regime based on the self-evident half-truth that all men are created equal will eventually founder because of its disregard of the many ways in which men are created unequal." (Jaffa was not pleased with this formulation, and naturally picked a fight with Mansfield over it.)

Is this a distinction without a difference? No—there is a strong case for each side of this argument, and someone better than me might be able to work out a harmonious middle ground. But in trying to referee this quarrel one would miss the larger point behind it: the battleground of this feud changed conservatism, and may yet save the country. Intellectual arguments like this tend never to be settled fully, and working the scorecard overlooks the fact that this entire line of argument brought a new richness to conservative engagement with the Constitution and filled in some serious gaps in conservative constitutionalism. While Jaffa and Berns clashed directly (with a sidebar skirmish involving Mansfield), the other key figures in the story are Martin Diamond, Herbert Storing, and Robert Goldwin, though this list could include several other worthy thinkers.

Walter Berns's patriotism may have been "bred in the bone," as the Elizabethan-era saying goes, and it certainly came out in the flesh. He recalled the deep impression of seeing Civil War veterans of the Union army on parade in Chicago when he was a young boy in Illinois (like Ronald Reagan at about the same time). Berns also liked to recall meeting an elderly man who had known James Madison, a little detail that gives both his patriotism and his later scholarship an aspect of apostolic succession. He thought it also indicated how young our country is in many ways.

A number of parallels turn up between Berns and Jaffa, who were born eight months apart in 1919. Like Jaffa, Berns was athletic. Jaffa was an avid cyclist well into middle age; Berns had been a football lineman in college and was, by his own description, "a serious tennis player." He lettered in both sports. During and shortly after his graduation from the University of Iowa in the late 1930s, between sets among his circle of tennis partners "more and more the talk turned to America going into the war. . . . At a certain point in my own experience, after France had fallen and the prospect arose of England being invaded, I realized that was a horrible possibility. I realized the heritage, the connection we had with Britain. We read our textbooks in English, I had learned to memorize Shakespeare, Eliot. There was never any question of [whose] side we would go with."[4] And, he added, there was "no question" that he'd join the armed forces and fight. Berns served in the Navy for the duration of World War II. He signed up for the Navy *before* Pearl Harbor.

His mention of Shakespeare and Eliot shows that Berns shared Jaffa's literary inclination, but Berns took his literary passion further—at least at first. After the war, Berns worked as a waiter in Taos, New Mexico, where somehow he befriended Frieda Lawrence, the widow of D.H. Lawrence; he soon began frequenting Lawrence's ranch outside Taos, delighting in meeting many of the illustrious guests who visited her there, including Stephen

Spender and Leonard Bernstein. Berns at that time was ambitious to become a novelist, but Frieda, "among others," Berns wrote, convinced him "that I would never become a writer," and so in 1949 Berns left Taos for the University of Chicago, "and became, of all things, a political scientist."

I'm not so sure Berns was correct that he wasn't cut out to be a literary figure. Unlike most political scientists, his writing is clear, direct, and jargon free. It contains a dry wit that matched the dry martinis he favored, and at times he could hit quiet poignant notes that remind us of no one so much as Flannery O'Connor. (See his short memoirs of Frieda Lawrence and Herbert Storing as examples.[5]) Then there was his obvious indignation at injustice. There was nothing understated about that.

A good example of both Berns's patriotism and his storytelling ability is the example he liked to give of the reflexive anti-Americanism of the Cornell faculty:

> It was the 4th of July celebration in the stadium with fireworks; the townspeople and the college faculty got together for this event. At a cocktail party later one professor's wife was asked in my presence whether she enjoyed the celebration. "Yes," she said, "but I could have done without all the flag waving." I thought of that old song that was around when I grew up, "if you don't like my peaches, why do you shake my tree?" In other words, what did she expect at a 4th of July celebration! But that was typical of universities when I taught there.[6]

Berns took a circuitous route to his mature views about the Constitution. His very first scholarly publication, in the *Western Political Quarterly* in 1953, was about the notorious 1927 Supreme Court decision in *Buck v. Bell*, which upheld a Virginia statute that authorized involuntary sterilizations of the "feeble-minded."[7] This is the case in which Justice Oliver Wendell Holmes, writing for the majority, asserted that "three generations of imbeciles are enough," and afterward boasted to friends that the decision gave him real pleasure and pride. He wrote to Harold Laski that he felt "I was getting near the first principle of real reform."

Buck v. Bell was an odd case in that it had no dissenting opinion, although one justice, Pierce Butler, voted against the majority. Berns's article, based on his master's thesis at Chicago, could be thought of as the "missing dissent." There is nothing cautious or detached about Berns's treatment of the case and its wider implication for due process of law. His moral indignation bristles from every page, and he does not hedge his contempt for Holmes. "[T]here are some things which decent government simply should not do," Berns wrote; "One of these is to perform compulsory surgical operations in order to satisfy the racial theories of a few benighted persons. To reduce the due process clause to a guarantee of prescribed procedures is to permit more than the public control of grain elevators." After demolishing Holmes's shoddy legal reasoning, Berns reviewed the still strong and disgusting ideology and practice of eugenics even after World War II: "The present writer believes it important to reveal just what it was these men wanted." (In a footnote, Berns tallied up the thousands of forced sterilizations still taking place in the United States in the early 1950s, and pointed out how several of the leading American eugenicists expressed their sympathy for Nazi eugenic theory as late as the middle of World War II.)[8]

Berns concluded by quoting a leading constitutional legal figure of the period, A.T. Mason, who approved of the Supreme Court jettisoning "the dogmas of eighteenth century individualism, faithfully performing what it conceived to be its historical function of protecting the individual against arbitrary action of legislative majorities." To which Berns responded: "But *Buck v. Bell* illustrates the need for some body to perform precisely this function. . . . In the end, *procedural* due process is a *substantive* right which is denied everyone to whom injustice is done." Later, in *Freedom, Virtue and the First Amendment,* Berns would write: "The question arises whether it is ever possible for a Supreme Court justice to write an opinion without basing it on an extra-constitutional 'spirit.' The answer is, of course, yes; but some of these mechanical decisions prove that Lincoln was right when he interpreted the Constitution according to natural justice."[9]

One would not have expected Berns to elaborate on this closing challenge in the scope of a short journal article, but it opens the door to one of the largest questions that divides conservative constitutionalism today: how to understand—and apply—the idea of the original intent of the Founders in jurisprudence. Part of the controversy is about just what *was* the original intent of the Founders. One school of originalist thought, which Jaffa's followers especially champion, argues that the philosophy of natural law and natural right as expressed in the Declaration ought to have authoritative status in jurisprudence. (Libertarian legal thinkers, like Richard Epstein and Randy Barnett, share a version of this view.) The contrary school of original intent jurisprudence holds a narrower text-based view: courts should strike down laws only where there is a clear clause in the Constitution to provide a basis for rejecting the legislative act of a duly constituted majority. Advocates of this view include Robert Bork, William Rehnquist, Antonin Scalia—and the later Berns.

Berns's 1953 article seems to tilt in favor of the first school of thought, which could be called "conservative substantive due process." But to invoke this term shows the difficulty: "substantive due process" was the orientation of the liberal rights revolution, starting with the Warren Court; ever since then, liberal jurists have been discovering unenumerated "rights" in the "emanations and penumbras" of the Constitution, most of which conveniently intersect with a modern egalitarian agenda (such as "welfare rights"). Berns's article on *Buck v. Bell,* and his first book, *Free-*

dom, Virtue and the First Amendment, appeared before the Warren Court began its rampage in earnest. When asked later about his flirtation with "substantive due process" in that early article, Berns said, "I changed my mind."

———

How did Berns come to change his mind? This issue is, to borrow Lincoln's phrase, "piled high with difficulty." Before sorting it out, it is worth digressing briefly to point out why this controversy over the original intent is so significant, regardless of which side you find more compelling. The work of Berns and his colleagues, starting in the 1950s, represented something new and significant. While Jaffa was working on the importance of Lincoln and the Civil War, several of his contemporaries, including Berns, turned their constitutional gaze directly at jurisprudence and the Supreme Court.

Berns's first book, published in 1957, critiqued the Supreme Court's modern First Amendment jurisprudence. But from the title itself you can see something new and startling; the book is called *Freedom, Virtue, and the First Amendment*. Virtue? Here is a word unheard of in both political science and jurisprudence. The premise of the book is that freedom is not simply the absence of restraint and cannot be disconnected from a substantive understanding of individual virtue. Berns's special target is ACLU-style "libertarianism," as he calls it, which can find no restraining principle against obscenity, for example. Berns argued powerfully that the "clear and present danger" tests and other improvisations of the Court were inadequate, incoherent, and beside the point. Given that the worst examples of First Amendment permissiveness lay in the future, the book is a remarkable exercise in foreseeing the consequent logic of free speech absolutism.

The influence of Strauss is evident throughout, as is the fact that Berns at the time still considered himself to be a liberal, as did Strauss and most of the Straussian circle. In the preface, Berns wished to make it clear that he is no conservative and didn't think much of the emerging conservatism of the 1950s:

> The term liberal is used throughout this study in its true sense, which I mention here in order to declare my innocence of any charge that I am interested in contributing to the growing, partisan literature of anti-liberalism. While I agree with those few constitutional lawyers who have shown the inadequacies of libertarian ideas, this does not compel any of us to ally ourselves with the so-called conservative movement. The contemporary political theory of conservatism may be characterized by the fact that it concludes its inquiry at the point where, historically, political philosophy began. Its contributions to our political understanding may be judged accordingly.[10]

In other words, don't mix me up with Russell Kirk or that *National Review* crowd.

But even if Berns still considered himself to be a liberal Democrat at this point, in this early work he marked out a number of perspectives that would remain front and center for his later work, and that find distinct echoes in his final book, *Making Patriots*. (Berns never abandoned thinking of himself as a liberal "in its true sense," despite the commonplace perception of liberalism that was taken on in the last half of the twentieth century.) Absolutist free speech jurisprudence, he argued, "foreclosed from permitting the exercise of the political virtue, practical wisdom or prudence, by the Supreme Court justice. . . . [W]hether by design or oversight, liberalism ignores the problem of virtue."[11]

You might even make this out as the case for "judicial statesmanship," though Berns did not use that term. There is a parallel with Jaffa's understanding of Lincoln's constitutionalism, especially the sequence where Berns writes that "it does not follow that it would be un-American to heed the advice Charnwood attributes to Lincoln and construe the Constitution, including the First Amendment, so as to 'render it agreeable to natural justice.'"[12] (The quotation Berns ends with here comes from a fragment in one of Alexander Hamilton's notebooks on the law, which reads "construction may be made against the letter of the statute to render it agreeable to natural justice." Lord Charnwood somehow plucked that phrase out of obscurity to explain and justify Lincoln's controversial measures, such as his suspension of *habeas corpus*.) As with his outrage over *Buck v. Bell*, Berns points to cases whose outcome he describes as "technically correct" on due process grounds but nonetheless "monstrous" to any person of common sense.

Berns rests his case for judicial statesmanship on the ground that "the formation of character is the principal duty of government" (statecraft as soulcraft?), but he begs the question of just where he derives the authority for this conclusion. Virtue is not mentioned in the Constitution, which is silent on education of any kind. It might be observed that, strictly speaking, education and morals are understood as state responsibilities, as can be seen, for example, in the language of the Northwest Ordinance of 1787. And the public language of the Founders, such as George Washington's previously mentioned comments, buttresses Berns's case.

Notwithstanding these clear currents, under Berns's early view, either virtue has to be imported into constitutional law, or the judiciary has to be understood as more of a political branch than a narrowly legal branch that merely "applies" the law in morally neutral ways. Of course, that is exactly what many of its critics today think the judiciary has become—"politicians in robes," with the balance of political power favoring the left for several decades now.

My theory of Berns's change of mind is simple: as the judicial predations of the Warren Court era accelerated in the 1960s and

1970s, Berns tilted toward Lockean legislative supremacy, toward which he had tentatively nodded in several places in *Freedom, Virtue and the First Amendment*. By the 1980s, Berns was arguing against natural law jurisprudence and aligning himself with the textual originalists. His embrace of textual originalism can be understood or defended as a prudential judgment—as the only means of preventing the Supreme Court from getting worse. In other words, it was an entirely understandable attempt to keep the "living Constitution" from becoming so alive that it became a Frankenstein monster at the hands of liberal social engineers.

Berns's subsequent detailed inquiries about the Hobbesian and Lockean roots of the Founding led him to a much more confined understanding of judicial review. As he wrote in 1983: "This doctrine of natural rights has no room for judicial review. In fact, judicial review is likely to prove a threat to the civil society built on natural rights. . . . There is no room for judicial review in Locke's system."[13] This led to the further conclusion that a natural rights jurisprudence would open a "bottomless well" or "Pandora's box." Berns, Bork, and other critics of natural law jurisprudence have in mind the gross abuses of the Fourteenth Amendment.

A regard for textual originalism is not entirely absent from Berns's early work, but he is less than clear on the matter. There is this admonition in *Freedom, Virtue and the First Amendment*: "It deserves mention that fidelity to the original text would have avoided the era of 'substantive due process' and its progeny, 'substantive equal protection.' . . . It would have spared us a generation of constitutional lawyers who feel obligated to spin out elegant (but obviously absurd) theories in the vain attempt to provide some valid textual basis for the Court's Fourteenth Amendment jurisprudence. Best of all, it would have made it easier to preserve the public's esteem for the Constitution as fundamental law."

By the 1980s, however, the ambiguities in Berns's early position were gone: "Anyone who argues that the Founders intended the courts to exercise a natural law–natural rights jurisdiction must come to terms with the fact that the original and unamended Constitution contains precious few provisions for such courts to work with."[14] By the mid-1990s Berns would write an essay bearing the unambiguous title, "The Illegitimacy of Appeals to Natural Law in Constitutional Interpretation."[15]

———

Here I should step back for a moment and take in the wider scene before introducing a new complication. Prior to the late 1950s when Berns and others began their work in this field, serious conservative constitutionalism could be summarized very quickly by saying that there wasn't much. There were lots of political complaints about the Supreme Court's shocking about-face starting in 1937 that erased the limits of the Commerce Clause and has enabled New Deal liberalism and its successors to flourish ever since, but, in fact, what might be called constitutional originalism had been in shards for decades by that time. If one had been asked in 1950 to point to a body of academic literature contesting this state of affairs in some fundamental way, the bookshelf would have been pretty bare. The inventory, such as it was, perhaps included Edward Corwin's famous book, *The "Higher Law" Background of American Constitutional Law*, and Charles Howard McIlwain's *Constitutionalism Ancient and Modern*, but both of these slender books were dated by the 1950s and didn't match up very well with the fast-moving scene in legal thought.

The conservative counterrevolution in political thought that helped generate a new constitutional originalism is part and parcel of the audacious project that held the American Founding should be taken seriously on its own terms, and not just as an obsolete station in a historical process that blesses the current intellectual fashion. It is revealing to pore through the political science journals of the mid-twentieth century and see how few articles there were, for example, on *The Federalist*, or how few books were written about *The Federalist* during that period. I can find almost no articles of any substance on *The Federalist* in the *American Political Science Review* prior to 1959, when Martin Diamond published "Democracy and *The Federalist*: A Reconsideration of the Framers' Intent."[16] Diamond's article was a seminal event on par with Friedrich Hayek's 1945 essay in the *American Economic Review* on "The Use of Knowledge in Society."[17] It single-handedly revived the serious study of *The Federalist* in political science. It is almost fitting to say that modern assessments of *The Federalist* should be dated "BD" or "AD": "Before Diamond, After Diamond."

Diamond was yet another example of the extraordinary impact of the Strauss circle and also a highly idiosyncratic character. Born in 1919, the same year as Berns and Jaffa, Diamond dropped out of college to join the merchant marine in World War II, after having spent his early adulthood as a socialist rabble-rouser on the streets of New York. After the war, he worked for the socialist presidential candidate Norman Thomas. "We were self-made, windy and largely phony intellectuals," Diamond told *Time* magazine in 1966, when it included him in a cover story about the best professors in America, "but there's really something to be said for getting hit over the head by a policeman."[18]

Maybe those truncheon blows shook loose some synapses. "As a socialist, I was as utopian as anyone could be," Diamond recalled, "but I finally learned that society can't be made perfect by any social arrangement."[19] Somehow he was admitted to the graduate program at the University of Chicago on the basis of his self-education alone, something that would be unheard of today. "I needed a place to stop spinning my wheels and think things out anew," he explained. After Chicago, he made his way to Claremont Men's College, where he was Jaffa's colleague for many years. When Leo Strauss heard that Diamond had been named chairman of the political science department, he gave a broad smile and said, "At last, I am now a teacher of statesmen!" It is widely recalled around Claremont that Diamond enjoyed his students needling him about his youthful radicalism.

In addition to correcting the distorted historical record about what the Founders were up to, Diamond offered the bold assertion that *The Federalist* offered timeless political wisdom, and was a relevant teaching for our own time: "[I]t may be that they possessed wisdom, a set of political principles still inherently adequate, and needing only to be supplemented by skill in their proper contemporary application." There is a clear parallel here to Strauss's emphasis on returning to the classics to recover true political wisdom, for Diamond argued that we should "return to [the Founders'] level of thoughtfulness about fundamental political alternatives, so that we may judge for ourselves wisely regarding the profound issues that face us."[20]

And if we're going to cast a look back to *The Federalist*, shouldn't we also have a close second look at the Anti-Federalists? As history's losers, the Anti-Federalists have always tended to get the short end of the stick, and they had the defect of having more and disparate voices than the three authors of *The Federalist*. It fell to Herbert Storing, another of the Strauss circle in the 1950s, to revive the serious study of the Anti-Federalists, culminating ultimately in *The Complete Anti-Federalist*, an annotated seven-volume work.

While the Anti-Federalists lost the political fight, their arguments in favor of a Bill of Rights carried the day, a fact that had important implications for jurisprudence because it controverted Alexander Hamilton's argument, in *Federalist* 84, that a Bill of Rights was not only unnecessary but might even be *dangerous*. Coupled with Hamilton's prior argument in *Federalist* 78 that the judiciary would be "the least dangerous" branch to the rights of the people, and the fact that the power of judicial review of legislation is nowhere specifically stated in the text of the Constitution, the

Anti-Federalist concern looks much the stronger. Not even the best talent of Broadway theater can rescue Hamilton from the view that he was naïve about the prospect that the new Constitution would allow the government to encroach on individual rights in the absence of express prohibitions. Herbert Storing sympathized with this view.[21]

And yet, when the paradoxes and subtleties of the arguments over the Bill of Rights are probed, it is less clear that Hamilton's argument was without sense, which brings us back to the current question of whether a strict textual originalism is a sufficient defense of the Constitution or limited self-government. It is necessary, though, to mark out the two parts of Hamilton's argument. First, in *Federalist* 84, Hamilton resists the call for a Bill of Rights with the argument that the Constitution has no express power to invade individual rights such as freedom of the press, because under the Constitution "the people surrender nothing." That is, the people retain all of their natural rights and don't need express reservation in the text as a safeguard, which throws some shade on the strict compact interpretation that the Constitution converts our natural rights into civil rights. More:

> Here is a better recognition of popular rights, than volumes of those aphorisms which make the principal figure in several of our State bills of rights, and which would sound much better in a treatise of ethics than in a constitution of government.

If there's one proposition today that could find nearly unanimous agreement between left and right, it would be "thank God they didn't take Hamilton's advice!" (I say "nearly" unanimous agreement, since many on the left would like to make the Second Amendment disappear, and have lately added repealing the First Amendment to their list so they can regulate politics and elections more directly.)

But the second part of Hamilton's argument has some staying power: a Bill of Rights would be dangerous because it would mis-instruct Americans as to the ground of their rights, and narrow our understanding of rights the government is meant to protect. As Hadley Arkes likes to point out, nothing is more typical today than to hear citizens say that their rights belong to them "because of the Bill of Rights," rather than recurring to the understanding of the Declaration that their rights are "inalienable," that is, not theoretically dependent on positive law. As Hamilton put it, "They [bills of rights] would contain various exceptions to powers not granted; and, on this very account, would afford a colorable pretext to claim more than were granted." In other words, any right that was unenumerated in the Bill of Rights would be inversely presumed to be fair game for government legislation and control. And sure enough, the constitutional status of whether there is a right to earn a living is a tangled mess; in the past, wage and price controls have been found permissible because of the lack of a tex-tual prohibition against them. Or, to take the example on the minds of many right now, the Supreme Court found it easy to expand the taxing power to uphold the individual mandate of Obamacare, while at the same time found itself unable to uphold a property tax on oil tankers in Alaska because it ran afoul of the Constitu-tion's "tonnage clause" in Article I, Section 10 ("No State shall, without the Consent of Congress, lay any Duty of Tonnage").[22]

The first Congress, in writing the Bill of Rights, recognized this problem and thought they had a remedy for it—the Ninth Amendment, which says that "The enumeration in the Constitu-tion, of certain rights, shall not be construed to deny or disparage others retained by the people." What are these "certain" rights, if not the natural rights comprehended in the Declaration of Inde-pendence? But, like the "republican guarantee clause" of Article IV ("The United States shall guarantee to every State in this Union a Republican Form of Government"), is the Ninth Amendment justiciable? A few concurring opinions of the Supreme Court have cited it, but, in general, judges have been reluctant to dilate upon its practical meaning. Robert Bork was so allergic to the Ninth Amendment that he compared it to an "inkblot"—"Nobody has ever to my knowledge understood precisely what the Ninth Amendment did mean and what it was intended to do," Bork told Senator Joseph Biden during Bork's dismal confirmation hearings in 1987. Much of Bork's dislike of the Ninth Amendment stemmed from its use by Justice Arthur Goldberg as the basis for discovering a "right to privacy" in *Griswold v. Connecticut*, the precursor case to *Roe v. Wade*. But can it really be that a passage of the Constitution is practically meaningless, that there are rights which judges are powerless to protect? Were the Founders bad draftsmen?[23]

To repeat a previous point, declining to employ the Ninth Amendment on behalf of natural rights can be defended as a prudential judgment that opening the door to natural law reasoning is a game that favors the Left in its endless invention of new rights that are really claims and duties to be imposed on others. It is not hard to find good evidence in support of this prudence. See, for example, Daniel A. Farber's *Retained by the People: The "Silent" Ninth Amendment and the Constitutional Rights Americans Don't Know They Have*, where the Ninth Amendment is employed as a basis for gay marriage, universal health care, and virtually the entire egalitarian wish list.[24] All to be achieved by a court injunction, one supposes.

Storing thought better of the second Hamilton argument, and offers the heterodox speculation that we might be better off without the Bill of Rights after all. It is worth citing Storing at length:

It is interesting to consider what our constitutional law would be like today if there had been no Bill of Rights. Its focus would presumably be to a far greater extent than it is today on the powers of the government. We might expect a more searching examination by the Supreme Court of whether federal legislation that seems to conflict with cherished individual liberties is indeed "necessary and proper" to the exercise of the granted powers. We might expect a fuller articulation than we usually receive of whether, in Marshall's terms, "the end" aimed at by given legislation "is legitimate." Might this not foster a healthy concern with the problems of *governing*, a healthy sense of responsible self-government? . . .

. . . Any formulation of the standard of natural rights is problematic and obscure. . . . Without a bill of rights our courts would probably have developed a kind of common law of individual rights to help to test and limit governmental power. Might the courts thus have been compelled to confront the basic questions that "substantive due process," "substantive equal protection," "clear and present danger," etc. have permitted them to conceal, even from themselves? Is it possible that without a bill of rights we might suffer less of that ignoble battering between absolutistic positivism and flaccid historicism that characterizes our constitutional law today?[25]

Maybe Broadway is unwittingly onto something more than it knows with its glowing celebration of Hamilton.

———

But if jurisprudence is to be guided by a strict textual originalism that emphasizes legislative supremacy, the door is left ajar once again to unqualified majoritarianism, or at least to a serious confusion about constitutional principles. At the root of the problem is that a strict textual originalism is indistinguishable from positivism. That's the prospect that launched Jaffa into near-Earth orbit.

The trouble is that for a long time legal education has neglected to teach the role of the natural law tradition in the evolution of the Anglo-American legal world. With few exceptions, such as

Catholic law schools (Ave Maria University comes to mind) or the rare conservative law professor here and there, law students are taught only the positivist basis of law. Constitutional law in most law schools is shockingly narrow, as it is overwhelmingly taught from a practitioner's viewpoint, that is, how the case law has unfolded and how you need to deploy the precedents and doctrines to argue constitutional cases today. While this is obviously necessary for the practice of law in the courtroom, it has created several generations of lawyers who are mere constitutional technicians rather than *constitutionalists*. While a law student will learn constitutional law, he or she won't learn *constitutionalism*. It could be compared training a surgeon without ever pondering the Hippocratic Oath.

As such, even conservative-minded law students will not have much exposure to the full range of constitutional philosophy, and this can be seen in the surprising, if not shocking, things some conservative judicial heroes have said. In 1976 future Chief Justice William Rehnquist gave a major lecture aimed at the worthy goal of turning back the worst abuses of the "living Constitution," rightly seeing it as a doctrine that unleashes judges to implement their own political and social views.[26] Among Rehnquist's observations:

A mere change in public opinion since the adoption of the Constitution, unaccompanied by a constitutional amendment, should not change the meaning of the Constitution. A merely temporary majoritarian groundswell should not abrogate some individual liberty truly protected by the Constitution.

So far, so good. But then there's this:

The third difficulty with the . . . notion of the living Constitution is that it seems to ignore totally the nature of political value judgments in a democratic society. If such a society adopts a constitution and incorporates in that constitution safeguards for individual liberty, these safeguards indeed do take on a generalized moral rightness or goodness. They assume a general social acceptance neither because of any intrinsic worth nor because of any unique origins in someone's idea of natural justice but instead simply because they have been incorporated in a constitution by the people. . . . The laws that emerge after a typical political struggle in which various individual value judgments are debated likewise take on a form of moral goodness because they have been enacted into positive law. It is the fact of their enactment that gives them whatever moral claim they have upon us as a society, however, and not any independent virtue they may have in any particular citizen's own scale of values.

Immediately after this passage, Rehnquist cites approvingly Holmes's famous attack on natural law.

This is no good. It is pure positivism. Here Jaffa is entirely correct in arguing that "No one can at one and the same time be a legal positivist and an adherent to the original intentions of the Framers." The principles of the Declaration of Independence, and hence the Constitution, are not conceived as "value judgments." Would Rehnquist actually rewrite the Declaration, "We hold these value judgments to be what we hold, because a majority has declared it so . . ."? As Jaffa pointed out, the majority in 1787 included safeguards for the owners of slaves. Did these "safeguards" also "take on a generalized moral rightness" because "they have been incorporated into a constitution by the people"?

To be fair, the balance of Rehnquist's argument is on the side of legislative supremacy and against a "living Constitution" that would provide "an end run around popular government." A good deal of Rehnquist's jurisprudence on the Supreme Court rested on deferring to the popular branches of government, which as a practical matter is defensible—up to a point. But along the way in his lecture he mangles the due process issue in the *Dred Scott* case and gets the *Lochner* case completely wrong, and so we shouldn't be surprised to see his protégé, Chief Justice John Roberts, base much of his dissent in the *Obergefell* case that legalized gay marriage on the argument that the decision represents a return to *Lochner*-style jurisprudence.[27] (I'll mention in passing that more than twenty years ago I had a vigorous argument about Rehnquist's disputable originalism with one of his very smart law clerks; his name was Ted Cruz.)

Justice Antonin Scalia, whose textual originalism was consistent and powerfully argued both in Court opinions and in his books (especially *A Matter of Interpretation*) voiced a similar bent toward unqualified majoritarianism in a 1996 speech:

> The whole theory of democracy . . . is that the majority rules; that is the whole theory of it. You protect minorities only because the majority determines that there are certain minority positions that deserve protection. . . . [Y]ou either agree with democratic theory or you do not. But you cannot have democratic theory and then say, but what about the minority? The minority loses, except to the extent that the majority, in its document of government, has agreed to accord the minority rights.[28]

In Scalia's defense it must be recognized that he faced a regular onslaught of cases that, as he pointed out in many passionate dissents, seemed to have as their object "a major, undemocratic restructuring of our national institutions and mores," and undoubtedly sought the most effective way to counterbalance the feeblemindedness especially of fellow Republican justices such as Harry Blackmun, John Paul Stevens, David Souter, and Anthony Kennedy. He was absolutely on target with his criticisms against using legislative histories in construing *statutes*. He also said separately that "A Bill of Rights that means what the majority wants it to mean is worthless."[29]

On the other hand, in casual conversation, Scalia, despite his devout Catholic faith, would express scorn for the place of natural law (or common law, for that matter) in jurisprudence. In his book *A Matter of Interpretation*, Scalia all but joins the Kendall-Diamond "no guidance" school about the Declaration of Independence:

> If you want aspirations, you can read the Declaration of Independence, with its pronouncements that "all men are created equal" with "unalienable Rights" that include "Life, Liberty, and the Pursuit of Happiness." Or you can read the French Declaration of the Rights of Man. [T]here is no such philosophizing in our Constitution, which, unlike the Declaration of Independence and the Declaration of the Rights of Man, is a practical and pragmatic charter of government.[30]

It is one thing to say that, strictly speaking, there is no philosophizing *in* the Constitution's text, but can or should the Constitution be understood as a philosophically empty or neutral vessel? And if we are not satisfied with the "glittering generalities" of the Declaration (as they are often dismissed), we might inquire about what more extensive legal philosophy the Founders did read. Immediately you come to William Blackstone, who was fully suffused with the necessity of natural law as the cornerstone for legal reasoning.

If you want to find a Supreme Court justice who holds that the Declaration and its philosophy of natural law and natural right should be an authoritative source for interpreting the Constitution, you have to look to Clarence Thomas. Unsurprisingly, at the time of Thomas's nomination to the Supreme Court in 1991 the left attacked Thomas for his previous public speeches embracing the natural rights philosophy of the Founding. (Among other things, the attempt led the comical Joe Biden, then chair of the Senate Judiciary Committee, to lecture Thomas on the distinction between "good" natural rights and "bad" natural rights—good ones being the welfare rights beloved of the left, and "bad" ones being those that protect property and economic liberty. Biden opened Thomas's confirmation hearing by holding aloft Richard Epstein's fine book on property rights, *Takings*, and essentially demanding of Thomas, "Are you now or have you ever been a reader of this book?")

It was a great surprise, however, to see Thomas attacked from the *right* at the time of his nomination. *Human Events* ran a full-page editorial on Thomas's "unsettling" view of natural rights:

> What has sent up caution flags is Thomas's embrace, in some of his writings and speeches, of a controversial position promoted by the disciples of the late political theorist Leo Strauss—including Prof. Allan Bloom of the University of Chicago and perhaps most notably Prof. Harry Jaffa of Claremont College in California—which asserts that the Constitution includes protections for "natural rights," abstract moral principles not specifically set out in the document or its amendments. . . .
>
> Not surprisingly, the revelations of Thomas's natural-rights approach have aroused considerable discomfort among conservative legal scholars. One of them, Bruce Fein, told the *Washington Post*: "If he got up there [at confirmation hearings] and said he believes in the natural-rights theory, I would write a column that says he should not be confirmed."[31]

Never mind that the article completely mangled Jaffa's (and Thomas's) actual views, though Jaffa's rejoinder had some nice zingers in it. (Regarding one gross mischaracterization of Jaffa's viewpoint, Jaffa wrote to the editors: "I find it incomprehensible that anyone, not functionally illiterate, could have discovered this 'thesis' in anything I have written."[32]) The point is to see how this issue divides the right, though surely those who doubted Thomas ought today to admit at least to some embarrassment, given his sterling record on the Court, and inquire further as to why his record has been so sterling, noting especially how he has cited the Declaration of Independence as an authoritative source for legal reasoning in numerous opinions from the bench.[33] Neither Scalia nor Robert Bork deny or oppose the ideas of natural law or natural rights (although I have heard several second-hand reports of Scalia dismissing the Founders' views on natural rights); they think that it is a bad idea for the judiciary to protect unenumerated rights or for judges to employ natural law as a jural tool. On principle, Rehnquist argues, using natural law opens the door to imposing one's own moral views in the cloak of judicial review. In practice, he thinks it is a game that favors the left. Bork thought the origin of the "judicial activism" that modern conservatives deplore is much older than the New Deal or the Progressive Era. Bork made out the appeal to natural law that appeared in one of the earliest Supreme Court decisions, *Calder v. Bull* in 1798, as the "poisoned apple" of judicial activism. In *Calder*, Justice Samuel Chase appealed to "the great first principles of the social compact"—meaning the Declaration of Independence—as ground for limiting legislative power. Bork's imagery stands in a stark contrast to Lincoln's famous description of the Constitution as the "frame of silver" for the "apple of gold"—the Declaration of Independence.

Judicial modesty is a worthy position and also a prudent policy for many cases and controversies that come before the courts. Rehnquist, Scalia, and their many allies are surely correct that many controversial issues such as abortion and gay marriage would be better left to the popular branches of government to resolve, usually on a state-by-state basis. They are likewise correct that the left can invent new rights endlessly, and that turning back these claims in the current intellectual environment is the judicial equivalent of the Dutch boy running out of fingers to put in the leaky dike. My favorite at the time of this writing is the federal lawsuit arguing that action against climate change is required under the Constitution's guarantees of "life, liberty, and property." One wonders what a federal judge can do by injunction that the Environmental Protection Agency isn't already attempting on its own contestable authority.

At the same time, it should be acknowledged that understanding the Constitution as simply an act of majoritarian will, and the concession to positivism it involves, makes us into moral mutes, and therefore ill-equipped to argue against the assertive and unending demands of the left couched in the language of "rights." Jaffa's robust view of the character of the Founding, and the essential connection to the reasoning of the Declaration of Independence, is unquestionably subtle and hard to grasp, and this brief survey of the intellectual battlefield barely scratches the surface of the arguments on both sides. (Readers should see Jaffa's complete treatment of the issue in *Original Intent and the Framers of the Constitution: A Disputed Question*, which includes lengthy responses from three of Jaffa's critics, plus his rebuttals.[34])

If Jaffa's perspective about the high moral character of the Founding, which took him years to work out, is forbidding or inaccessible, it should be noted that Berns's attempt to maintain the connection between the Declaration and the Constitution by confining the concepts of natural right within a strictly Hobbesian interpretation is no less subtle or challenging to understand and apply.

Perhaps I can do no better than to make a plea for a restoration of Lincoln's style of constitutional *sensibility*, which will by no means resolve the arguments outlined here. One of the defects of our age is the tendency, frequently reinforced by the Supreme Court and the legal guild, to regard the Constitution as the near-exclusive property of lawyers rather than of all citizens, as the preamble should remind us.[35] Citizens should contest about the meaning of the Constitution just as much as lawyers do. Constitutional government cannot be restored by legal action alone.

CHAPTER 8

Extremism in
Defense of Liberty

*Writing as I do, about the Civil War, and the American
Revolution, both as events in the past, and as elements
of an "eternal present," is of the essence of my project.*

HARRY JAFFA, 1982

*I would remind you that extremism
in the defense of liberty is no vice.
And let me remind you also that moderation
in the pursuit of justice is no virtue.*

BARRY GOLDWATER, 1964

In 1965, Oxford University Press published Jaffa's second book, a collection of essays and lectures from the previous decade, entitled *Equality and Liberty: Theory and Practice in American Politics.* Among the disparate essays were original treatments of the dynamics of party politics, the deeper meaning of "consensus" in American history, the reciprocal nature of civil and religious liberty, still more on the Lincoln-Douglas debates and the Civil War, and serious attacks on current trends in political science methodology. Jaffa's great range was on full display.

Commentary magazine, then still a liberal journal, assigned George Kateb, then at Amherst College, to review the book. He produced a long review, almost none of it about the contents of the book. Instead, he couldn't get beyond a big stumbling block. Best to let Kateb explain it in his own words:

> Eyebrows were raised last summer when the *New York Times* reported that Harry Jaffa was writing campaign speeches for Barry Goldwater. How could it be that this student of Professor Leo Strauss, this ardent author of a brilliant book on the slavery controversy in the 1850's, this respected teacher of political theory, would lend his intelligence to such a cause? It is bad enough that professors should be partisans; worse that professors of political theory should be partisans. But there must be limits: working for Goldwater—not just for the Republican party, at a decent remove from its temporary leader, but for the leader himself—must surely be beyond reasonable limits. Especially, one would have thought, for somebody like Jaffa. In none of his writing was there anything to prepare his readers for the news of his behavior.... [W]hat should we, familiar with Jaffa's work and impressed with the intelligent idealism behind it, and now apprised of his specific views on party, think of his attachment to Goldwater? What should we make of it?[1]

Could there be anything more *outré* than working for the "extremist" Barry Goldwater, who most academics would have thought makes Donald Trump look moderate and statesmanlike? As you can see from Kateb's incredulity, it was questionable to be a Republican at all. (Jaffa got his revenge on Kateb years later when, at a conference, Jaffa told him: "George, I have an apology to make. You were right about my politics in 1964. I should never have supported a man who promised to keep us out of a land war in Asia.")

To be sure, Jaffa grew up and remained a New Deal Democrat well into adulthood, and in fact didn't become a Republican until

1962—the same year Ronald Reagan formally switched parties. President John F. Kennedy's weakness, especially as revealed in the Bay of Pigs fiasco, was the turning point for Jaffa. Despite the internationalism of Eisenhower, throughout the 1950s Jaffa continued to regard the Republican Party as being in the thrall of Taft-style isolationism. As he explained to Henry Regnery in a letter in the late 1980s:

> The dilemma of where to turn was also mine for a number of years. My political peregrination resembles Ronald Reagan's— we both joined the Republican Party in 1962, after having been New Deal Democrats in the 1930s. In 1946 I remember reading Hayek's *Road to Serfdom*, and being converted into a thorough-going anti-socialist. But the isolationism of the Republican Party remained a stumbling block, long after I preferred Republicans to Democrats on every domestic issue.[2]

The reference to Friedrich Hayek is interesting because the Straussian community mostly ignores or overlooks Hayek, even though much of Hayek's early and middle work (especially *The Constitution of Liberty*) is harmonious with the work of many Strauss followers, and Strauss and Hayek were acquainted, serving on at least one dissertation committee together.[3] Jaffa offered public praise for Milton Friedman many times, but said, "I won't call myself a free market economist because I'm not an economist at all. I am however a devotee of the free market as a most desirable ground for constitutional government."[4] That's not far from how Hayek might have explained himself if the question had been put to him the right way. (About Ayn Rand, however, Jaffa had no hesitation. After hearing from students of her growing popularity in the 1960s, he read some of Rand's philosophical essays and pronounced: "In a world filled with intellectual lightweights, Ayn Rand has a firm grasp on the lowest rung.")

But if Jaffa thought Goldwater's anti-Communism was more robust than the Democrats', there was still the difference between him and Goldwater on a significant issue: civil rights. Jaffa strongly supported the Civil Rights Act of 1964 and later the Voting Rights Act of 1965, seeing them as "the long delayed fulfillment of promises embodied in the 13th, 14th, and 15th Amendments." Jaffa actually argued that the Voting Rights Act should have been passed first, which would have enabled Southern blacks to have a political voice first through elections rather than through judicial and federal bureaucratic avenues. Goldwater voted against the Civil Rights Act. It bears pointing out, though, that Goldwater, who had voted for previous civil rights legislation and spearheaded the desegregation of Phoenix as a member of the city council in the 1950s, objected only to Title VII of the Act, which dealt with employment discrimination, and Goldwater thought it was unconstitutional and unenforceable. Given the more than forty years of instability in Title VII, as seen in the number of cases reaching the Supreme Court, Goldwater had a point. I never heard Jaffa mention this difference of opinion with Goldwater, but later Jaffa changed his mind about Title VII; he was persuaded by Richard Epstein's 1992 treatise *Forbidden Grounds* that Title VII in action has led directly to the world of quotas and reverse discrimination. "Professor Epstein has convinced me that the abuses of the antidiscrimination laws are so intimately connected with misconceptions in the law themselves, that any benefits from them will always be far outweighed by the harm that they do."[5] Count this as yet another vindication of Goldwater.

Jaffa's affinity for *The Road to Serfdom* explains the compelling factors that outweighed his difference over civil rights. Jaffa explained in 1980 that the liberal ideology of the early 1960s was aiming to claim a larger share of the fast-growing prosperity of the nation: "[w]e Goldwaterites knew—and said as loudly as we could—that under the Democrats, the prosperity of the economy would become an excuse for vast *new* government programs. . . . We knew that such a 'war' [on poverty] would be nothing but a vast federal program, designed to soak up the federal revenues that a prospering free market economy was producing." More than this, Jaffa reasoned, it would involve centralizing more power in Washington. While not the "road to serfdom," it was the road to the administrative state, the topic I'll return to in the next chapter.

It took some prescience to anticipate exactly how liberalism would unfold if it was able to work its will—a foresight that, besides Goldwater, only Ronald Reagan seemed to have had at the time, as seen in his famous "Time for Choosing" speech later in that ill-fated campaign. Goldwater's leading rivals for the nomination in 1964, Governor William Scranton of Pennsylvania and Governor Nelson Rockefeller of New York, were the epitome of "me-too" Republicans, whose idea of "moderation" was to offer essentially low-budget liberalism as an alternative to the Democrats' high-octane version. Why this was thought attractive to voters is high in the catalogue of why Republicans were called "the Stupid Party." Why vote for cut-rate liberalism when you can get the real thing?

In those days, the "conservative Republican alternative program" was known by the obvious acronym CRAP. Despite the erudition of the *National Review* circle, conservatism in the early 1960s still seemed a marginal political force with limited popular appeal. What appeal it did have was regarded as residual McCarthyism, made still more obscurantist by the cranky conspiratorial stylings of the John Birch Society, at the time the most prominent right-wing organization in the nation. Many political figures close to Goldwater and his campaign were either supporters or sympathizers of the John Birch Society, which created a practical difficulty for Goldwater in 1964, as it did briefly for Ronald Reagan in California in 1966.

Jaffa, then teaching at Ohio State University, was recruited in

1963 for a project that became *The Conservative Papers*, a book published in 1964 that was intended as a means for conservatives to step up their game as a serious intellectual and policy force. Contributors included Milton Friedman, Edward Banfield, Edward Teller, and Henry Kissinger. Jaffa's essay, "On the Nature of Civil and Religious Liberty," made a serious theoretical case in favor of banning the Communist Party, though—like Reagan in the late 1940s during the controversy over the Hollywood Ten—Jaffa argued that as a prudential matter it was unnecessary to do so.[6] As the Goldwater campaign began to gain steam, he turned to the American Enterprise Institute as a brain trust, which in turn recruited Jaffa and put him on the AEI payroll to work on the GOP platform.

As the GOP convention opened in San Francisco, Governor Scranton, in an eleventh-hour bid to derail Goldwater, sent a letter challenging Goldwater to a floor debate. The letter was not confined to the debate invitation, but included every wild liberal charge against Goldwater in the most insulting language imaginable, such as: "Goldwaterism has come to stand for a whole crazy-quilt collection of absurd and dangerous positions that would be soundly repudiated by the American people in November." Scranton later denied having seen the letter—he claimed it was drafted and sent by an aide—and it was widely thought to have been a gambit to ensure that the convention didn't try to draft him as Goldwater's running mate, which would have gone some distance in healing party factions.

Goldwater was outraged, and, sensing that the intemperate letter would backfire on Scranton, ordered it circulated to every delegate at the convention with the terse comment that "I consider it an insult to every Republican in San Francisco." Jaffa had argued in a memo for a more conciliatory response to Scranton's provocation. He suggested that Goldwater make a magnanimous statement and borrow Abraham Lincoln's response to an editorial attack from Horace Greeley: "If there be perceptible in it an impatient and dictatorial tone, I waive it in deference to an old friend, whose heart I have always supposed to be right." Goldwater didn't go for it, but something else in a Jaffa memo to the platform committee caught his approving eye: extremism in the defense of liberty is no vice; moderation in the defense of justice is no virtue.

The Scranton provocation led Goldwater to say to one of his aides, "Christ, we ought to be writing a speech telling them to go to hell." Goldwater signaled that he thought his acceptance speech should indicate that his nomination and campaign marked a "historic break" for the Republican Party. It is also likely that Goldwater wanted to keep faith with "the people who brung him," as the old country saying goes. He asked that Jaffa work with his chief speechwriter, Karl Hess, to revise his acceptance speech, and include the infamous "extremism" line.

For a candidate whose chief vulnerability was his supposed extremism, praising extremism seemed the height of imprudence. It did not matter that the statement's intellectual pedigree stretched back to Aristotle and Cicero. Theodore White recorded the shock of a fellow reporter: "My God, he's going to run as Barry Goldwater." There was going to be no "tacking to the center," as is the commonplace strategy of presidential campaigns. Goldwater's defense of "extremism" opened the floodgates for his foes and the media to engage in a *reductio ad Hitlerum*.

Jaffa would later say the "extremism" line was "imprudent," but at the time he was enthusiastic, and he would also offer a comprehensive defense of Goldwater's speech as a whole. Jaffa explained in a 1980 interview:

> I wrote that statement, in part, as a repudiation of the critique of extremism that was made by Rockefeller and Scranton witnesses before the [platform] committee. Sometimes these things

get out of hand. They are like letters you do not intend to send. But they blow out the window and somebody picks them up and they are delivered. And this one was delivered to the Senator, who fell in love with it and ordered that it be incorporated in his Acceptance Speech. . . . It was not my political judgment that the thing be used in the speech at all, although I must say that I was flattered at the time and didn't think too much of what the consequences would be. . . . The Senator liked it because he had been goaded by mean-spirited attacks through the long months of the primaries. Nothing in the political history of the country surpasses in fundamental indecency the kind of attacks that were made on Goldwater by Nelson Rockefeller and his followers. . . . But I was not asked for the extremism statement; I had written it as an in-house memorandum, and it was appropriated. I'm not making an excuse for myself in saying I wasn't responsible for it. I was certainly enthusiastically in favor of it at the time.[7]

Over the years there has been some confusion about the authorship of that line, since the libertarian-leaning Karl Hess was more widely known as Goldwater's chief campaign speechwriter, but in fact a close reading of the speech shows Jaffa's unmistakable thought and style throughout. I don't know if a first draft of Goldwater's acceptance speech survives somewhere in Goldwater's papers—supposedly a draft had been written before the convention—but the speech bears Jaffa's imprint so strongly that a first draft would seem to have been totally transformed.

In the full context of that bitter campaign, we can make out how Goldwater's speech connected his supposed "extremism" with both the historical cause and disposition of the Republican Party going back to its roots and the cause of constitutionalism itself. Goldwater might well have added that the Republican Party was branded as an "extremist" party in 1857, when the *Dred Scott* decision held that the central purpose of the new party was unconstitutional. Moreover, much of the speech departs from the mode of most nomination acceptance speeches of recent decades in either party in offering a history lesson of the party's core principles. The speech has references to private property, federalism and decentralized control, the separation of powers, and, above them all, the Constitution. It invokes the "laws of nature and nature's God" from the Declaration, and offers a rehabilitation of the idea of equality: "Equality, rightly understood as our founding fathers understood it, leads to liberty and emancipation of creative differences; wrongly understood, as it has been so tragically in our time, it leads first to conformity and then to despotism." Above all, read as a whole, the speech makes a serious argument about how to understand "extremism" and "moderation" as they ought to be understood. In other words, Goldwater's speech, as Jaffa transformed it, is arguably the most Aristotelian nomination speech ever delivered.

Jaffa later compared Goldwater's campaign and the "extremism" passage to Lincoln's "House Divided" speech of 1858 and the clash with Republican "moderates" in the pre–Civil War crisis, noting that Lincoln's "house divided" image was heavily criticized at the time for being dangerous and divisive rhetoric. Jaffa argued:

> The eastern leaders of the party in both cases had, in effect, identified "moderation" with their own *policies*, as distinct from the philosophical balance between dangerous or vicious extremes. . . . For Senator Goldwater to have adopted the definition of moderation proposed to him by the eastern Republicans who have succeeded those of 1858, the ones who wished to reject the leadership of Lincoln, would have meant to abandon his extreme defense of constitutionalism. Yet constitutionalism *means* the embodiment of philosophical moderation in practice; just as communism embodies the essence of its rejection.[8]

Goldwater had marked out his departure from the dominant moderate wing of the GOP in his best-selling 1960 book, *The Conscience of a Conservative* (ghostwritten for him by Brent Bozell). *Conscience* deplores not just the liberalism of the Democratic Party, but the weak sisters in Goldwater's own party, which both "propound the first principle of totalitarianism: that the State is competent to do all things and is limited in what it actually does only by the will of those who control the State." The Constitution, Goldwater reminds us, "*is a system of restraints against the* natural *tendency of government to expand in the direction of* absolutism."

Even though many of the worst expressions of the modern Administrative State lay ahead in 1964, Goldwater warned that our government was tending toward "Leviathan, a vast national authority out of touch with the people, and out of their control. This monolith is bounded only by the will of those who sit in high places." *Conscience* culminated in a rallying cry that has come back into fashion among conservatives in recent years:

> I have little interest in streamlining government or in making it more efficient, for I mean to reduce its size. I do not undertake to promote welfare, for I propose to extend freedom. My aim is not to pass laws, but to repeal them. It is not to inaugurate new programs, but to cancel old ones that do violence to the Constitution, or that have failed in their purpose, or that impose on the people an unwarranted financial burden. I will not attempt to discover whether legislation is "needed" before I have first determined whether it is constitutionally permissible. And if I should later be attacked for neglecting my constituents' "interests," I shall reply that I was informed their main interest is liberty and that in that cause I am doing the very best I can.

In light of Goldwater's rhetoric in *Conscience*, the famous "extremism" aphorism shouldn't have come as a shock or surprise. Implicit in Goldwater's rhetoric is that liberalism entailed a departure from the Constitution by necessity, and that the accommodationists among Republicans weren't just conceding to bad policy, but to bad constitutionalism as well. *Conscience of a Conservative* might well be regarded as the first Tea Party manifesto.

The prologue to the "extremism" passage in Goldwater's acceptance speech is vintage Jaffa:

> Back in 1858 Abraham Lincoln said this of the Republican Party, and I quote him because he probably could have said it during the last week or so: "It was composed of strained, discordant, and even hostile elements." End of quote.
>
> Yet all of these elements agreed on one paramount objective: to arrest the progress of slavery, and place it in the course of ultimate extinction. . . .
>
> Anyone who joins us in all sincerity we welcome. Those who do not care for our cause, we don't expect to enter our ranks in any case. And let our Republicanism so focused and so dedicated not be made fuzzy and futile by unthinking and stupid labels.
>
> I would remind you that extremism in the defense of liberty is no vice.
>
> And let me remind you also that moderation in the pursuit of justice is no virtue.

As Jaffa explained, in an essay reflecting on the speech thirty years later:

> It may be asserted with some confidence that the Senator's intention was to rid the campaign, once and for all, of the elements of dangerous irrationality with which abuse has imbued

these terms. While the immediate reaction may suggest to some that the Senator only made a bad situation worse, the longer-range results may yet vindicate him. Like a dangerous cyst that had to be lanced by the surgeon's scalpel, the poisonous passions involved in the offending words are escaping from the diseased core of misunderstanding.[9]

Jaffa observed that two sentences after the offending passage Goldwater said, "We must not see malice in honest differences of opinion, no matter how great, so long as they are not inconsistent with the pledges we have given to each other in and through our Constitution."

In more modest moments, Jaffa would often joke that his chief contribution to future Republican presidential campaigns would be to refrain from writing any more speeches, so long as candidates took his advice.[10] According to one apocryphal story, a friend sent Jaffa a telegram that read: "Great speech. Nothing wrong with it that 10,000 carefully chosen words couldn't explain." But was the "extremism" line, in retrospect, a grievous mistake? Goldwater was not alone in knowing prospectively that his chances of defeating Lyndon B. Johnson were somewhere between slim and none, coming in the aftermath of John F. Kennedy's assassination less than a year before. The "extremism" line surely made no difference to the outcome of the election, given the media hostility and demagogic campaign the Democrats ran against him. Meanwhile, the "extremism" line is the best-recalled passage of any nomination acceptance speech (rivaled only by William Jennings Bryan's "Cross of Gold" speech in 1896) and, taken in full, is a serious defense of constitutionalism and limited government as *the* cause of the Republican Party. How many Republican politicians today are as clear about this?

It is commonplace among liberals today to say that the Republican Party has shifted to the right over the last two decades, but there is little in today's supposed "extremist" party that is not present here in Goldwater's speech. The significance of the Goldwater campaign is that, as Lee Edwards wrote, "for the first time in thirty years, a presidential candidate was challenging the basic assumptions of the welfare state." Liberals were used to dismissing conservatism as the lunatic conspiracy ravings of the John Birch Society (still very prominent in 1964), and simply wouldn't take Goldwater's substantive challenge seriously. The premises of the welfare state were so axiomatic among liberals as not to require any articulation or defense. Goldwater's themes were simply brushed aside with a wave. "Whether government should or should not tamper with the private economy," economist Robert Lekachman wrote during the campaign, is an "obsolete question"—a dismissal that recalls Carl Becker's famous dismissal of the Declaration of Independence mentioned in chapter 5 ("To ask whether the natural rights philosophy of the Declaration of Independence is true or false is essentially a meaningless question").

Goldwater's intent, then, of reorienting the Republican Party and propelling the conservative movement to the fore was the more significant deed. The more serious question is whether the entire Goldwater candidacy was a mistake, and not the single line for which he is best remembered. David Frum has written that the Goldwater nomination should be regarded as a catastrophe for Republicans and conservatism, because "Goldwater's overwhelming defeat invited a tsunami of liberal activism. . . . Suppose somebody other than Sen. Goldwater had won the Republican presidential nomination. Suppose his narrower margin of defeat had preserved those 36 Republican seats in the House. . . . Under those circumstances, the legislation of 1965 might have looked a lot more like the more moderate legislation of 1964."[11]

Counterfactuals like this cannot be proved or disproved; what is, is singular, Churchill once remarked, while what might have been is infinite. The bookend of the Goldwater campaign was

Ronald Reagan's "Time for Choosing" speech, delivered in the closing hours of the doomed campaign, which would propel Reagan's subsequent political career. Without Goldwater, Reagan's rise might well never have happened. And would a putative "moderation" of Johnson's Great Society legislation have left the Republican Party invigorated? It is hard to see. Eugene McCarthy once remarked that the chief purpose of moderate Republicans is to shoot the wounded after the battle is over. Absent Goldwater, it is less than clear that Republicans would ever have entered many battles at all. Here a paraphrase of both halves of Goldwater's couplet seems fully vindicated: moderation in the pursuit of electoral viability is no virtue. Just ask Bob Dole, Mitt Romney, and John McCain.

Goldwater wrote to Jaffa in 1994:

> How well I remember that night we were putting together the finishing touches on the acceptance speech, and you called your wife back in Columbus, and told her precisely where a book would be, and told her the page to turn to, and what to read. That became the basis for the best speech I ever made, the one on "extremism in defense of liberty is no vice." I'd love to make that speech three times a day for the rest of my life.[12]

Another important long-term consequence of Jaffa's role in the Goldwater campaign is that Jaffa caught the eye of Henry Salvatori, one of Goldwater's backers, who also played a central role in arranging Reagan's "Time for Choosing" broadcast that fall. Salvatori was a major donor to Claremont Men's College and helped arrange for Jaffa to leave Ohio State and come to Claremont the following year; he ultimately endowed the chair that Jaffa held until his retirement from teaching in the late 1990s. More than a decade later, Salvatori provided substantial seed funding for the

Claremont Institute, publisher of the *Claremont Review of Books* and the home base, so to speak, of the "West Coast Straussian" perspective that emanates from Jaffa's work. Jaffa would likely have developed in exactly the same way had he stayed at Ohio State or another Midwestern university, but it is less certain that his ideas would have reached a critical mass of students or that a "Claremont school" (the alternative designation of "West Coast Straussianism") would come into being.

It is just a coincidence that the recognition of "West Coast Straussianism" occurred at roughly the same time that the "West Coast offense" emerged in the NFL and transformed football, but there are some stylistic similarities. Wikipedia defines "West Coast offense" as "more of a philosophy and an approach to the game than it is a set of plays or formations" that aims to disrupt defenses with daring, open-ended passing plays. There's a double irony here in that Jaffa was very close to Ohio State's legendary football coach Woody Hayes. But Hayes was the champion par excellence of the "three-yards-and-a-cloud-of-dust" school that conceived of football as primarily a ground game. Hayes, for whom General George Patton was a hero, compared football to an infantry operation.[13] This can be taken as a metaphor of academic scholarship in general. The typical mode is for knowledge to advance by small increments, like a ground game marching down the field to score in sixteen plays over ten minutes. Jaffa's style of argument is certainly more wide open, disruptive of cautious conventions in political philosophy, and aims for quick scoring.

Beyond his feuds with other students of Strauss about Lincoln and the nature of the American Founding, there is one other way in which Jaffa and his circle disrupted the conservative understanding of American government—one that has come into much sharper focus and widespread acceptance in the last decade. While the argument will drag on about whether America is theoretically closer to a classical than an Enlightenment liberal regime, there is one sense in which American government today is tending away from being either, and it represents a crisis of the regime every bit as serious as the Founding Era itself and the Civil War. Jaffa and his students are not the only thinkers to be aware of this crisis, but they were among the first to perceive it and diagnose its roots. That's the next chapter.

CHAPTER 9

The Administrative State and the End of Constitutional Government

[The King] has erected a multitude of New Offices, and sent hither swarms of Officers to harass our people, and eat out their substance.

DECLARATION OF INDEPENDENCE

The free constitutional regimes of the West are thus being drawn inexorably towards unfreedom by the most powerful intellectual force in their midst.

HARRY V. JAFFA

When William F. Buckley Jr. was looking for a description for himself in his sensational debut book *God and Man at Yale* in 1951, he didn't use the term "conservative." In those days, "conservative" was, George Will recalls, "a disparaging epithet" and "at best, an eccentricity." Buckley chose "Christian individualist" instead, seeing this combination as the most sensible opposite to the secularism and socialist collectivism he found pervasive at Yale in the late 1940s. Partly this reflected Albert Jay Nock's residual influence on Buckley, and partly it reflects the fact that the unorganized right at the time could be described mostly as a reactionary movement against Communism abroad and socialism at home, even if American "socialism" was of the relatively mild New Deal variety.

When Buckley founded *National Review* in 1955, however, he fully embraced the label "conservative," in part because he thought it was a "broader" term than individualism, and because he wanted *National Review* to be an intellectually eclectic journal of opinion, since rightists came in so many varieties. But in truth the early *National Review* could be regarded more as a reactionary journal (in the non-pejorative sense of "reactionary"), because many of its senior staff were ex-Communists or ex-socialists rather than conservatives by prior conviction, like Russell Kirk. Whittaker Chambers, for example, disdained the term "conservative" in favor of "man of the right," self-consciously reacting against modernity. As ex-leftists, many of the senior editors were well versed in radical ideology but, with the exception of Willmoore Kendall, only lightly acquainted with American political thought. Not surprisingly, editors and contributors such as Willi Schlamm, Max Eastman, John Dos Passos, Frank Meyer, and James Burnham, as well as Chambers, had a more European sensibility, which meshed well with Buckley's Roman Catholic sensibilities. This meant, inter alia (as Buckley liked to write), that this pro-America magazine was ironically weak on American ideas.

Today the crisis of American government is expressed in an ungainly phrase that rarely appeared in conservative vocabulary in the 1950s and 1960s—the "administrative state," by which is meant the independent "fourth branch of government" that fits nowhere within the scheme of the Constitution as understood by its authors. Conservatives were slow to perceive the full nature and origins of the administrative state. They saw Marxism and radicalism as wholly foreign in character, and the character of the Progressive Era and New Deal bureaucracy as primarily economic and narrowly constitutional in nature. They missed the benign-sounding homegrown versions of deeply radical political philosophy behind the administrative state, especially the key role of Woodrow Wilson and similar Progressive Era intellectuals. Paul Eidelberg, another of Leo Strauss's students, was one of the first to argue in the early 1970s (relatively late in the scheme of things) that "underlying Wilson's politically neutral science of administration is a revolutionary teaching having the profoundest moral significance."[1] But there was very little recognition of this in conservative popular or academic literature in the 1940s or 1950s. If Wilson was mentioned at all, it was usually with a shrug or mild approval of his conventional expressions of Christian faith. In *Crisis of the House Divided*, Harry Jaffa wrote approvingly, albeit briefly, of Wilson's fondness for Lincoln and accepted Wilson's profession of continuity between them. Only later did the decisive break from Lincoln and the Founding that Wilson represented become evident to Jaffa and other conservatives.

It didn't much matter at the time that the modern conservative movement was gaining traction. The urgency of the Cold War dominated the attention of conservative intellectuals and activists alike; with the predations of the New Deal fresh in mind, it was understandable that the conservatism of that time would set the New Deal as the horizon line for their attack on current American politics. To the extent that conservative intellectuals at *National Review* and elsewhere in the 1950s concerned themselves with theoretical questions, they tended to concentrate on how to reconcile libertarianism and traditional Burkean-style conservatism. A lot of the frustration that 1950s-era conservatives had with President Eisenhower and the mainstream of the Republican Party was their conscious accommodation of the New Deal. Only slowly did it come into focus that the New Deal was not the key turning point toward liberalism, and that socialism was not the chief threat to constitutional government and individual liberty.

"Administrative state" is not a new or recent phrase: it has been around for several decades, but its nature and depth has only recently been more fully appreciated. Once confined chiefly to scholars and policy wonks, the term is now in widespread popular use. George Will attacks the administrative state frequently in his columns; ditto Jonah Goldberg. The administrative state is not the same thing as bureaucracy, with its connotations of wastefulness, inefficiency, red tape, and rule-bound rigidity, nor it is limited to the post–New Deal welfare and entitlement state. Its character is best described in Tocqueville's famous chapter on "What Sort of Despotism Democratic Nations Have to Fear"; Tocqueville, after struggling over what to call it, could do no better than "soft despotism."[2]

The administrative state represents a new and pervasive form of rule and a perversion of constitutional self-government. It has deep theoretical roots that were overlooked for a long time, roots inimical to the Constitution; it thereby provides a lesson in the importance of understanding the principles of the Constitution. A chief feature of the administrative state is its relentless centralization: "the brute fact of political power snatched and torn from its local roots and centralized in Washington" as Jaffa put it, but with a reciprocal effect: its mandates, regulations, distorting funding mechanisms, and elitist professionalism have corrupted our political culture all the way down to local government. It is the chief reason why Americans increasingly have contempt for government.

Dwight Waldo, a political scientist prominent from the 1940s to the 1970s, may have been the first thinker to use the phrase "administrative state" in its modern sense. His 1948 book, *The Administrative State: A Study of the Political Theory of American Public Administration*, was a revision of his 1942 doctoral dissertation at Yale, which was supervised by Francis Coker and Harvey C. Mansfield Sr., both coincidentally Harry Jaffa's principal undergraduate teachers and advisers at Yale. Though dated,

Waldo's thorough survey of the subject is still very much worth reading today. Nothing can induce narcolepsy faster than the phrase "public administration." Waldo's account arguably suffers from being too wide-ranging and detailed, but he was writing at a time when we were trying to sort out many of the practical problems arising from the rapid expansion of regulation and government agencies in the New Deal, whose improvisations and arbitrariness demanded some kind of confinement or reform. These problems were the focus of the Hoover Commission and the Brownlow Committee, and culminated in the Administrative Procedure Act of 1946, sometimes called the "constitution of the administrative state." But in trying to create a stable political and legal equilibrium for the new regulatory state, the deeper issues of public philosophy were left behind.

Good as it is, Waldo's account vastly understates the violence done to the Constitution and its underlying principles by Progressivism. This story, especially Woodrow Wilson's role, became better understood only by degrees, but has been very well told more recently and won't be repeated in detail here beyond the briefest sketch.[3] Unlike the Progressive attacks on the Constitution from Beard, Smith, Parrington, and other historians mentioned in chapter 5, who portrayed the Constitution as an antidemocratic fraud, the most potent part of Progressivism, and its chief legacy for today, was its *theoretical* attack on the Founding. Progressivism proposed that the principles of the American Founding were wrong for the twentieth century and needed to be discarded. The swirling currents of Darwinism, Hegelian historicism, and scientific hubris all combined, in the summation of Harvey Mansfield Jr., to make Wilson "the most powerful intellect in the movement" and "the first American president to criticize the Constitution."[4]

What bothered Wilson the most was one of the central features of the logic of the Constitution as explained especially in *The Federalist*: the separation of powers.[5] Wilson laid out his criticism of the separation of powers in his famous chapter in *Constitutional Government in the United States*, where he argued in favor of a "Darwinian" Constitution. Government, he argued, is not a machine, but a living, organic thing. And "No living thing can have its organs offset against each other as checks, and survive. . . . You cannot compound a successful government out of antagonisms."[6] Wilson thought the conditions of modern times demanded that government power be unified rather than fragmented and checked. His great confidence in the wisdom of science and the benevolence of expert administrators led him to view the Founders' worries about concentrated power as obsolete. Wilson exhibited the combination of love for power and unbounded paternalism that is the hallmark of the administrative state today. In *Congressional Government*, he wrote, "I cannot imagine power as a thing negative and not positive," and, on another occasion, noted that "If I saw my way to it as a practical politician, I should be willing to go farther and superintend every man's use of his chance."[7] This stance is quite a contrast from James Madison's views on the permanent reasons for suspicion of government power, expressed in *Federalist* 51, as well as his specific understanding of the separation of powers, expressed in *Federalist* 47: "The accumulation of all powers, legislative, executive, and judiciary, in the same hands, whether of one, a few, or many, and whether hereditary, self appointed, or elective, may justly be pronounced the very definition of tyranny." Wilson explained once that the increased role of the national government could be accomplished "only by wresting the Constitution to strange and as yet unimagined uses. . . . As the life of the nation changes so must the interpretation of the document which contains it change, by a nice adjustment, determined, not by the original intention of those who drew the paper, but by the exigencies and the new aspects of life itself."[8] The legal academy was happy to oblige. Roscoe Pound, for example, remarked that "No one will assert at present that the separation of powers is part of the legal order of nature or that it is essential to liberty."[9]

The main reason Progressives like Wilson no longer shared the older liberal suspicion of government power was the new view that politics and administration could be neatly and cleanly separated, with administration entrusted to scientifically trained and disinterested experts, who by their very expertise should be insulated from political pressure. Frank Goodnow, a prominent political scientist of the Progressive Era and one of Wilson's teachers, provides the best short summary of this view:

> The fact is, then, that there is a large part of administration which is unconnected with politics, which should therefore be relieved very largely, if not altogether, from the control of political bodies. It is unconnected with politics because it embraces fields of semi-scientific, *quasi*-judicial and *quasi*-business or commercial activity—work which has little if any influence on the expression of the true state will. For the most advantageous discharge of this branch of the function of administration there should be organized a force of government agents absolutely free from the influence of politics. Such a force should be free from the influence of politics because of the fact that their mission is the exercise of foresight and discretion, the pursuit of truth, the gathering of information, the maintenance of a strictly impartial attitude toward the individuals with whom they have dealings, and the provision of the most efficient possible administrative organization. The position assigned to such officers should be the same as that which has been by universal consent assigned to judges. Their work is no more political in character than is that of judges.[10]

There is something almost charming as well as comic about this level of naïveté, except that so many people in the administrative apparatus of government still believe it.

Blasting apart the separation of powers is the single most important change that enabled the rise of the administrative state—much more important even than the income tax. In recent years, a number of leading legal scholars, such as Richard Epstein and Philip Hamburger, have said openly what would once have been unthinkable and unsayable in serious company: the modern administrative state is unconstitutional.[11] Writing in the *Harvard Law Review* in the early 1990s, Gary Lawson of Boston University School of Law puts the proposition with admirable directness and concision: "The modern administrative state is not merely unconstitutional; it is anti-constitutional. The Constitution was designed specifically to prevent the emergence of the kinds of institutions that characterize the modern administrative state." And, he says, "the destruction of this principle of separation of powers is perhaps the crowning jewel of the modern administrative revolution."

Lawson offers this illuminating one-paragraph description of the administrative state in action:

> Consider the typical enforcement activities of a typical federal agency—for example, of the Federal Trade Commission. The Commission promulgates substantive rules of conduct. The Commission then considers whether to authorize investigations into whether the Commission's rules have been violated. If the Commission authorizes an investigation, the investigation is conducted by the Commission, which reports its findings to the Commission. If the Commission thinks that the Commission's findings warrant an enforcement action, the Commission issues a complaint. The Commission's complaint that a Commission rule has been violated is then prosecuted by the Commission and adjudicated by the Commission. This Commission adjudication can either take place before the full Commission or before a semi-autonomous Commission administrative law judge. If the Commission chooses to adjudicate before an ad-

ministrative law judge rather than before the Commission and the decision is adverse to the Commission, the Commission can appeal to the Commission. If the Commission ultimately finds a violation, then, and only then, the affected private party can appeal to an Article III court. But the agency decision, even before the bona fide Article III tribunal, possesses a very strong presumption of correctness on matters both of fact and of law.[12]

While legal scholars and policy wonks are devoting increased attention to the structure and methods of the administrative state, the idea that its suspect constitutional foundations will lead to any meaningful rollback has little or no purchase in contemporary jurisprudence. The main reason for this sorry state is that the roots of the problem go deeper than decades of bungled Supreme Court opinions, aggressive presidents, and a complacent or negligent Congress. The problem of the administrative state goes beyond a failure to internalize the insights of public choice theory, the restraints of economic cost-benefit analysis, or the erosion of the nondelegation doctrine. It is another example of what happens when first principles are forgotten or obscured. And the bitter irony of it is how conservatives unwittingly assisted in this demolition job.

———

Wilson and most other leading Progressives hated the Declaration of Independence for its principle of individual rights rooted in "the laws of nature and nature's God." The central philosophical proposition of "Progressivism" is that History with a capital "H" or "Progress" with a capital "P" had replaced nature as the ground of political life. Wilson said he just about wore out a German dictionary reading Hegel and adapting Hegelian historicism for his own understanding of politics.

It is possible to trace back the idea of History or Progress to any number of individual thinkers or schools of thought, such as

Bacon's science for the relief of man's estate, Comte's positivism, Condorcet's perfectionism, Bentham's utilitarianism, as well as Hegel's idealism, Darwin's evolutionism, and Marx's dialectical materialism.[13] It is not essential to sort out which is the most important or dominant strain to understand the political effects. As implausible as it might seem today, the idea that science would unlock Newtonian "laws of motion" for history, thus making the course of the future as predictable as the acceleration of a falling object, was surprisingly widespread. And if history is scientifically predictable, it is controllable. The world of chance and accident could be conquered. "Progress!," Wilson wrote; "No word comes more often or more naturally to the lips of modern man."[14]

The State, now with a capital "S" to go along with capital "H" History and capital "P" Progress, is the agent of purposeful change. Hegel was direct in seeing History replace the Christian idea of Providence, with the State taking the place of God: "The State is the Divine idea as it exists on earth. We have in it, therefore, the object of History in a more definite shape than before."[15]

Out of this progressive philosophy, the modern understanding of "political leadership" was born—the necessity of what George H. W. Bush unwittingly but correctly mocked as "the vision thing." The term "leadership" was almost wholly absent from the vocabulary of the Founders. Modern "leadership" is distinct from the older understanding of statesmanship. A progressive leader sees ahead, and thus forces the pace of change, whereas statesmanship is more anchored in the understanding of the limits of politics. In a remarkable 1890 essay entitled "Leaders of Man," Wilson set out a bold and frequently shocking account of modern political leadership:

> The competent leader of men cares little for the interior niceties of other people's characters: he cares much—everything for the external uses to which they may be put. His will seeks the

lines of least resistance; but the whole question with him is a question *of the application of force*. There are men to be moved: how shall he move them? He supplies the power; others supply only the materials upon which that power operates. The power will fail if it be misapplied; it will be misapplied if it be not suitable both in kind and method to the nature of the materials upon which it is spent; but that nature is, after all, only its means. It is the *power* which dictates, dominates: the materials yield. Men are as clay in the hands of the consummate leader.[16]

There is much else of this ominous character throughout this long and confusing essay, including a studied disavowal that he is any kind of radical or socialist. At the heart of Progressivism is a confusion and contradiction that has always made Progressivism a vague and tricky creed to sort out. Progressivism saw itself as the moderate alternative to revolutionary socialism, but its economic inclinations certainly tended toward the kind of central authoritarian control of the economy that is nearly indistinguishable from socialism. It was not explicitly utopian, but its underlying philosophy ran in that direction. The Progressives were always imprecise about how much or how far human nature might be malleable and they were more reticent than the Europeans, such as Nicolas de Condorcet for example, with regard to the prospect of the perfection of man. But the limits to the Progressive project were unspecified.[17]

But by far the greatest contradiction was the idea that Progressivism would be more populist and elitist at the same time. Practical democratic reforms—such as the direct election of senators, initiatives and referendums, and so forth—were intended to give more voice to the people, while the doctrine of scientific administration sought to seal off a larger and larger portion of government from the people. "Administrative questions are not political questions," Wilson wrote.[18] Progressivism represented the American domesticated version of the phrase attributed to Friedrich Engels and Henri de Saint-Simon that "the government of men will be replaced by the administration of things." The Progressive attempt to resolve this contradiction involved supercharging the distinction between means and ends—popular politics would allow the public to speak about the *ends* of government, while the means would be left to the expert administrators. But, because the *ends* of Progressive politics were severed from the old liberal understanding of protecting individual natural rights and were now open-ended, this distinction collapses instantly.

Between the ideology of Progress as understood by the visionary "leader" and the doctrine of scientific administration, a new understanding of the difference between the Ruler and the Ruled took hold—and it isn't good news for the Ruled. Despite his frequent obscurity and paeans to democracy and the "will of the people," Wilson argues at one point in "Leaders of Men" that the "vision" of Progress is the new supreme force in politics:

> [L]eadership does not always wear the harness of compromise. Once and again one of those great Influences which we call a *Cause* arises in the midst of a nation. Men of strenuous minds and high ideals come forward, with a sort of gentle majesty, as champions of a political or moral principle. They wear no armour; they bestride no chargers; they only speak their thought, in season and out of season. But the attacks they sustain are more cruel than the collisions of arms. Their souls are pierced with a thousand keen arrows of obloquy. Friends desert and despise them. They stand alone: and oftentimes are made bitter by their isolation. They are doing nothing less than defy public opinion, and shall they convert it by blows? Yes. Presently the forces of the popular thought hesitate, waver, seem to doubt their power to subdue a half score stubborn minds. Again a

little while and those forces have actually yielded. Masses come over to the side of the reform. *Resistance is left to the minority, and such as will not be convinced are crushed.* (Emphasis added.)

Notice especially this last sentence, and recall how often it is today that "progressives," such as President Obama, will criticize the minority who resist the latest Progressive advance such as gay marriage or degendered bathrooms with the telltale phrase, "on the side of history." It is the leading slogan of the soft despotism of our age, all the more confident and aggressive for its presumption that its goals need not be rationally justified through argument or persuasion.

Progressivism surely did not understand itself as tyrannical, and on the surface it eschewed utopian ideology, but its premises were metaphysically identical to utopian ideologies that invariably end up tyrannical in practice. There was sufficient ambiguity in Progressive thought to muddy up the picture, and even Wilson's strongest critics disagree about how to understand his brand of Progressivism. Not all Progressives joined Wilson in attacking or rejecting the Declaration of Independence. (Albert J. Beveridge, for example, frequently invoked the Declaration in its original meaning.) But overall the dominant Wilsonian variety of Progressivism amounted to a revolution, a refounding of the country in which all of the old terms—liberty, equality, consent, rights, and freedom—were retained, but with wholly new meanings. (Wilson advocated for what he called "mature freedom," which was very different from traditional understandings of liberty.)

The first World War and its sequels put an end to the easygoing assumption of inevitable or irreversible progress, but the residue of Progressive theory—most especially the idea of the scientifically managed administrative state—was firmly in place, to be picked up and expanded by the New Deal after the brief interregnum of the "return to normalcy" in the 1920s. It didn't take long during the

New Deal to recognize that the idea of "neutral" or "disinterested" expert administrative government was a farce, that in practice independent bureaucratic entities would become the active agents for discrete interests and ideological impulses, the overwhelming majority being client groups of one party. That bureaucratic government is the partisan instrument of the Democratic Party is the most obvious, yet least remarked upon, trait of our time (though this lack of public identification can be taken as additional evidence of the incompetence of the Republican Party).

Economists tended to call this phenomenon "agency capture," and, while accurate, the term goes nowhere near the heart of the matter. A central aspect of so-called expert administration beyond organizational self-interest and clientism is the deliberate gnosticism of its operation. Max Weber, the preeminent early theorist of bureaucratic government as well as a progenitor of modern social science, foresaw this in the nineteenth century:

> Every bureaucracy seeks to increase the superiority of the professionally informed by keeping their knowledge and intentions secret. Bureaucratic administration always tends to be an administration of 'secret sessions': in so far as it can, it hides its knowledge and action from criticism. . . . In facing a parliament, the bureaucracy, out of a sure power instinct, fights every attempt of the parliament to gain knowledge by means of its own experts or from interest groups. . . . Bureaucracy naturally welcomes a poorly informed and hence a powerless parliament—at least in so far as ignorance somehow agrees with the bureaucracy's interests.[19]

While Weber thought bureaucracy was necessary or unavoidable for government in advanced industrial nations, he had misgivings about its effects, worrying that the rationalistic oligarchy it empowered represented a new "iron cage" that would dehumanize both the rulers and the ruled. Anticipating what contemporary scholars in public choice and other schools of thought have explained in detail but with more vivid imagery, Weber foresaw "mechanized petrifaction, varnished by a kind of convulsive sense of self-importance," that bureaucrats would become "specialists without spirit or vision and voluptuaries without heart." The tragedy of Weber was his inability to shake loose from his positivist fact-value distinction, despite signs that he recognized the inadequacy of a world without the ability to make rational, objective moral judgments and politics without great statesmen. Weber's tragic position took on poignancy with his famous post–World War I valedictory lecture, "Politics as a Vocation," in which he recognizes the necessity of the prudence of the statesman while being unable to provide guidance about how to acquire the necessary wisdom to inform that prudence because it is beyond the grasp of human reason.[20]

American Progressives had none of Weber's honest doubts and anguish, chiefly because of their total absorption of historicism (and also because Weber's works were mostly unknown in America at the time). If Progress and History soon waned as a dominant, driving foundation for Progressive politics, the positivist distinction between *facts* and *values*, which corresponds to the distinction between administrative questions and political questions, endured. By mid-century the behavioral revolution came to dominate political science just as much as the rest of social science, replacing History as the ground of mastery. Political philosophy was declared to be dead. Behaviorism was an even more explicitly deterministic outlook than Progress, but it shared with Progressive historicism the same convenient but self-contradictory trait that it preserves freedom of choice and action for the rulers alone. The "scientific" elites of the administrative state were still in business.

While behaviorism provoked furious debates about methodology and the place of political philosophy in political science around mid-century, it soon waned, too. It is embarrassing now to look back upon the cartoonish rigidity of the fact-value distinction and the confidence that science was on its way to unlocking causation in humans and human affairs, while openly placing questions of "value"—or the *ends* of politics—beyond the reach of human reason. One of Leo Strauss's signal contributions was explaining how Weber's fact-value distinction was, in the end, indistinguishable from nihilism, despite the futile attempt of Weber and his successors to preserve some sphere of objective reality for "values."

The behaviorism of mid-century has been replaced by regression modeling, which is scarcely better, though it is more modest in its pretensions. The salient point here is that Strauss's leading students all came of age during the heyday of behaviorism, and they directed considerable follow-on firepower to Strauss's critique of social science. The core of the critique was the simple understanding that the value-free approach to political science is distinctly *antipolitical*. Edward Banfield asked, "Would anyone maintain that in the Convention of 1787 the Founders would have reached a better result with the staff of model builders?" Walter Berns thought the detachment from taking moral questions and human excellence seriously made behavioral political science diabolical: "It would be ironic if the science that once made man free, were now to become the instrument of his enslavement." Few put it with the directness and pungency of Martin Diamond: "[T]o teach our students that there is no cognitive basis for ultimate questions and answers about political health and excellence, is to make them scientifically armed philistines, armed by us with a scientific defense against all the pain and beauty of truly political, which is to say human inquiry. And it is thereby to make them vulnerable to those who offer a cheap substitute for that pain and beauty—modern armed messianism."[21]

This wasn't just a critique of narrow specialization, of "knowing more and more about less and less," as Strauss put it. Lots of "mainstream" and left-leaning political scientists also decried the fact-value distinction, precisely because of the moral relativism it imposes like a straitjacket, and the self-limiting obscurity of increasingly technical specialization.[22] In fact, it is hard to say whether the revolt against the fact-value distinction was stronger from the right or the left.

None of the current categorical imperatives of the left can be traced back to a ground of fundamental principle beyond a vague and unlimited egalitarianism, which constantly requires ever-increasing political exertions to achieve. Instead, as noted previously, the moral ground is the "side of history." In other words, what has happened is a revival of the earlier Progressive historicism of Woodrow Wilson, only with objectives borrowed chiefly from Marxism. The return of historicism, along with the revival of the "progressive" label, is not a coincidence.

One might wonder whether we weren't better off in the bad old days of behaviorism and the fact-value distinction. In the new horizon of today's historicism, not only is there no rational basis for values but also *facts* are not faring very well either. It is a hard call, as the progressive impulse of our time ends up being just as deterministic as behaviorism. The "side of history" may be a gauzy, low-grade form of determinism, but, like all determinisms, it is the ground of despotism. Diamond's phrase about "armed messianism" is apt, as today's progressives evince the same attitude as Wilson: "*Resistance is left to the minority, and such as will not be convinced are crushed.*"

The impulse goes much deeper than the censorious castigation of "hate speech" and the open attacks against freedom of speech that have been steadily gaining ground. The frontier of leftist "critical thinking" questions language itself, holding that language is a subjective and arbitrary tool of power and control, rather than *the* tool of human reason and deliberation. This is an indirect way of saying that reason and objectivity are impossible, a view leftists tend to conceal or obscure if they can. (I have occasionally baited leftist "critical theorists" by asking, "If language is merely an arbitrary tool of power detached from any objective reality, is it right to wonder not only *why* we are having this conversation, but also *how* we are having this conversation?")

Debunking language itself attacks the very root of human freedom, because it is through speech that we reason together and form opinions on what is just and unjust, good and bad, high and low. Reason expressed through speech sets humans apart from the lower animals. Denying the metaphysical nature of speech derives from denying the idea of human nature. (Or, if there is a human nature, progressives are intent on changing it.) If language and speech can be detached from reason, there is no reason to believe in individual liberty. Walter Berns defended the older understanding—Plato's understanding—back in the early 1960s before the attacks on language became so popular: "With his speech he imitates the language of nature; he apprehends things as they are, not by means of his sense but in and through speech. . . . The freedom of speech *is* essential, because of the possibility that through speech we can discover nature."[23]

The doctrine of power combined with the revived doctrine of History as Progress gives us the insatiable and unlimited administrative state we see today. The heart of the administrative state is now aimed less at correcting market failures than moral failures. Thus the federal bureaucracy without hesitation extends the Civil Rights Act of 1964 to tell North Carolina that it cannot have single-sex bathrooms and Title IX is extended well beyond legislative intent to institutionalize the radical feminist ideology of "rape culture," heedless of either facts or due process of law. This process is not limited to government bureaus. Just as James Burnham's theory of how the "managerial society" would come to permeate the world of "private" business as much as government, we can see this mentality in the case of Brendan Eich, hounded out as CEO of Mozilla for having once held the same position on gay marriage that President Obama and Hillary Clinton held at the same time; or in the number of corporations that announced they would cut back business activity in North Carolina over the bathroom bill. *"Resistance is left to the minority, and such as will not be convinced are crushed."* And this project is self-perpetuating. As Jaffa put it: "The practical aim of a Skinnerian or a Marxist-Leninist 'educational' process must always come to this: to induce in the subjects of the government a kind of behavior that will keep the government and its coopted successors permanently in office."[24]

Today's progressives do not think of themselves as tyrants any more than the Progressives of Wilson's time, but the underlying doctrines are metaphysically identical to totalitarianism. The Progressivism of the Progressive Era was modest and relatively restrained compared to its present-day manifestations. At least the Progressives of the Theodore Roosevelt–Wilson era were setting after genuine social ills—child labor, workers' compensation, substandard housing, public health and safety, economic monopoly power (even if badly misunderstood). If there was a tendency toward utopianism, it was tempered by the perception that socialism didn't fit the American character. Today's progressives are more fully utopian, though their utopianism is diffuse or shrouded by deliberately obscure theory, and, above all, they hate any conception of American exceptionalism.

The point is, the problem of the administrative state is much more than a problem of economic illiteracy, decayed constitutionalism, or modernization, which is why the numerous gimmicks to restrain or reform it, such as cost-benefit analysis, affirmative congressional consent to new regulations, rolling back judicial deference, or other legal fixes will not do very much to change the direction of rule today. The problem is more serious than bad policy and bad law. If it is not stopped and reversed, however, it will result in the end of limited constitutional government.

As I suggested at the outset of this chapter, the modern conservative movement was slow to recognize Progressivism in its fullness. It is clear in hindsight that everyone, especially conservatives, made a mistake twenty-five years ago in thinking that the collapse of the Soviet Union and the eclipse of Marxism meant that liberal democracy, individual rights, and open markets had achieved an enduring triumph—the famous "end of history" thesis. At the time, Jaffa was one of the few voices dissenting from the widespread triumphalism; he foresaw that, to the contrary, the threats to human freedom might become more dangerous precisely because radical thought would metastasize into new forms even more remote from reason and objectivity. In a lecture delivered at the end of 1991, Jaffa argued that the end of Marxism changed nothing:

> The revolutionary goal of a classless society of altruists has survived. It has survived, detached from any foundation in rational analysis, such as Marx claimed for himself. For what else is the movement for "consciousness raising," but a renamed version of the demand for "socialist man"? What is the conflict between the property rights of individuals and global environmentalism, but another chapter in the conflict between bourgeois man and socialist man? "Diversity" is demanded by those who will tolerate no deviation from the "politically correct." And what is "political correctness" but another name for "the party line"? It is Leninism-Stalinism without Lenin or Stalin.

Thus Jaffa reached the conclusion mentioned back in chapter 1:

> The defeat of communism in the USSR and its satellite empires by no means assures its defeat in the world. Indeed, the release of the West from its conflict with the East emancipates

utopian communism at home from the suspicion of its affinity with an external enemy. The struggle for the preservation of Western civilization has entered a new—and perhaps far more deadly and dangerous—phase.[25]

This was not a new theme for Jaffa at this point. By the mid-1970s, he had come to see that the denial of human nature and the idea of scientific administration would become the motive force of the administrative state, and also the defining characteristic of the privileged attitude of bureaucratic government. More and more regulation today has a *moral* purpose rather than an economic purpose. This fundamental change, argued John Wettergreen, Jaffa's first graduate student, is a recipe for "total regulation."[26] Jaffa made this a recurrent theme, writing, for example, in 1981:

> In the name of equality of opportunity, there will be a privileged bureaucratic elite choosing its successors according to its whim. . . . It cannot be emphasized too strongly that Marxist-Leninists and western behavioral scientists do not differ in what is most essential to the development of their doctrine and their practical influence: the conviction that there is no human nature properly so called, and that what is called human nature is an unintended by-product of a blind evolutionary-historical process. In differing (but ultimately unimportant) ways they think that man can now take control of his own destiny by making his own nature the supreme object of his policy. . . . The very nature of this new science of politics results in the bifurcation of mankind into two "natures"; that of the scientific rulers, and that of the ruled. . . . The free constitutional regimes of the West are thus being drawn inexorably towards unfreedom by the most powerful intellectual force in their midst.[27]

Jaffa was not the first to notice the homegrown roots of the administrative state in the Progressive Era, nor were the Strauss-influenced thinkers the only ones who figured it out. Vincent Ostrom noted the importance of Wilson's Progressive philosophy in *The Intellectual Crisis in American Public Administration* in the early 1970s, and even Dwight Waldo acknowledged that "public administration is not a scientific discipline." I'm not sure who was the first conservative thinker to shine a spotlight on Progressivism in a sustained way. Paul Eidelberg's work in the early 1970s, mentioned previously, may have been the first, but other scholars who began to expand on the significance of the Progressive Era in deforming American politics around that time include Harvey Mansfield Jr., James Ceaser, and Charles R. Kesler; in recent years a flood of academic work in this vein has been produced, most of it from the next generation of students of Jaffa, Berns, Mansfield, Kesler, and Ceaser.

The combination of Progressivism's embrace of historicist philosophy and positivist scientism is neither an exhaustive nor exclusive account of what ails America. Fred Siegel and other historians rightly point to literary and social currents of the time that simply despise middle-class American life and consciously seek its destruction for reasons unrelated to formal nihilism.[28] It is also hard to disentangle from this story other imported and adapted ideologies, such as the Frankfurt School, French linguistics, deconstructionism, and so forth, which have done for American intellectual culture what the British invasion did for rock and roll.[29] But it is hard to see the constitutional deformations succeeding to the extent they did over the last century, the crisis of the Great Depression notwithstanding, in the absence of the conscious Progressive assault on the American Founding. It makes clear that restoring the American republic to something resembling the nation the Founders designed requires fighting back through Progressivism at the level of basic political philosophy.

That is a tall order, and not an easy case to make on the retail level. On the one hand, the ordinary or commonsense understanding of change and "progress" provides today's progressives with a superficial rhetorical home-field advantage. On the other hand, public confidence in American government is at an all-time low, in part because the administrative state is incompetent in pursuing its increasingly ambitious ends, and as its increasingly arbitrary character becomes more evident. Leo Strauss might be said to have predicted this more than fifty years ago, when he commented in *The City and Man* about the public alienation that comes about "when the citizens' understanding of political things is replaced by the scientific understanding."[30]

There is also the intellectual exhaustion of the Left. While the Left still has its celebrity intellectuals—the Zizeks and Badious—the deliberate obscurity of their thought limits their broader public appeal. The least that can be said of the Progressives and their immediate successors is that they had a number of prominent public intellectuals. The late sociologist Robert Nisbet observed: "Royce, James, Dewey, and Russell were household names. Who at this moment would have the slightest interest in what a living philosopher had to say on any subject, cosmological, moral, political, or social?"

Given that the Left today is explicitly obsessed with power, perhaps it no longer needs a pseudo-rational foundation, or feels a need for serious philosophical engagement. But this attitude is among the reasons for the decline of the humanities in higher education, of the evident and growing boredom among the dwindling number of non-radicalized students who wander haplessly into classrooms in the humanities and social sciences, and sensibly come away with the impression that there is nothing important to learn.

The modern rejection of political philosophy is that it cannot settle "close calls," which is one reason for concentrating on the prudence of the statesman in politics. A great example of the poverty of moral philosophy today is the popularity of the "runaway trolleycar" thought experiment, first introduced in American classrooms in the 1970s.[31] This simple, if not simpleminded, exercise in comparing utilitarian versus essentialist moral principles is wildly popular with students, which shows how superficial and unserious moral education has become. Yet this lack of seriousness provides hope that a return to the older way of studying political things would find a large and eager audience. (In fact, it is not unusual to find that political science is a leading major at colleges and universities that teach the subject the "old-fashioned way.")

Leo Strauss liked to rebut the simple rejection of moral reasoning on account of the impossibility of rational agreement on specific moral conflicts (abortion is a good example) with the observation:

> If we cannot decide which of two mountains whose peaks are shrouded by clouds is higher than the other, cannot we decide that a mountain is higher than a molehill? If we cannot decide, regarding a war between two neighboring nations which have been fighting each other for centuries, which nation's cause is more just, cannot we decide that Jezebel's action against Naboth was inexcusable?[32]

The road back might begin with questions like this. But hardly anyone dares to ask them this way anymore.

CHAPTER 10

Political Philosophy in an Anti-Philosophic Age

Europe was created by history.
America was created by philosophy.

MARGARET THATCHER

In the final analysis, not only American politics,
but all modern politics, must be clarified on the
basis of classical political philosophy.

HARRY JAFFA

When the University of Chicago Press decided in the mid-1980s to produce a new, third edition of *History of Political Philosophy*, a popular multiauthor reader edited by Leo Strauss and Joseph Cropsey and first published in 1963, Jaffa picked another fight. Cropsey, Jaffa's old boyhood friend, had decided the third edition should include some new essays on several additional thinkers: Thucydides, Xenophon, Edmund Husserl, Martin Heidegger, and Leo Strauss himself. Jaffa had been the author of the well-regarded essay on Aristotle in the first two editions, but when asked for permission to use the essay again in the third edition, Jaffa made his approval conditional on including new chapters on Shakespeare, Churchill, and Lincoln. Cropsey declined, and the third edition went forth with a new chapter on Aristotle from Carnes Lord.

The final irony of this episode is that Jaffa was enthusiastic about the new chapter on Strauss written by Nathan Tarcov and Thomas Pangle, saying effusively that it could have been written by someone from Claremont. Having tangled with Pangle several times in the 1980s over how to understand Strauss's legacy, Jaffa suspected the chapter would have an "eastern Straussian" perspective portraying Strauss as philosophically detached from political life, disdainful of democracy, indifferent to the American Founding, and neglectful of statesmanship. But the Strauss of Tarcov and Pangle was largely harmonious with Jaffa's outlook, seeing modern democracy as necessarily partaking of the civic republicanism of antiquity:

> [Democracy] therefore continues to require, Strauss insisted, some version (an attenuated version, to be sure) of the Greco-Roman ideal of an active, proud citizenry imbued with knowledgeable respect for outstanding statesmanship. Strauss consequently deplored the influence of those thoughtlessly egalitarian historians who debunk, rather than make more intelligible, the greatness of statesmen.[1]

The centrality of the statesman at the intersection of philosophy and political life was the ground on which Jaffa thought Lincoln and Churchill deserved inclusion alongside Plato, Aristotle, Hegel, Burke, and the rest in a reader devoted to a Straussian perspective on political philosophy. It is certainly possible to find support for this thought from Strauss, in particular the eulogy to Churchill that he delivered in class the day after Churchill's death in 1965. In that compact observance, Strauss sees the unity of the thought and deeds of Churchill, or the translation of thought *into* deeds. As mentioned in chapter 4, Strauss thought Churchill's

Marlborough was an "inexhaustible mine of political wisdom" that should be required reading of all students of political science. While Strauss found Churchill to be an example of "political greatness, human greatness, of the peaks of human excellence," Strauss also pointed to Churchill's *failures*—especially his inability to prevent the Cold War that he had foreseen—as a further lesson in the limitations of politics and therefore the need of prudence and moderation. Whatever the substantive differences were between ancient and modern political philosophy, Strauss made out a straight line between the classical Aristotelian perspective and the possibility of modern statesmanship with his remark in a letter to Karl Lowith that "A man like Churchill proves that the possibility of *megalophysis* [the great-souled man] exists today *exactly* as it did in the fifth century B.C."[2]

The case for Shakespeare's inclusion among the canon of great political philosophers gets to the heart of the ancient quarrel between philosophy and poetry—the contest for supremacy regarding wisdom. This is another tension, like reason and revelation, that is badly distorted in modern thought, but which Strauss-trained political scientists believe is very much still alive in the same form that it was 2,500 years ago.

Jaffa noticed that at the end of Plato's *Symposium*, Socrates fleetingly mentions the possibility of the same person writing both comedy and tragedy, and that it was the same art. Plato's account does not expand on Socrates' argument. Aristodemus, the narrator of the *Symposium*, says only that "the chief thing we remembered was Socrates compelling the other two [Aristophanes and Agathon] to acknowledge that the genius of comedy was the same with that of tragedy, and that the true artist in tragedy was the artist in comedy also."

This was a heterodox proposition in classical Greek thought, and Jaffa argued that "we do not know, to this day, of any great poet who has written both tragedy and comedy. That is to say, we do not know of any such poet, except William Shakespeare. Shakespeare is the greatest—perhaps he is the only—poet to have practiced the art referred to by Socrates at the end of the *Symposium*."[3] Today Shakespeare has become politicized with all of the usual filters of postmodern ideology, and it is not certain whether to greet with dismay or relief the news that a startlingly high number of university English literature departments nowadays de-emphasize Shakespeare. (Some colleges no longer require a single course on Shakespeare for English majors.) Meanwhile, in political science departments where conservatives have a strong presence, it is common to find popular courses on Shakespeare as a political thinker. Allan Bloom justified the enterprise in a manner that would not be uncongenial to the great Shakespearean scholar Harold Bloom (who was no relation to Allan):

> Shakespeare devotes great care to establishing the political setting in almost all his plays, and his greatest heroes are rulers who exercise capacities which can only be exercised within civil society. To neglect this is simply to be blinded by the brilliance of one's own prejudices. As soon as one sees this, one cannot help asking what Shakespeare thought about a good regime and a good ruler. I contend that the man of political passions and education is in a better position to understand the plays than a purely private man. With the recognition of this fact, a new perspective is opened, not only on the plays but also on our notions of politics. . . . The poet can take the philosopher's understanding and translate it into images which touch the deepest passions and cause men to know without knowing that they know.[4]

Today, however, you're more likely to get something like this about Shakespeare's politics from literature departments, such as this passage from an actual book:

The development of cultural materialism in relation to Renaissance literature has been fairly recent although there is already a diverse and developing field of work relating literary texts to, for example, the following: enclosures and the oppression of the rural poor; State power and resistance to it; reassessments of what actually were the dominant ideologies of the period and the radical countertendencies to these; witchcraft; the challenge and containment of the carnivalesque; a feminist recovery of the actual conditions of women and the altered understanding of their literary representations which this generates; conflict between class factions within the State and, correspondingly, the importance of a non-monolithic conception of power.[5]

In the pages of the book where this passage appears, *Political Shakespeare*, the Bard and his characters completely disappear from view for many pages at a time.

Bloom and Jaffa published major articles on Shakespeare's political teaching in the unlikely venue of the *American Political Science Review* in 1957 and 1960, when the *APSR* was under the general editorship of Harvey C. Mansfield Sr.[6] It is likely not a coincidence that, while a few short reviews of books about Shakespearean political themes appear from time to time, there haven't been any main articles on Shakespeare in the *APSR* since 1960.

On the surface it might seem strange that Shakespeare could be considered as meaningful to political thought as he is (or was) for literature, but, as Bloom argued, it is perhaps only in political science today that "Shakespeare is taught as though he *said* something." Jaffa put it succinctly: "Shakespeare's theater and Plato's cave are closely related. . . . Shakespeare was the great vehicle within the Anglo-American world for the transmission of an essentially Socratic understanding of the civilization of the West." Jaffa argued further that Shakespeare was one of only two writers who absorbed the full impact of Machiavelli's teaching.[7] (He thought the other was Strauss.)

Grasping the relevance of Shakespeare as a source of political wisdom involves looking no further than Lincoln, whose command of *Macbeth* was so complete that he pointed out minor errors to actors after seeing live performances. Lincoln regarded *Macbeth*—"nothing equals *Macbeth*" he said—as a profound teaching of the problem of tyranny. Both Jaffa and Walter Berns make special note of Lincoln's interest in *Macbeth*, how he apparently saw himself as Duncan, twice quoting after the Confederate surrender at Appomattox: "Duncan is in his grave . . . nothing can touch him further."

Jaffa's interest in Shakespeare united his study of political philosophy with his early interest in literature, and he found Shakespeare to be as worthy a guide as Aristotle to the "moral order of the universe." By contrast, Jaffa argued, the predominant effect of modern literature was the "corruption of the moral consciousness," a deliberate weakening of the ground of morality.[8] Jaffa delivered a series of lectures on Dostoyevsky and Camus that argued this theme in the early 1970s. Of Camus's *The Stranger*, Jaffa concluded:

> By the art of Camus we are led to admire his hero, Meursault; young people especially tend to identify with him. What kind of hero is Meursault? He is utterly indifferent to morality and cannot understand what others mean when they say they love other human beings. In the story, he kills a man and is sentenced to be executed, in part because he did not weep at his mother's funeral. Meursault becomes passionate in the end: but the only passion he ever experiences is the passionate revulsion against the idea of human attachment. He thinks no one had a right to expect him to weep at his mother's funeral, or for anyone else to weep at her funeral. By Camus's hero we are taught to be repelled by those who (he believes) falsely teach us that

there is any foundation for human attachments, or that there is anything in the universe that is lovable. The benign indifference to the universe is the only form of the benign, of goodness itself, in the universe. To imitate the indifference of the universe to good and evil is to live life at its highest level.[9]

This erosion of morality is simply a symptom of the abolition of the objective ground of truth in modern philosophy. In exasperation, Jaffa once asked, "How do you talk to these people?"

In other words, Jaffa was a moralist, and so was Walter Berns. While it is surprising that Berns, the one-time aspiring novelist, never wrote much sustained literary criticism, his indignation at the moral decay of modernity was evident in much of his writing—and certainly in casual conversation! For Walter, the adjective "indecent" was not subjective. His moral bearing is perhaps best seen in his 1979 book *For Capital Punishment*, which defended the death penalty on *moral* grounds rather than the typical utilitarian ground of deterrence.[10] In his culminating argument that abolishing the death penalty would be *immoral*, Berns illustrates the nature of modern nihilism with a chapter that was his most extensive excursion into literature, which began with explicating the teaching of . . . *The Stranger*. His analysis and description of Camus is identical to Jaffa's:

A moral community is not possible without anger and the moral indignation that accompanies it, which is why the most powerful attack on capital punishment was written by a man, Albert Camus, who denied the legitimacy of anger and moral indignation by denying the very possibility of a moral community in our time. . . . Meursault is an "outsider" not because he is an inhuman man in a human world, but because he is the only honest man in a world of hypocrites. He alone understands that the universe provides no support for what men in their ignorance persist in regarding as the human things, say, love and justice.[11]

From here, Berns's argument moves on to the moral reasoning to be found in . . . *Macbeth*. Once again, his argument parallels Jaffa closely. Jaffa: "The lesson of the play is the inexorable and inescapable vindictive power of the moral universe."[12] Berns: "In *Macbeth* the majesty of the moral law is demonstrated to us. . . . [I]t teaches us the awesomeness of the commandment, thou shalt not kill."[13]

None of this is to suggest in the slightest that Berns borrowed from Jaffa, or vice versa. In fact, Jaffa's 1973 lecture from which the selections here are taken was not published until many years after Berns's book appeared, and in the middle of Berns's chapter a long footnote pays lavish tribute to Jaffa's *Crisis of the House Divided*.[14] Rather, these parallels let us observe again the similarity in the modes of thinking and essential *agreement* between these two giants, and thus to regret anew that they fell into such a bitter personal feud.

What, finally, accounts for the feud? Partly it was a matter of style and temperament. Jaffa's stubbornness and intransigence was of a piece with his exacting analysis and devotion to principle, and, as Churchill liked to say, you have to take the rough with the smooth. A less combative Jaffa wouldn't have been Jaffa. Berns was equally stubborn, if less prideful and gratuitous. Jaffa was faulted, often by his own students, for personalizing his disagreements. Berns once attempted a direct personal rebuke. In his last private letter to Jaffa in 1981—a letter that, Berns lamented, "I have no reason to believe will do any good"—Berns called out Jaffa's "overweening vanity" but went on to charge Jaffa with squandering his genius:

> In the current atmosphere of this country, you could have become the great historian and poet of the American regime. Are you pleased with what you have done instead? Even after 22 years, the promised second Lincoln volume, *The New Birth of Freedom*, has not appeared, and, because you fritter away your

great gifts on petty, vain, and vindictive projects, will never appear. And that is a terrible loss to your friends and to the country.

I have not enjoyed writing this letter.[15]

The tragic dimension of this letter is unavoidable, for it is easy to see that underneath Berns's indignation at Jaffa's repeated provocations is an ungrudging recognition of Jaffa's brilliance. You can mark out the case with syllogistic precision: Berns says Jaffa could have been "America's poet"; separately, as I noted earlier, he had lauded Jaffa as "Lincoln's poet;" a chapter of his last book, *Making Patriots*, is called "Lincoln, Patriotism's Poet." Q.E.D.

Although it is unmentioned, the influence of Jaffa's understanding of Lincoln appears on every page of this chapter in Berns's *Making Patriots*—in contrast to Berns's laudatory references to Jaffa's insights about Lincoln in his book on capital punishment, which came out before the two men were estranged. Berns's chapter on Lincoln in *Making Patriots* shows Berns at his literary best, and is superior to Jaffa's demanding treatment on that score. A sober contrast between the style and temperament of the two men offers a useful instruction on why it was not possible even for a genuinely neutral observer to break the enmity between these two giants. Ohio State literature professor Sigurd Burckhardt, responding to the aforementioned Bloom and Jaffa articles on Shakespeare in the *American Political Science Review* in 1960, put his finger on the essence of Jaffa's "strongly scholastic flavor" and "too-too-solid logical structure." "Accept his premises," Burckhardt wrote, "and the conclusions will follow, most of the time, with the inexorability of a syllogism. The reasoning is so well sustained that a real mental effort is demanded to break through the web of argument; if we don't make this effort, we find ourselves, in the end, rubbing our eyes in disbelief at what we have been made to agree to."[16] I suspect Burckhardt may have experienced Jaffa firsthand at some Ohio State faculty meetings (where, among other causes, Jaffa liked to defend Woody Hayes and the Ohio State football team from the faculty's malice), but in any case isn't this mode what you'd expect of someone whose very first book was an extraordinary close study of Thomas Aquinas's interpretation of Aristotle? Lincoln's understanding of the Declaration, Constitution, and the slavery question, while expressed by Lincoln in Euclidean logic, take on a Thomistic quality in Jaffa's hands.

But one reason Berns's Lincoln is more poetic and less lawyerly than Jaffa's is that patriotism is a matter of heart, though it can—and must—be informed by the mind. "Love and rational judgment are not irreconcilable," Berns wrote at the end of his Lincoln chapter, "but are they different?" Berns then offers an interesting contrast between the Jefferson and Lincoln Memorials on the Mall in Washington—a contrast that, while likely unintentional, illuminates why Jaffa's approach does not catch on with everyone. The inscriptions on the Jefferson Memorial include his famous statement, "I have sworn upon the altar of God eternal hostility against every form of tyranny over the mind of man," and also excerpts from the Declaration of Independence, the Virginia Statute for Religious Freedom, and his *Notes on the State of Virginia*. All good and memorable words. But do they stir the patriotic soul? Berns writes: "But his words alone, even those of the Declaration, are not likely to call forth our love, either for him or for the nation he helped to found."[17]

The Lincoln Memorial includes the Gettysburg Address and his second inaugural address, where "Lincoln speaks only as a great poet can speak. . . . Ordinary Americans are moved by these words, sometimes to tears; I have seen it happen." I suspect this gruff Navy combat veteran was among them, and that, had he been a general in World War II, he would have privately cried over casualty reports as General George Patton did. Berns also captured the theological dimension of Lincoln more capaciously than Jaffa. He shared the view that Lincoln was "the martyred

Christ of democracy's passion play." Jaffa saw the second inaugural more in Old Testament terms: "The story of Israel as the Lord's Suffering Servant, retold as the story of America, will find its final form in the second inaugural. There it will come as an explanation, within the framework of biblical teaching, of the terrible suffering of the war. In Philadelphia [in 1861] Lincoln says, 'there is no need of bloodshed and war.' In the second inaugural he will say there was such a need."[18]

Jaffa was no less patriotic than Berns, and his own formulations and concern for the soul of individual students as well as the nation as a whole could be deeply moving at times. Perhaps I've reached the point where it is suitable to invoke the closing of *Federalist* 43, where Madison, in justifying the "delicate" problem of the Philadelphia convention departing from the prescribed terms for amending the Articles of Confederation, says "The time has been when it was incumbent on us all to veil the ideas which this paragraph exhibits," certain aspects of which "forbids an over-curious discussion of it." (This was a favorite passage of Jaffa's defense of the statesmanship of the founders.)

And yet . . .

Beyond the personal rancor, their particular disagreements about Locke, natural rights, and the Declaration of Independence, Jaffa and Berns maintained an additional serious argument that is harder to understand, for it connects ultimately to the deep ground of American patriotism. It concerns the role of political philosophy itself and its relationship to patriotism fully understood.

In one of their last public spats in 1982, Berns argued that Jaffa was misrepresenting or exaggerating Strauss and, worse, being unphilosophical:

> Strauss did not believe he, or political philosophy, could save Western civilization (or reverse "the decline of the West"). It is precisely hopes of this kind that distort the quest for truth.

Eternity, not history, is the theme of philosophy, which Strauss believed, must beware of wishing to be edifying. Jaffa, like Marx, wants to change the world, not to interpret it; he does nothing but edify.[19]

This is a curious and enigmatic thing to say, and it is tempting to understand it as a high rebuke against what Harvey Mansfield Jr. called Jaffa's "excess of fighting spirit." One could imagine this complaint against Jaffa coming from a Strauss follower such as Seth Benardete or Lawrence Lampert, whose scholarly investigations could be considered more purely philosophical and largely disengaged from contemporary political questions. But it is an odd argument coming from Berns, given his own deep political engagement and moral indignation, which he expressed throughout his writings. Berns's spiritedness about current political questions, and about political science itself, was at least the equal of Jaffa's, as can be seen, for example, in his early critiques of the political science methodology of voting behavior and his repeated jeremiads against world government. Wasn't Berns also hoping to change the world—to be "edifying"?

Back in his first book, *Freedom, Virtue, and the First Amendment*, Berns had held up political philosophy as the one thing most needful for America:

Political philosophy is therefore concerned with political life; it rises out of and seeks a superior understanding of the problems encountered in political life, in order to guide political life. Ideologies, not political philosophy, are imposed on political life. Political philosophy is needed in a community, or at least the need becomes more urgent, to the extent to which that community is faced with political problems. We can rejoice with Professor Boorstin that Americans have rejected Fascism and Communism, but we cannot rejoice in the fact that Americans have rejected political philosophy, particularly at a time when America faces so many political problems, some of them for the first time. One of these is the problem of freedom.[20]

Certainly Berns agreed with Jaffa and Strauss that the pervasive nihilism of modern times constituted the crisis of the West. The crux of the argument is that Jaffa's partisanship or excessive spiritedness caused him to abuse or distort political philosophy by turning Strauss's challenges into an *ideology*—ideology being the enemy of true philosophy, not to mention decent politics. Berns wrote that Jaffa was "a textbook case of someone converting philosophy into ideology, of abusing theoretical teachings . . . for practical ends. . . . Jaffa did not learn from his teacher Leo Strauss, that moral indignation is the greatest enemy of philosophy."[21] In other words, Berns thought Jaffa's view that America represented the classical ideal of best regime might be too close to the "spurious utopianism" that Strauss criticized.

Berns's warning against philosophy as a source of edification refers to a sentence from Hegel's *Phenomenology*—"philosophy must beware of wishing to be edifying"—which Strauss had quoted at the very end of his *Thoughts on Machiavelli*. In *Natural Right and History* Strauss had warned, "Let us beware of the danger of pursuing a Socratic goal with the means, and the temper, of Thrasymachus," which certainly describes how Marx turned Hegel on his head with his ideological dialectic of class struggle. But does the complete sentence from Strauss suggest a reading contrary to what Berns gives it?

It would seem that the notion of the beneficence of nature or of the primacy of the Good must be restored by being rethought through a return to the fundamental experiences from which it is derived. For while "philosophy must beware of wishing to be edifying," it is of necessity edifying.[22]

Jaffa certainly thought so, replying, as always, that he considered Berns's criticism to be a compliment, albeit a "hyperbolic" compliment. Jaffa had celebrated that he was "bringing philosophy down from the heavens and into the city—making it practical and political."[23]

Berns's challenge to Jaffa presents three serious issues to be sorted out. The first concerns the intent and legacy of Leo Strauss himself, which leads immediately to a second question: the relation of political philosophy to philosophy proper. As Berns mentions, eternity is the theme of philosophy, but in political philosophy as Jaffa understood it, the practical wisdom (*phronesis*) of the statesman is higher than the contemplative theoretical wisdom (*sophia*) of the philosopher, even though Aristotle said the opposite, at least in *The Politics*. The third question concerns the compatibility of philosophy with the informed patriotism that Berns and Jaffa both saw as the most needful thing of our time.

In direct contradiction to what Berns wrote, Jaffa argued that "Leo Strauss's life and work had a motive that was not less political than philosophic. The political motive was to arrest and reverse 'the decline of the West.' That decline consisted in the West's loss of a sense of purpose." But did Strauss think that a return to a classical political regime or outlook was possible? Jaffa thought so. He straightforwardly claimed in his 1973 eulogy of Strauss that "Strauss also thought that American politics, at its best, showed a practical wisdom that owed much to a tradition older than Locke."

As always with Strauss's careful and often indirect writing, where it is often difficult to tell when he is speaking in his own voice or dilating the views of other philosophers under discussion, he can be cited on all sides of this question. It is one thing to expose the fatal defects and contradictions of modern social science and philosophy, but is it possible to, as the critics would put it, "turn the clock back"?

The argument against a "return" per se is found in the introduction to *The City and Man*, where Strauss says:

We cannot expect that a fresh understanding of classical political philosophy will supply us with recipes for today's use. For the relative success of modern political philosophy has brought into being a kind of society wholly unknown to the classics, a kind of society to which the classical principles as stated and elaborated by the classics are not immediately applicable. Only we the living today can possibly find a solution to the problems of today.[24]

The immediate sequel suggests that the classics may be a *starting* point for an adequate analysis of current politics, and "for the wise application, to be achieved by us, of these principles to our task." But it would take a lot more than this brief and typically inconclusive comment to validate Jaffa's project of seeing a harmony between Aristotle and Locke, and that America really *is* the best regime in a classical sense.

There are other witnesses on Berns's side of this question, such as Harvey Mansfield Jr., who characterizes the difference among Strauss's students between west and east as the "west coast wanting politics to be more like philosophy—to be best friends of philosophy, indeed identical twins perhaps, to go that far," while the East Coast believes in "maintain[ing] a certain estrangement [between philosophy and politics] even in such a wonderful country as America, and such a wonderful philosopher as Aristotle." ("The east coast—that's where I am," Mansfield added.[25])

A more curious case is Yale's Steven B. Smith, author of *Reading Leo Strauss: Politics, Philosophy, Judaism*, one of the better recent books about Strauss.[26] Smith discusses at length the "deep rift" between the so-called East Coast and West Coast followers of Strauss about the character of the American republic, and, while he aligns himself with the "eastern" view of America as a "low but solid" modern Lockean regime, in a separate review article in the *New York Times Book Review* he portrays himself as a moderate between Jaffa and other figures, such as Lampert, who believe that Strauss's teaching must be completely severed from politics.[27]

In the *Times* review, Smith wrote, "Jaffa's peculiar genius—and I use that word advisedly—was to apply Strauss's understanding of political philosophy as the study of high statesmanship to the theory and practice of American politics." In his book, however, Smith says that "Strauss would have found laughable the attempt to bathe the American founding in the warm glow of antiquity," and that "Strauss explicitly claimed that philosophic knowledge is unnecessary for sound policy and the guidance of practical conduct." His chief evidence for this conclusion is a 1942 lecture Strauss delivered at the New School entitled "What Can We Learn from Political Theory?" After reviewing one of Strauss's observations about Churchill and the implication that Churchill's statecraft and aims did not need illumination from political philosophy, Smith quotes Strauss as saying that the modern statesman "does not need a single lesson in political philosophy."

Strauss never published this lecture during his lifetime, though it finally appeared in the *Review of Politics* in 2007—the year after Smith's book was published—and there are additional passages in the spirit of Smith's summary, such as this:

> As Hegel said, the owl of Minerva starts its flight at dusk, philosophy *always* comes too late for the *guidance* of political action; the philosopher *always* comes *post festum*; philosophy can merely *interpret* the result of political action; it can make us *understand* the State: it cannot teach us what should be *done* with regard to the State. One may wonder whether there are

any significant political concepts, or ideas, which are the product of political philosophy: all political ideas seem to go back to political fighters, statesmen, lawyers, prophets.[28]

It appears, however, that Smith has misread or hastily mischaracterized the lecture. Both the quotation immediately above and the passage Smith cites come in an early section where Strauss sets out a three-part case against political philosophy, whereupon the rest of the essay is a *refutation* of these objections. To be more direct about the conclusion of someone I generally admire, the lecture as a whole says exactly the *opposite* of what Smith says.

Along the way, however, Strauss sheds some useful light on the point of dispute about being cautious with regard to the edifying capacity of philosophy, so this is not an open-and-shut case. As usual with Strauss, there is much subtlety involved. It is clear that the main intention of the lecture was to caution against utopianism, the perennial vice or weakness of political philosophy that loses sight of the inherent limits of political life and therefore of the necessity of moderation and prudence. Strauss comments directly on the famous passage that Berns alludes to in charging that Jaffa was "like Marx" in wanting to change the world:

[W]hat is more utopian than the implication of Marx's famous sentence: "Hitherto, the philosophers have limited themselves to *interpreting* the world; what matters is that the world be *changed*." For *why* did the philosophers limit themselves to interpreting the world? Because they knew that the world in the precise, unmetaphoric sense of the term, the universe, cannot be changed by man. Marx's innocent looking sentence implies the substitution of the little world of man for the real world, the substitution of the whole historical process for the real whole, which by making possible the whole historical process sets absolute limits to it. This substitution, a heritage from Hegel's idealistic philosophy, is the ultimate reason of Marx's utopian hopes. For is it not utopian to expect a *perfect* order of society, which is essentially *perishable*?[29]

Strauss also dismisses the argument from the earlier part of the lecture about the relation of the great tradition of classical political philosophy to Churchill's statecraft:

> We do not need lessons from that tradition in order to discern the soundness of Churchill's approach, e.g., but the cause which Churchill's policy is meant to defend would not exist but for the influence of the tradition in question. This tradition is menaced today by a spurious utopianism. No one will deny that the basic impulse which generated that utopianism was generous. Nevertheless, it is bound to lead to disaster because it makes us underestimate the dangers to which the cause of decency and humanity is exposed and always *will* be exposed. The foremost duty of political philosophy today seems to be to counteract this modern utopianism.[30]

Finally, in his typically compact and rich manner, Strauss offers this coda of the centrality of engaged political philosophy as a necessary bulwark against the anti-philosophical and antirational current of our era:

> As long as philosophy was living up to its own innate standard, philosophers as such, by their merely being philosophers, prevented those who were willing to listen to them from identifying *any actual* order, however satisfactory in many respects, with the *perfect* order: political philosophy is the eternal challenge to the philistine. There never has been, and there never will be a time when the medicine administered by political philosophy has been and will be superfluous, although it must always be

administered, as all medicine must, with discretion. This holds true in particular of our time; for in our time, we are confronted not merely with the Philistines of old who identify the good with the ancestral, but with the Philistines of progress who identify the good with the new and the future.[31]

This passage, and many others that can be drawn from the essay, directly oppose Smith's conclusion that Strauss was "deeply skeptical of whether political theory had any substantive advice or direction to offer statesmen." A skeptic might point to the fact that Strauss never published this lecture during his lifetime as evidence that it does not represent his mature thought, though parts of this lecture appear in places in *The City and Man* and other later works. Other critics of Jaffa's position argue that these and similar Strauss formulas that indicate sympathy for the audacious idea of restoring a classical outlook on political life are merely *exoteric*— that is, superficial statements that Strauss didn't believe.

The most famous of these is his remark in the opening pages of *Thoughts on Machiavelli* that "The United States may be said to be the only country in the world which was founded in explicit opposition to Machiavellian principles. . . . At least to the extent that the American reality is inseparable from the American aspiration, one cannot understand Americanism without understanding Machiavellianism which is its opposite."[32] Given that Strauss thought Machiavellianism marked the key dividing line between classical and modern liberal understandings of politics, this would seem to indicate that Strauss had some sympathy with the idea of America as a regime that embodied classical virtue of some kind.

But, in addition to the placement of this passage at the beginning of the book where it might be dismissed as "exoteric" teaching, in typical fashion Strauss complicates the issue by partially taking back his initial proposition in the immediate sequel—a passage that Walter Berns sometimes pointed out to inquisitive

students: "Machiavelli would argue that America owes her greatness not only to her habitual adherence to the principles of freedom and justice, but also to her occasional deviation from them.
He would not hesitate to suggest a mischievous interpretation of
the Louisiana Purchase and of the fate of the Red Indians."[33] It is
possible to divine a harmony out of this ambiguity by recourse to
Strauss's intention to recover the latitude of statesmen discussed
in chapter 4, but there is no getting around the fact that this ambiguity looms large throughout Strauss's writings and that this
controversy will never be resolved.

Jaffa liked to point to Strauss's essay "On Classical Political
Philosophy" as a defense of his (Jaffa's) proposition that classical
political philosophy could be edifying *today*. This essay is Strauss's
most forward statement in favor of the superiority of the practical
wisdom (*phronesis*) of the statesman over the theoretical wisdom
(*sophia*) of the pure philosopher:

> Thus the attitude of classical political philosophy toward politi-
> cal things was always akin to that of the enlightened statesman;
> it was not the attitude of the detached observer who looks at
> political things in the way in which a zoologist looks at the
> big fishes swallowing the small ones, or that of the social "en-
> gineer" who thinks in terms of manipulating or conditioning
> rather than in terms of education or liberation, or that of the
> prophet who believes that he knows the future. . . . The politi-
> cal philosopher first comes to sight as a good citizen who can
> perform this function of the good citizen in the best way and
> on the highest level.[34]

Another piece of evidence in favor of the classical thesis comes
from the passage in *The City and Man*, mentioned above, where
Strauss added that a return to classical political philosophy was
"necessary" though "tentative or experimental," because, as he ex-

plained elsewhere, "all solutions are questionable." Strauss's most challenging approach to this question is found in a lecture he delivered before a Jewish audience at Hillel House of the University of Chicago in the mid-1950s, entitled "Progress or Return?"[35] There Strauss wrote, "The crisis of modernity on which we have been reflecting leads to the suggestion that we should return. But return to what? Obviously, to Western civilization in its premodern integrity, to the principles of Western civilization." Yet in addressing a Jewish audience, Strauss was fixed on one of his central interests—the conflict between reason and revelation in the West, which he thought was not only the secret of the West's vitality but also an irresolvable conflict. "Philosophy and the Bible are the alternatives, or the antagonists in the drama of the human soul."[36] Jaffa thought the American Founding had solved the practical political conflict between civil and religious authority by its grounding of civil and religious liberty in individual natural rights.

Strauss might not have fully accepted Jaffa's understanding of the American solution to the problem of religious conflict, which Jaffa didn't fully work out until after Strauss died. This was one of the points of contention between Jaffa and Berns in the mid-1980s. Berns argued that the founders were nominal Christians at best—a popular view nowadays, with which Jaffa disagreed vigorously—and that "the very idea of natural rights is incompatible with Christian doctrine." This argument turned in part on Strauss's notice that the idea of "nature" was foreign to the Old Testament, while it is central to political philosophy.

At least in the context of Jewish assimilation, Strauss offered this reflection in "Progress or Return?":

It is very far from me to minimize the difference between a nation conceived in liberty and dedicated to the proposition that all men are created equal, and the nations of the old world, which certainly were not conceived in liberty. I share the hope in America and the faith in America, but I am compelled to add that that faith and that hope cannot be of the same character as that faith and that hope which a Jew has in regard to Judaism and which a Christian has in regard to Christianity. No one claims that the faith in America and the hope for America are based on explicit divine promises.[37]

Yet "divine promises" are certainly one basis for American patriotism, as Ronald Reagan, to mention one prominent recent example, demonstrated.

I'll have to set aside a complete treatment of the large and important question of religion and the American Founding for some other time, and confine myself to the narrower issue of whether and how to find the basis for American patriotism from the tradition of classical political philosophy, for this was the heart of the work Jaffa and Berns carried forth from Strauss. Strauss was not unique in thinking that the secular individualism of modern liberalism makes a return to a premodern orientation impossible. This is one of the things he meant by speaking of the "relative success" of modern political philosophy, by which he meant the Lockean materialist individualism at the heart of Enlightenment and post-Enlightenment liberalism. The penultimate sentence of *Natural Right and History* joins the issue directly: "The quarrel between the ancients and the moderns concerns eventually, and perhaps even from the beginning, the status of 'individuality.'"[38] This is why Strauss respected the more serious leftists who criticized the insufficiency of individualism, such as C. B. Macpherson and Alexandre Kojève. Strauss understood precisely what R. H. Tawney meant with his remark that Karl Marx was the last of the Thomistic "Schoolmen," and that the primary attraction of Marxian socialism was not economic, but moral. Jaffa noted this in various ways over the years, writing to Henry Salvatori, for example, that "'metaphysical despair' is genuine, and will always lead 'the best and the brightest' on toward Marxism-Leninism, if not something worse, unless they can be led towards a universe that seems to hold some promise of meaning for their lives."[39] However, the postulates of dead-end individualism (Strauss ultimately reduced liberal individualism to "the joyless quest for joy") are so embedded in our times—and are such a potent force behind conservative and especially libertarian political activism—that appeals to the classical principle that the creation and maintenance of virtue should be of prior importance to individual freedom—that duties are prior to rights—is a difficult proposition.

Berns was not alone in wondering whether Jaffa's project was to create a "myth" to make America different or better.[40] And Berns wasn't the only person to fight with Jaffa over this point. Thomas Pangle, with whom Jaffa once clashed in person over Socrates' attachment to Athens (Pangle had shocked Jaffa with the proposition that "Socrates didn't give a shit about Athens"), argued that Jaffa's "obscurantist" myth-making was exactly the kind of Philistinism that Strauss warned against. "A complete American patriot," Pangle wrote in *National Review*, "is likely to pass through a stage of serious skepticism about America. . . . To a degree rarely seen in history we are asked to love our country while at the same time purifying our ardor by cultivating an awareness that our country may not be the best, certainly not the best conceivable, political order."[41] Modern America, he went on to say, did not make the kinds of material and moral demands "as harsh as those imposed by earlier, and in many ways nobler, republics."

The parsing of the theoretical strands between ancient and modern can, and hopefully will, go on as long as America exists. Pangle is correct in saying that the constant reargument about the fundamental principles that is almost entirely unique to America is a source of America's strength and vitality, similar to how Strauss understood the tension between reason and revelation as a source of strength and vitality of the West in general. (The obsolescence of that tension is one of the reasons for the lassitude of Europe today.)

But another piece of evidence ought to be weighed in the argument. Aristotle noted that the true test of the character of a regime is what kind of human types it generates. This is something Martin Diamond observed: "Now, the interesting thing is that however much we are not a regime in the ordinarily recognizable Aristotelian sense, we are emphatically so in one regard: we form a distinctive being, the American, as recognizably distinctive a human product as that of perhaps any regime in history." As an empirical matter, Pangle is correct that America does not today make the kind of "harsh" demands of all of its citizens that classical republics did. On the other hand, the kind of American soldiers—volunteers all—who have fought in large numbers over the last fifteen years surely compare favorably with any Spartan corps for their courage, discipline, self-sacrifice, loyalty, and patriotism. Nothing could less describe these Americans than "commercial self-interest" or preoccupation with comfortable self-preservation. Thomas Paine worried in 1776 about "the summer soldier and the sunshine patriot who will shrink from the service of their country." This has not come to pass, either in the Civil War or in our current wars. As I mentioned in the Preface, this expression of American vigor during the difficult military campaigns of the last decade, against all of the undercurrents of our time, encouraged Berns to discern that the latent patriotism of the American character was durable.

At the end of *Making Patriots*, Berns worried about the powerful and menacing anti-American strains of thought within our own intellectual class, which beg for a more assertive resistance than is currently being offered. But as much as intellectuals stress the importance of ideas and principles, the example of the American soldier is worth a thousand political philosophers. William Allen asked Jaffa, not long before Jaffa died, if a philosopher can be a hero in the same way as a statesman. Jaffa said the answer was no; the statesman pursues honor, while the philosopher pursues wisdom. Certainly in his honorable character, the contemporary American soldier is a statesman in microcosm—and is the kind of human being loathed on most college campuses today.

Despite his worries, Berns concluded that Lincoln's understanding of America as "the last, best hope of Earth" was still very much alive in the way Lincoln meant it. Maybe Jaffa's "excess of fighting spirit" is needed, along with his argument that America has deeper roots in the highest reaches of human excellence than the standard accounts perceive. I think Berns's final thoughts on America implicitly concede some of Jaffa's case, and that John Agresto was right to say that, in the end, they didn't fundamentally disagree. In any case, Tocqueville's observation largely remains true: "There is nothing more annoying in the habits of life than this irritable patriotism of the Americans. A foreigner would indeed consent to praise much in their country; but he would want to be permitted to blame something, and this he is absolutely refused."[42]

To paraphrase what Berns said in *Making Patriots*, while patriotism is a matter of the heart, American patriotism needs to be informed by rational judgment. As Steven B. Smith rightly puts it, "Patriotism is not just a moral but also an intellectual virtue. The proper love of country is not something we inherit, it must be taught."[43] Beyond the complicated depths treated all too briefly in this account, I hope one thing is clear: the capaciousness, profundity, and grasp of political things by thinkers like Berns, Jaffa, and their friends and students stand far above the general run of political thinkers and what is taught in political science today. In the current atmosphere of this country, it is the kind of argument that is most needed.

ACKNOWLEDGMENTS

The very first person to thank for this project is Roger Kimball, the courageous publisher of Encounter Books, for taking a flyer on this unusual project. Confessing that he knew very little about the two figures at the center of this book, he immediately and enthusiastically signed off on what I regarded as a very speculative idea.

I received encouragement and, more important, great insight along the way from Michael Uhlmann, who is one of the few people of our generation who knew both Jaffa and Berns well. A number of old friends shared their recollections and, in some cases, their letters and papers from Jaffa with me, including Ken Masugi, Daniel Palm, Richard Reeb, Dennis Teti, and Matthew Spalding. The Claremont Institute and especially its energetic chairman, Thomas Klingenstein, were important sources of information and encouragement.

The story could not have been told at all without my many classmates, now old friends, from those long-ago days in graduate school and my early years at the Claremont Institute. They are too numerous to mention, but it should be said that a critical mass of such spirited students, who found that what happened in the classroom extended far into the rest of our daily lives, is a rare thing in academia these days.

NOTES

PREFACE

1. John Agresto, *Rediscovering America: Liberty, Equality, and the Crisis of Democracy* (Los Angeles: Asahina & Wallace, 2015), 16.

2. Michael Uhlmann, interview with author, July 8, 2015.

3. If you think this is some kind of exaggeration, just take in this sentence from Harvey C. Mansfield Jr.'s very fine study of executive power, *Taming the Prince*: "The history of executive power depends on its prehistory, and we must consult Aristotle at length, paradoxically because he devotes so little space to it." This actually makes perfect sense, but still. See *Taming the Prince: The Ambiguity of Modern Executive Power* (New York: Free Press, 1989), 25.

4. Herbert Storing, "The Achievement of Leo Strauss," in *Toward a More Perfect Union: Writings of Herbert J. Storing*, edited by Joseph M. Bessette (Washington, D.C.: AEI Press, 1995; originally published in *National Review*, December 7, 1973), 445–446.

5. Readers curious about these controversies should see any of the several good recent books about Strauss, especially Catherine Zuckert and Michael Zuckert, *Leo Strauss and the Problem of Political Philosophy* (Chicago: University of Chicago Press, 2014), and the Zuckerts's previous offering, *The Truth about Leo Strauss: Political Philosophy and American Democracy* (Chicago: University of Chicago Press, 2006); Steven Smith, *Reading Leo Strauss: Politics, Philosophy, Judaism* (Chicago: University of Chicago Press, 2006); Thomas Pangle, *Leo Strauss: An Introduction to His Life and Legacy* (Baltimore: Johns Hopkins University Press, 2006); Nathan Tarcov and

Thomas L. Pangle, "Epilogue: Leo Strauss and the History of Political Philosophy," in *History of Political Philosophy*, edited by Leo Strauss and Joseph Cropsey, 3rd ed. (Chicago and London: University of Chicago Press, 1987).

6. Storing, "American Statesmanship, Old and New," in *Toward a More Perfect Union*, 403.

7. Harry V. Jaffa, *Crisis of the House Divided: An Interpretation of the Issues in the Lincoln-Douglas Debates*, 3rd ed. (Chicago: University of Chicago Press, 1982; originally published 1959), 2–3.

8. Walter Berns, "Ancients and Moderns: The Emergence of Modern Constitutionalism," in *Democracy and the Constitution: Essays by Walter Berns* (Washington D.C.: AEI Press, 2006), 5.

9. Peter Evans and Helen Evans, "Interview with Walter Berns," August 4, 2004, http://www.renewamerica.com/columns/evans/040804.

10. Dennis Teti, private communication with author, December 18, 2015.

11. Walter Berns, *Making Patriots* (Chicago: University of Chicago Press, 2001), 9.

12. Walter Berns, *Freedom, Virtue and the First Amendment* (Baton Rouge: Louisiana State University Press, 1957), 221, 225.

13. Ibid., 221.

14. Harry V. Jaffa, "'Terminator' IRS Hounded Joe Louis into Poverty," *Claremont Review of Books* online, January 13, 2015, http://www.claremont.org/crb/basicpage /terminator-irs-hounded-joe-louis-into-poverty/.

15. Harry V. Jaffa, *American Conservatism and the American Founding* (Durham, N.C.: Carolina Academic Press, 1984), 156.

16. Walter Berns, "How to Talk to the Russians," in *In Defense of Liberal Democracy* (Chicago: Gateway, 1984; originally published in *The American Spectator*, July 1983).

CHAPTER 1. "A LITTLE TOUCH OF HARRY IN THE NIGHT"

1. Thomas Jefferson, letter to William Stephens Smith, November 13, 1787.

2. Joseph Cropsey, private letter to Harry V. Jaffa, July 1, 1984.

3. Harry V. Jaffa, private memorandum to Dan Mazmanian, November 11, 1988, copy on file with author.

4. Dennis Teti, private communication with author, December 18, 2015.

5. Walter Berns, "Oliver Wendell Holmes, Jr.," in *American Political Thought: The Philosophic Dimension of American Statesmanship*, edited by Morton J. Frisch and Richard Stevens (New York: Charles Scribner's Sons, 1971), 170.

6. See Walter Berns, "The New Pacifism and World Government," in *In Defense of Liberal Democracy* (Chicago: Gateway, 1984), 65–80.

7. William F. Buckley Jr., Foreword to Harry V. Jaffa, *American Conservatism and the American Founding* (Durham, N.C.: Carolina Academic Press, 1984), xi.

8. Edward Shils, *Portraits: A Gallery of Intellectuals*, edited by Joseph Epstein (Chicago: University of Chicago Press, 1997), 35.

9. Buckley, Foreword to Jaffa, *American Conservatism and the American Founding*, xi.

10. Michael Uhlmann's remarks at the memorial service for Jaffa, January 16, 2015, in Michael M. Uhlmann, Edward J. Erler, Thomas G. West, et al., "Harry V. Jaffa, 1918–2015," *Claremont Review of Books* 15, no. 1 (Winter 2014/15), available at http://www.claremont.org/crb/article/harry-v-jaffa-1918-2015/.

11. Michael Anton, "Harry V. Jaffa: An Appreciation," *Claremont Review of Books* 15, no. 1 (Winter 2014/15), http://www.claremont.org/crb/article/harry-v-jaffa-an -appreciation/.

12. Ken Masugi, "Harry Jaffa: An Inconvenient Thinker," LibertyLawForum, January 15, 2015, http://www.libertylawsite.org/2015/01/15/harry-v-jaffa-an-incon venient-thinker/.

13. I've actually started a Twitter feed for Jaffa's useable aphorisms: https://twitter .com/HarryVJaffa.

14. Harry V. Jaffa, "Political Philosophy and Political Reality," lecture delivered at Henry Salvatori Center, Claremont McKenna College, December 3, 1991, http://www.claremont.org/crb/basicpage/political-philosophy-and-political-reality/.

15. Norman Podhoretz, unpublished text, on file with author.

CHAPTER 2: "PATRIOTISM IS NOT ENOUGH"

Epigraph: D. W. Brogan, *Is Innocence Enough?* (London: Hamilton, 1941), 13.

1. Lerone Bennett Jr., "Was Abe Lincoln a White Supremacist?," *Ebony* (February 1968): 35–42.

2. Senator Bernie Sanders, remarks at Liberty University, September 14, 2015; "Bernie Sanders Says America Was Built on Racist Principles," *New York Daily News*, September 14, 2015.

3. Walter Berns, "On Patriotism," *The Public Interest* (Spring 1997): 19.

4. Walter Berns, *Making Patriots* (Chicago: University of Chicago Press, 2001), 3.

5. Berns, "On Patriotism," 23.

6. Quoted in Ed Whelen, "Elena Kagan and the Declaration of Independence," Bench Memos, *National Review*, July 14, 2010, http://www.nationalreview.com /bench-memos/231046/elena-kagan-and-declaration-independence-ed-whelan.

7. Pauline Maier, *American Scripture: Making the Declaration of Independence* (New York: Knopf, 1997), 212.

8. See, in particular, George Nash, *The Conservative Intellectual Movement in America Since 1945* (New York: Basic Books, 1976); Angus Burgin, *The Great Persuasion: Reinventing Free Markets Since the Great Depression* (Cambridge: Harvard University Press, 2012); Patrick Allitt, *The Conservatives: Ideas and Personalities Throughout American History* (New Haven, Conn.: Yale University Press, 2010).

9. Leo Strauss, *Natural Right and History* (Chicago: University of Chicago Press, 1953), 2.

10. Leo Strauss, review of *German Philosophy and Politics*, by John Dewey, in *What Is Political Philosophy? And Other Studies* (New York: Free Press, 1959), 281.

11. There is also evidence that Strauss had carefully read and found insight in Lord Charnwood's *Abraham Lincoln* (New York: Henry Holt, 1917), still the best political biography of the Great Emancipator.

12. Gordon Wood, "The Fundamentalists and the Constitution," *New York Review of Books*, February 18, 1988.

CHAPTER 3. STARTING OVER:
SOMETHING HAS GONE WRONG...

Epigraphs: Peter Drucker, *Men, Ideas, and Politics* (New York: Harper and Row, 1971), 52. Arthur M. Schlesinger Jr., *The Vital Center: The Politics of Freedom* (New York: Riverside Press, 1949), 39. Leo Strauss, Preface to the English translation, *Spinoza's Critique of Religion*, trans. E. M. Sinclair (New York: Schocken Books, 1965), 31.

1. This was no isolated episode. Just as propaganda was instrumental to the rise of Nazi power inside Germany, Nazi Germany paid close attention to popular culture overseas. Hitler was reportedly obsessed with any Hollywood depiction of his regime, and the German consul general in Los Angeles made a point of lobbying studio heads. Ironically, criticism from Jewish leaders also played a role in killing *It Can't Happen Here*. See Ben Urwand, *The Collaboration: Hollywood's Pact with Hitler* (Cambridge, Mass.: Belknap Press of Harvard University Press, 2013).

2. Winston Churchill, "Hitler and His Choice," *Great Contemporaries*, edited by James W. Muller (Wilmington, Del.: ISI Books, 2012; originally published London: Butterworth, 1937), 467. This passage appeared in the original version of this article that Churchill published in *The Strand* magazine in 1935, but was omitted from the revised version published in all previous editions of *Great Contemporaries*.

3. See especially Karl Loewenstein, "Autocracy Versus Democracy in Contemporary Europe (II)," *American Political Science Review* 29, no. 5 (October 1935): 755–784.

4. Leo Strauss, *On Tyranny* (Chicago: University of Chicago Press, 2000; originally published Ithaca, N.Y.: Cornell University Press, 1961), 177.

5. See Karl Loewenstein, "Autocracy Versus Democracy in Contemporary Europe (I)," *American Political Science Review* 29, no. 4 (August 1935): 571–593.

6. Robert C. Brooks, "Reflections on the 'World Revolution' of 1940," *American Political Science Review* 35, no. 1 (February 1941): 1–28.

7. Walter Lippmann, quoted in Ronald Steel, *Walter Lippmann and the American Century* (Boston: Little Brown, 1980), 331.

8. Eric Voegelin, *Hitler and the Germans* (Columbia: University of Missouri Press, 1999), 229. He continued: "Again, that did not interest the jurists, but only whether this or that legal construction could be applied."

9. Albert Lepawsky, "The Nazis Reform the Reich," *American Political Science Review* 30, no. 2 (April 1936): 324–350.

10. Roger H. Wells, "Municipal Government in National Socialist Germany," *American Political Science Review* 29, no. 4 (August 1935): 658.

11. Arnold J. Zurcher, "The Hitler Referenda," *American Political Science Review* 29, no. 1 (February 1935): 91–99.

12. Eric Voegelin, *Autobiographical Reflections* (Columbia: University of Missouri Press, 2011), chapter 13, "Anschluss and Emigration."

13. Peter M. Rutkoff and William B. Scott, *New School: A History of the New School for Social Research* (New York: Free Press, 1986), 90.

14. Ibid., 107.

15. Strauss, Preface, *Spinoza's Critique of Religion*, 1.

16. Leo Strauss, "Existentialism," *Interpretation* 22, no. 3 (Spring 1995): 304, 306.

17. In fact Strauss did ignore Heidegger for many years, and avoided even the mention of his name in his mature works. Heidegger is not mentioned in Strauss's most famous work, *Natural Right and History* (Chicago: University of Chicago Press, 1953), despite unmistakable indirect references to Heidegger and his thought. Some of Strauss's students suggest Strauss thought it indecent to mention the name Heidegger.

18. Yale's Steven Smith observes: "It was Heidegger's concern for Being, rather than beings, that led to his indifference to the fact of tyranny." Steven Smith, *Reading Leo Strauss: Politics, Philosophy, Judaism* (Chicago: University of Chicago Press, 2006), 130.

19. Leo Strauss, "Liberal Education and Responsibility," in *Liberalism Ancient and Modern* (New York: Basic Books, 1968), 24.

20. See Martin Heidegger, "'Only a God Can Save Us': The *Spiegel* Interview," in *Heidegger: The Man and the Thinker*, edited by Thomas Sheehan (Chicago: Precedent Publishing, 1981; originally published in *Der Spiegel*, 1976), 55.

21. C. S. Lewis, *The Abolition of Man* (New York: HarperCollins, 2000; originally published 1944), 73.

22. Leo Strauss, "German Nihilism," *Interpretation* 26, no. 3 (Spring 1999): 363. Earlier in the lecture, Strauss captured the mood and outlook of young Germans: "What they hated, was the very prospect of a world in which everyone would be happy and satisfied, in which everyone would have his little pleasure by day and his little pleasure by night, a world in which no great heart could beat and no great soul could breathe, a world without real, unmetaphoric, sacrifice, i.e. a world without blood, sweat and tears. What to the communists appeared to be the fulfillment of *the* dream of mankind, appeared to those young Germans as the greatest debasement of humanity, as the coming of the end of humanity, as the arrival of the latest man."

23. Leo Strauss, *The City and Man* (Chicago: University of Chicago Press, 1963), 11.

24. Leo Strauss, "Progress or Return?," in *The Rebirth of Classical Political Rationalism: An Introduction to the Thought of Leo Strauss*, edited by Thomas L. Pangle (Chicago: University of Chicago Press, 1989), 260.

25. Leo Strauss, "The Intellectual Situation of the Present," in *Reorientation: Leo Strauss in the 1930s*, edited by Martin D. Yaffe and Richard Ruderman (New York: Palgrave Macmillan, 2014), 242, 245.

26. Alexis de Tocqueville, "On the Philosophic Method of the Americans," in *Democracy in America*, translated and edited by Harvey C. Mansfield and Delba Winthrop (Chicago: University of Chicago Press, 2000), vol. 2, book 1, chapter 1.

27. Harry V. Jaffa, *Crisis of the Strauss Divided: Essays on Leo Strauss and Straussianism, East and West* (Lanham, Md.: Rowman and Littlefield, 2012), 2.

28. Arnold Brecht, *The Political Education of Arnold Brecht: An Autobiography, 1884–1970* (Princeton, N.J.: Princeton University Press, 1970), 187. It is probably not a coincidence that Justice Robert Jackson, whose most famous dictum on the Supreme Court was that "the Constitution is not a suicide pact," had presided at Nuremburg, and learned firsthand of the constitutional defects that had contributed to the German catastrophe.

29. Ibid., 198–199.

30. Ibid., 408.

31. Arnold Brecht, *Political Theory: The Foundations of Twentieth-Century Political Thought* (Princeton, N.J.: Princeton University Press, 1959), 8–9.

32. Ibid., 8.

33. Ibid., 124–125.

34. Ibid., 265.

35. In his autobiography, Brecht resisted appeals to natural law as the basis for opposing Nazism in Germany: "The story of the Hitler regime has led to grave objections against the whole positivistic doctrine according to which a judge is bound to apply any law the passing of which had been formally correct, irrespective of moral considerations. I, too, have combatted this doctrine, in particular in my essays on legal philosophy. . . . I consider it erroneous, however, to base objections against legal positivism on attempts to derive 'scientific' proof for the validity of moral principles from 'nature.' This could be done successfully, without going in vicious circles, only when the divine origin of nature could be proved scientifically. I hold that it is quite unnecessary to claim *scientific validity* for the thesis that certain moral axioms are absolutely valid, in order to deny *legal validity* to atrocious government decrees. Which governments are considered legitimate, and which of their orders *legally* valid, legally binding, and which not, is in ultimate analysis a decision of human volition." Brecht, *The Political Education of Arnold Brecht*, 433–434.

36. Leo Strauss wrote a critique of Brecht's discussion in "Relativism," in *Relativism and the Study of Man*, edited by Helmut Schoeck and James W. Wiggins (Princeton, N.J.: Van Nostrand, 1961), 141–145. Curiously, the version of this Strauss essay selected and later published by Thomas L. Pangle in *The Rebirth of*

Classical Political Rationalism: An Introduction to the Thought of Leo Strauss (Chicago: University of Chicago Press, 1989) omits Strauss's discussion of Brecht.

37. Strauss, "German Nihilism," 363.

38. Harry Jaffa, interview with Edward J. Erler, 2003, Liberty Fund Intellectual Portrait Series, http://oll.libertyfund.org/titles/jaffa-the-intellectual-portrait-series -a-conversation-with-harry-v-jaffa.

39. The three best examples of Jaffa's literary criticism are "Macbeth and the Moral Universe," *Claremont Review of Books* 8, no. 1 (Winter 2007/08), http:// www.claremont.org/crb/article/macbeth-and-the-moral-universe/; "Tom Sawyer: Hero of Middle America," *Interpretation* 2, no. 3 (Spring 1972); and "The Limits of Politics: *King Lear*, Act I, Scene 1," *American Political Science Review* 51 (June 1957).

40. Jaffa, interview with Edward J. Erler, 2003.

41. Jaffa, *Crisis of the Strauss Divided*, 7.

42. Jaffa, interview with Edward J. Erler, 2003.

43. Jaffa, *Crisis of the Strauss Divided*, 8.

44. Ibid., 12.

45. Harry V. Jaffa, "Joseph Cropsey, Rest in Peace," http://www.claremont.org /basicPageArticles/joseph-cropsey-rest-in-peace/.

46. See Joseph Cropsey, *Polity and Economy: With Further Thoughts on the Principles of Adam Smith*, rev. ed. (South Bend, Ind.: St. Augustine's Press, 2001). This passage from the introduction displays Cropsey's congruence with Jaffa's outlook: "In one sense liberalism has succeeded so well that we have lost sight of some of its problematic aspects. We have too much ceased to question the practical possibility of freedom as we know it, perhaps because the apparent success of liberalism seems to have done away with the question. Ceasing to question, we have ceased to consider that freedom exists upon a substructure of necessary conditions. We recapture some sense of this when we recur to the literature of a time when modern liberalism was viewed as an experiment. That time is not remote from us. The nobility of the Gettysburg Address is so moving that it sometimes blinds us to the theme upon which Lincoln spoke: can a nation conceived in liberty and dedicated to the proposition that all men are created equal, long endure. Abraham Lincoln solved the problem in a political way by vindicating the principle that freedom is not introspective, cannot deliberate its own existence, and does not include the freedom to destroy itself. A nation so conceived and so dedicated depends for its endurance upon its vigor (and its prudence) in suppressing the element of freedom that would divert the nation into slavery. But something more is needed than a principle that makes it illegal for freedom to murder itself. What is needed at the very minimum is a feasible and satisfactory substitute for strong authority, which is yet compatible with good order and good living in society. Whether, and wherein, such a substitute exists, is the lasting problem of freedom."

47. Joseph Cropsey, *Political Philosophy and the Issues of Politics* (University of Chicago Press, 1977), 13.

48. Strauss, *The City and Man*, 3.

49. Harry V. Jaffa, "Is Political Freedom Grounded in Natural Law?," unpublished manuscript, February 1984, on file with author.

50. Harry V. Jaffa, *American Conservatism and the American Founding* (Durham, N.C.: Carolina Academic Press, 1984), 154.

CHAPTER 4. STATESMANSHIP AND THE RENEGADE REVIVAL

Epigraph: Leo Strauss, "What Is Liberal Education?," in *Liberalism Ancient and Modern* (New York: Basic Books, 1968), 8.

1. Abraham Lincoln, "Eulogy of Henry Clay," State Capitol, Springfield, Illinois, July 6, 1852, http://teachingamericanhistory.org/library/document/eulogy-of-henry -clay/.

2. Harry V. Jaffa, *Crisis of the House Divided: An Interpretation of the Issues in the Lincoln-Douglas Debates*, 3rd ed. (Chicago: University of Chicago Press, 1982; originally published 1959), 12.

3. A good account of the controversy within the discipline is David M. Ricci, *The Tragedy of Political Science: Politics, Scholarship and Democracy* (New Haven: Yale University Press, 1984).

4. Ezra Klein, "PolySci 101: Presidential Speeches Don't Matter, and Lobbyists Don't Run D.C.," *Washington Post*, September 12, 2010, http://www.washingtonpost .com/wp-dyn/content/article/2010/09/10/AR2010091002671.html.

5. Joseph S. Nye Jr., "Scholars on the Sidelines," *Washington Post*, April 13, 2009, http://www.washingtonpost.com/wp-dyn/content/article/2009/04/12/AR2009 041202260.html.

6. See Kristin Renwick Monroe, ed., *Perestroika! The Raucous Rebellion in Political Science* (New Haven: Yale University Press, 2005).

7. Aaron Wildavsky, *The Revolt Against the Masses, and Other Essays on Politics and Public Policy* (New York: Basic Books, 1971), viii.

8. Leo Strauss, "An Epilogue," in *Essays on the Scientific Study of Politics*, edited by Herbert Storing (New York: Holt, Reinhart and Winston, 1962), 327.

9. Ibid., 55.

10. Harry V. Jaffa, "What Is Political Science? How to Deal with the Lemming (Or Gadarene Swine) Instinct," pamphlet (Salvatori Center for the Study of Individual Freedom, 1988).

11. Edward C. Banfield, "Policy Science as Metaphysical Madness," *Here the People Rule: Selected Essays* (New York: Plenum Press, 1985), 146.

12. Angelo Codevilla, "DeGaulle: Statesmanship in the Modern State," in *Statesmanship: Essays in Honor of Sir Winston S. Churchill*, edited by Harry V. Jaffa (Durham, N.C.: Carolina Academic Press, 1981), 232.

13. Leo Strauss, *Natural Right and History* (Chicago: University of Chicago Press, 1953), 159.

14. Richard M. Weaver, *Ideas Have Consequences* (Chicago: University of Chicago Press, 1948), 60.

15. Allan Bloom, *The Closing of the American Mind* (New York: Simon & Schuster, 1987), 55.

16. Strauss, *Natural Right and History*, 162. The sequel is necessary to understand why Strauss isn't embracing moral relativism simply: "Not to repeat what has been indicated before, when deciding what ought to be done, i.e., what ought to be done by this individual (or this individual group) here and now, one has to consider not only which of the various competing objectives is higher in rank but also which is most urgent in the circumstances. What is most urgent is legitimately preferred to what is less urgent, and the most urgent is in many cases lower in rank than the less urgent. But one cannot make a universal rule that urgency is a higher consideration than rank. For it is our duty to make the highest activity, as much as we can, the most urgent or most needful thing. And the maximum effort which can be expected necessarily varies from individual to individual. The only universally valid standard is the hierarchy of ends. This standard is sufficient for passing judgment on the level of nobility of individuals and groups and of actions and institutions. But it is insufficient for guiding our actions."

17. Winston Churchill, *Marlborough: His Life and Times* (Chicago: University of Chicago Press, 2002), 1:569.

18. Churchill, *Marlborough*, 1:40.

19. Winston Churchill, speech to the House of Commons on Army Reform, May 13, 1901, http://www.winstonchurchill.org/resources/speeches/1901-1914-rising -star/108-army-reform.

20. Winston Churchill, "Shall We All Commit Suicide?," first published in *Nash's Pall Mall* in 1924, available now in *Thoughts and Adventures* (Wilmington, Del.: ISI Books, 2009; originally published London: Thornton Butterworth, 1932). In this essay Churchill speculates on nuclear weapons: "May there not be methods of using explosive energy incomparably more intense than anything heretofore discovered? Might not a bomb no bigger than an orange be found to possess the secret power to destroy a whole block of buildings—nay, to concentrate the force of a thousand tons of cordite and blast a township at a stroke?"

21. Churchill, *Thoughts and Adventures*, 275.

22. Harry V. Jaffa, "Can There Be Another Winston Churchill?," in *Statesmanship: Essays in Honor of Sir Winston S. Churchill*, edited by Harry V. Jaffa (Durham, N.C.: Carolina Academic Press, 1981), 39.

23. For a more extensive analysis of Churchill's statesmanship, see Larry P. Arnn, *Churchill's Trial: Winston Churchill and the Salvation of Free Government* (Nashville: Thomas Nelson, 2015), and Steven F. Hayward, *Greatness: Reagan, Churchill and the Making of Extraordinary Leaders* (New York: Crown Forum, 2006).

CHAPTER 5. THE VITAL CENTER CANNOT HOLD

Epigraphs: Arthur M. Schlesinger Jr., "The Causes of the Civil War: A Note on Historical Sentimentalism," *Partisan Review* 16, no. 10 (October 1949): 980. Harry V. Jaffa, *Crisis of the House Divided: An Interpretation of the Issues in the Lincoln-Douglas Debates*, 3rd ed. (Chicago: University of Chicago Press, 1982; originally published 1959), 45.

1. Richard Hofstadter, *The Progressive Historians: Turner, Beard, Parrington* (New York: Alfred A. Knopf, 1968).

2. Arthur M. Schlesinger Jr., *The Vital Center: The Politics of Freedom* (New York: Riverside Press, 1949), 39.

3. Oliver Wendell Holmes Jr., *Holmes-Laski Letters: The Correspondence of Mr. Justice Holmes and Harold J. Laski, 1916–1935*, edited by Mark DeWolfe Howe (New York: Atheneum Press, 1963), 1:19.

4. Oliver Wendell Holmes Jr., *Holmes-Pollock Letters: The Correspondence of Mr. Justice Holmes and Sir Frederick Pollock, 1874–1932*, edited by Mark DeWolfe Howe (Cambridge, Mass.: Belknap Press of Harvard University Press, 1961), 252.

5. Carl Becker, *The Declaration of Independence: A Study in the History of Political Ideas* (New York: Alfred A. Knopf, 1942; originally published 1922), 277.

6. Ibid., xvi.

7. Harry V. Jaffa discusses the deeper background of Becker and Becker's turn in chapter 2 of *A New Birth of Freedom: Abraham Lincoln and the Coming of the Civil War* (Lanham, Md.: Rowman and Littlefield, 2000), esp. 96–121.

8. Louis Hartz, *The Liberal Tradition in America* (New York: Harcourt, Brace, 1955), 273.

9. Ibid., 236.

10. Richard Hofstadter, *The American Political Tradition* (New York: Alfred A. Knopf, 1948), 16–17. Hofstadter also proves himself an epigone of Woodrow Wilson, who had criticized the Founders and the Constitution for hewing to a "Newtonian" philosophy. Hofstadter writes: "Madison spoke in the most precise Newtonian language when he said that such a 'natural' government must be so constructed 'that its several constituent parts may, by their mutual relations, be the means of keeping each other in their proper places.'" (ibid., 11.) But it is not necessary to reach for Newton to find inspiration for "balanced" government, nor did any of the writers of the Founding era ever reference Newton as a source of their views. This is like saying Nietzsche was the primary influence on Einstein's theory of special relativity.

11. Schlesinger, *The Vital Center*, 43.

12. Another gratuitous and partisan simplification of consensus liberalism can be seen in the ways both Hofstadter and Schlesinger interpreted Jackson and the Jacksonian era as a close precursor of New Deal liberalism, which ignores or badly distorts the dominant laissez-faire political economy at the heart of Jacksonian policy.

Hofstadter's account is slightly better than Schlesinger's *Age of Jackson*; Hofstadter says that "For those who have lived through the era of Franklin Roosevelt it is natural to see in Jacksonian democracy an earlier version of the New Deal." But eventually he comes around to recognizing that "it was essentially a movement of laissez-faire, an attempt to divorce government and business" (*The American Political Tradition*, 56).

13. Daniel J. Boorstin, *The Genius of American Politics* (Chicago: University of Chicago Press, 1953), 99–132.

14. Richard Hofstadter, *The Progressive Historians: Turner, Beard, Parrington* (New York: Alfred A. Knopf, 1968), 462.

15. Harry V. Jaffa, "Conflicts within the Idea of the Liberal Tradition," *Comparative Studies in Society and History* 5, no. 3 (April 1963): 274–278. This article, and Louis Hartz's reply in the same issue, were revised from a symposium at the Mississippi Valley Historical Association in the spring of 1962.

16. Harry V. Jaffa, *Equality and Liberty: Theory and Practice in American Politics* (New York: Oxford University Press, 1965), vii.

17. John J. Miller, "The House of Jaffa," *National Review*, June 14, 2013, http://www.heymiller.com/2013/06/harry-v-jaffa/, accessed March 9, 2016. See also Andrew Ferguson, "Saving President Lincoln," *The Weekly Standard*, January 26, 2015.

18. Jaffa, *Crisis of the House Divided*, 3.

19. Alasdair MacIntyre, *After Virtue*, 2nd ed. (South Bend, Ind.: University of Notre Dame Press, 1984), 278.

20. Arthur M. Schlesinger Jr., "The Causes of the Civil War: A Note on Historical Sentimentalism," *Partisan Review* 16, no. 10 (October 1949): 980.

21. Louis Hartz, "Comment: Conflicts within the Idea of the Liberal Tradition," *Comparative Studies in Society and History* 5, no. 3 (April 1963): 282.

22. Ibid., 274.

23. Boorstin, *The Genius of American Politics*, 126–127.

24. William Graham Sumner, "The Mores of the Present and the Future," in *On Liberty, Society, and Politics: The Essential Essays of William Graham Sumner* (Indianapolis: Liberty Fund, 1992), edited by Robert C. Bannister, 317–318.

25. Woodrow Wilson said, "[W]hat commends Mr. Lincoln's studiousness to me is that the result of it was he did not have any theories at all. . . . Lincoln was one of those delightful students who do not seek to tie you up in the meshes of any theory"; *Woodrow Wilson: Essential Writings and Speeches of the Scholar-President*, edited by Mario R. DiNunzio (New York: New York University Press, 2006), 102.

26. [Godfrey Rathbone Benson], Lord Charnwood, *Abraham Lincoln* (New York: Henry Holt, 1917), 162.

27. David Herbert Donald, *Lincoln* (New York: Simon & Schuster, 1995), 226. But is the inclusion of blacks in the Declaration really an "unresolvable historiographical problem"? Jaffa asserts: "I know of no evidence yet brought forward by anyone

to show that Jefferson or Adams or Franklin or any other subscriber among the Founders to the doctrine of universal human rights thought either that the Negro was not a man or that, being human, there was any argument which ought to have persuaded him to be a slave." Jaffa, *Crisis of the House Divided*, 14.

28. Donald, *Lincoln*, 227.

29. Winston S. Churchill, *The Gathering Storm* (Boston: Houghton Mifflin, 1948), 320.

30. Abraham Lincoln, Eulogy of Henry Clay, State Capitol, Springfield, Illinois, July 6, 1852, http://teachingamericanhistory.org/library/document/eulogy-of-henry -clay/.

31. Harry V. Jaffa, *How to Think About the American Revolution: A Bicentennial Cerebration* (Durham, N.C.: Carolina Academic Press, 1978), 3, 4.

32. Jaffa, *Crisis of the House Divided*, 365–366.

33. Ibid., 370.

34. Hofstadter, *The American Political Tradition*, 110.

35. Ibid., 116.

36. Jaffa, *A New Birth of Freedom*, 227–228.

37. Thomas Babington Macaulay, *The History of England from the Ascension of James II* (New York: Harper & Brothers, 1899), 3:90.

38. Jaffa, *A New Birth of Freedom*, 331.

39. Jaffa, *Crisis of the House Divided*, 45, 369.

40. Ibid., 370.

41. John Burt, *Lincoln's Tragic Pragmatism: Lincoln, Douglas, and Moral Conflict* (Cambridge, Mass.: Belknap Press of Harvard University Press, 2013), 9.

42. Diana Schaub offers what might be regarded as Jaffa's response by proxy in "Lincoln for Liberals," *Claremont Review of Books* 13, no. 4 (Fall 2013), http://www .claremont.org/crb/article/lincoln-for-liberals2/.

43. A good catalogue and analysis of the liberal understanding and use of Lincoln, and especially Obama's misuse of Lincoln, is found in Jason R. Jividen, *Claiming Lincoln: Progressivism, Equality, and the Battle for Lincoln's Legacy in Presidential Rhetoric* (DeKalb: Northern Illinois University Press, 2011.)

44. Llewellyn H. Rockwell Jr., "A Dissent on UNophilia," LewRockwell.com. December 1, 1990, https://www.lewrockwell.com/1990/12/lew-rockwell/a-dissent -on-unophilia/.

45. Richard Brookhiser, "Harry Jaffa, R.I.P.," *National Review*, January 12, 2015, http://www.nationalreview.com/corner/396197/harry-jaffa-rip-richard-brookhiser.

46. Harvey Mansfield, "Scholars of American Politics," *Weekly Standard*, February 9, 2015, http://www.weeklystandard.com/scholars-of-american-politics /article/831309.

CHAPTER 6. EQUALITY AS A PRINCIPLE AND A PROBLEM

Epigraph: Harry V. Jaffa, *Equality and Liberty: Theory and Practice in American Politics* (New York: Oxford University Press, 1965), 47.

1. Harry V. Jaffa, "Thomas Aquinas Meets Thomas Jefferson," *Interpretation* 33, no. 2 (Spring 2006): 177.

2. Harry V. Jaffa, "What Is Equality? The Declaration of Independence Reconsidered," in *The Conditions of Freedom: Essays in Political Philosophy* (Baltimore, Md.: Johns Hopkins University Press, 1975), 155–156.

3. Walter Berns, *Freedom, Virtue and the First Amendment* (Baton Rouge: Louisiana State University Press, 1957), 253.

4. Alexis de Tocqueville, *Democracy in America*, translated and edited by Harvey C. Mansfield Jr. and Delba Winthrop (Chicago: University of Chicago Press, 2000), 482.

5. Abraham Lincoln, Speech on the Dred Scott Decision, Springfield, Illinois, June 26, 1857, http://teachingamericanhistory.org/library/document/speech-on-the -dred-scott-decision/.

6. Garry Wills, *Lincoln at Gettysburg: The Words that Remade America* (New York: Simon & Schuster, 1992), 38.

7. John Murley, "On the 'Calhounism' of Willmoore Kendall," in *Willmoore Kendall: Maverick of American Conservatives*, edited by John A. Murley and John E. Alvis (Lanham, Md.: Lexington Books, 2002), 122.

8. Willmoore Kendall and George W. Carey, *The Basic Symbols of the American Political Tradition* (Washington, D.C.: Catholic University Press of America, 1995; originally published 1970), xvi.

9. Abraham Lincoln, *Collected Works of Abraham Lincoln*, 7:260, http://quod.lib .umich.edu/l/lincoln/lincoln7/1:566?rgn=div1;view=fulltext.

10. Barack Obama, remarks on Chicago Public Radio Station WBEZ, Sept. 6, 2001, http://www.wsj.com/articles/SB122515067227674187.

11. Willmoore Kendall, *The Conservative Affirmation in America* (Chicago: Regnery, 1963), 260.

12. Kendall, *Willmoore Kendall: Maverick of American Conservatives*, 214.

13. Ibid., 148.

14. Buckley told this story of Kendall many times. This version appears in his Foreword to Murley and Alvis, *Willmoore Kendall*, xi.

15. Willmoore Kendall, *Willmoore Kendall: Contra Mundum*, edited by Nellie D. Kendall (New Rochelle, N.Y.: Arlington House, 1971), 45.

16. Walter Berns, review of *A Program for Conservatives*, by Russell Kirk, *Journal of Politics* 17, no. 4 (November 1955): 683–686.

17. Willmoore Kendall, *John Locke and the Doctrine of Majority-Rule* (Urbana: University of Illinois Press, 1941). Leo Strauss told Kendall in a private letter (1960)

that "I do not know of any other theoretical study by a man born and trained in the U.S., in your or my generation which equals in value your work on Locke."

18. Willmoore Kendall, "Source of American Caesarism," review of *Crisis of the House Divided*, by Harry V. Jaffa, *National Review*, November 7, 1959.

19. Jaffa offers the powerful anti-anti-Locke case in an essay directed at Garry Wills, "Inventing the Past: Garry Wills's *Inventing America* and the Pathology of Ideological Scholarship," in Harry V. Jaffa, *American Conservatism and the American Founding* (Durham, N.C.: Carolina Academic Press, 1984), 76–109.

20. Kendall, *The Conservative Affirmation*, 85, 99. In *Inventing America: Jefferson's Declaration of Independence* (New York: Doubleday, 1978), Garry Wills argued the laughable proposition that Francis Hutcheson, not Locke, was the principal inspiration for the Declaration. In particular, Jaffa liked to note Jefferson's 1825 letter to Henry Lee, in which he specifically mentions Locke: "[I]t was intended to be an expression of the American mind, and to give to that expression the proper tone and spirit called for by the occasion. All its authority rests then on the harmonizing sentiments of the day, whether expressed in conversation, in letters, printed essays, or in the elementary books of public right, as Aristotle, Cicero, Locke, Sidney, &c."; May 8, 1825, http://teachingamericanhistory.org/library/document/letter-to-henry -lee/.

21. Jaffa put his disagreement this way: "It was, and is, an anachronism to assume that the founders read Locke through the eyes of Strauss! One is reminded of Shakespeare's *Troilus and Cressida*. Hector, himself a young man, denounces the elders of Troy, who are so bewitched by Helen's beauty that they are unwilling to return her to her husband, and thus save their city from destruction. 'You gloz'd [commented],' he said, '[like] young men whom Aristotle thought unfit to hear moral philosophy.' It seemed to me that imputing to the Founding Fathers Leo Strauss's esoteric interpretation of Locke would be not unlike finding the *Nicomachean Ethics* in Hector's library." Harry V. Jaffa, "Aristotle and Locke in the American Founding," *Claremont Review of Books* 1, no. 2 (Winter 2001), posted February 10, 2001, http://www.claremont.org/crb/article/aristotle-and-locke-in-the-american -founding/.

22. Leo Strauss to Willmoore Kendall, October 29, 1964, in Murley and Alvis, *Willmoore Kendall*, 251.

23. Kendall, *Willmoore Kendall: Maverick of American Conservatives*, 250.

24. Allan Bloom, "Justice: John Rawls versus the Tradition of Political Philosophy," in *Giants and Dwarfs: Essays 1960–1990* (New York: Simon & Schuster, 1990), 337. Another important exception to the neglect of Rawls among conservative political philosophers is David Lewis Schaefer, *Illiberal Justice: John Rawls vs. the American Political Tradition* (Columbia: University of Missouri Press, 2007).

25. For a critique of Wood, see my "The Liberal Republicanism of Gordon Wood," *Claremont Review of Books* 7, no. 1 (Winter 2006/07).

26. Harry V. Jaffa, *Crisis of the House Divided: An Interpretation of the Issues in the Lincoln–Douglas Debates*, 3rd ed. (Chicago: University of Chicago Press, 1982; originally published 1959), 317, 321.

27. Harry V. Jaffa, *Crisis of the Strauss Divided: Essays on Leo Strauss and Straussianism, East and West* (Lanham, Md.: Rowman and Littlefield, 2012).

28. Harry V. Jaffa, "Agrarian Virtue and Republican Freedom: An Historical Perspective," in *Equality and Liberty: Theory and Practice in American Politics* (New York: Oxford University Press, 1965), 46, 47.

29. Jaffa, "What Is Equality?," 150.

30. Thomas Jefferson, First Inaugural Address, March 4, 1801, http://teaching americanhistory.org/library/document/first-inaugural-address-8/.

31. The best explanation of this might be found in *Federalist Paper* 31, where Hamilton explains the nature of the taxation power with a long preface about the logic of morals. Moral principles, he wrote, "contain an internal evidence which, antecedent to all reflection or combination, commands the assent of the mind. Where it produces not this effect, it must proceed either from some defect or disorder in the organs of perception, or from the influence of some strong interest, or passion, or prejudice."

32. Leo Strauss, *Liberalism Ancient and Modern* (New York: Basic Books, 1968), 24.

33. Willmoore Kendall, "How to Read Richard Weaver: Philosopher," in *Willmoore Kendall: Contra Mundum*, 400.

34. Jaffa, "What Is Equality?," 156.

35. Harry V. Jaffa, "Political Obligation and the American Political Tradition," in *The Conditions of Freedom: Essays in Political Philosophy* (Baltimore, Md.: Johns Hopkins University Press, 1975), 114.

36. Ibid., 158.

37. Harry V. Jaffa to Ernest Fortin, private correspondence, August 24, 1992.

38. Thomas G. West, "Harry Jaffa and the Nobility of the American Founding," *The Federalist*, February 19, 2015, http://thefederalist.com/2015/02/19/harry-jaffa -and-the-nobility-of-the-american-founding/.

39. Jaffa, "Aristotle and Locke in the American Founding."

40. George Washington, First Inaugural Address, April 30, 1789, http://teach ingamericanhistory.org/library/document/first-inaugural-address/.

41. Harry V. Jaffa, *The American Founding as the Best Regime: The Bonding of Civil and Religious Liberty* (Claremont, Calif.: Claremont Institute, 1987), 17–18.

42. Harry V. Jaffa, "Humanizing Certitudes and Impoverishing Doubts: A Critique of *The Closing of the American Mind* by Allan Bloom," *Interpretation* 16, no. 1 (Fall 1988): 111–138.

43. George Will, remarks delivered at the American Political Science Association annual meeting, September 2000.

44. Walter Berns, "Equally Endowed with Rights," in *Justice and Equality Here and Now*, edited by Frank S. Lucash (Ithaca, N.Y.: Cornell University Press, 1986): 151.

CHAPTER 7. HOW TO THINK ABOUT
THE CONSTITUTION: TWO VIEWS

Epigraphs: Harry V. Jaffa, *A New Birth of Freedom: Abraham Lincoln and the Coming of the Civil War* (Lanham, Md.: Rowman and Littlefield, 2000), 170. Walter Berns, *Freedom, Virtue and the First Amendment* (Baton Rouge: Louisiana State University Press, 1957), 254.

1. Abraham Lincoln, Letter to Alexander Stephens, December 22, 1860, http://teachingamericanhistory.org/library/document/letter-to-alexander-h-stephens/.

2. George Washington, Letter of the President of the Federal Convention, to the President of Congress, Transmitting the Constitution, September 17, 1787, http://avalon.law.yale.edu/18th_century/translet.asp.

3. Thomas G. West, "Jaffa versus Mansfield: Does America Have a Constitutional or a 'Declaration of Independence' Soul?," *Perspectives on Political Science* 31, no. 4 (2002): 235–246.

4. Peter Evans and Helen Evans, "Interview with Walter Berns," August 4, 2004, http://www.renewamerica.com/columns/evans/040804.

5. These essays are collected, oddly enough, in Walter Berns, *Democracy and the Constitution* (Washington, D.C.: AEI Press, 2006).

6. Evans and Evans, "Interview with Walter Berns."

7. Walter Berns, "*Buck v. Bell*: Due Process of Law?," *Western Political Quarterly* 6, no. 4 (December 1953): 762–775.

8. Ibid.

9. Berns, *Freedom, Virtue, and the First Amendment*, 191.

10. Ibid., ix.

11. Ibid., 230.

12. Ibid., 197.

13. Walter Berns, "Judicial Review and the Rights and Laws of Nature," in *In Defense of Liberal Democracy* (Chicago: Gateway, 1984), 43.

14. Ibid., 56.

15. Walter Berns, *Democracy and the Constitution* (Washington, D.C.: AEI Press, 2006), 17–28.

16. Martin Diamond, "Democracy and *The Federalist*: A Reconsideration of the Framers' Intent," *American Political Science Review* 53, no. 1 (March 1959): 52–68.

17. A panel of prominent economists drawn from across the political spectrum recently included Hayek's seminal essay as one of the twenty most significant essays ever to have appeared in the *American Economic Review*, though without noting that such an essay would be unlikely to be published in the *American Economic Review*

today. I am not aware of any similar attempt to single out the most significant articles to have appeared in the *American Political Science Review*, but if such an inventory were ever attempted, Diamond's essay on *The Federalist* would be an obvious selection.

18. Martin Diamond, quoted in "To Profess with a Passion," *Time*, May 6, 1966, 85.

19. Ibid.

20. Diamond, "Democracy and *The Federalist*," 68.

21. Herbert J. Storing, *What the Anti-Federalists Were FOR* (Chicago: University of Chicago Press, 1981), 64–70.

22. *Polar Tankers Inc. v. City of Valdez* (2009).

23. Berns thought that the Ninth Amendment is the real point of contact between the Constitution and the Declaration of Independence, and is merely a planted reminder of the right of revolution in the Declaration, that is, a reminder of the ultimate sovereignty and power of consent held by the people. He explains this view in "The Illegitimacy of Appeals to Natural Law in Constitutional Interpretation," in *Natural Law, Liberalism, and Morality: Contemporary Essays*, edited by Robert P. George (Oxford: Oxford University Press, 1996, 2001), 181–194.

24. Daniel A. Farber, *Retained by the People: The "Silent" Ninth Amendment and the Constitutional Rights Americans Don't Know They Have* (New York: Basic Books, 2007).

25. Herbert J. Storing, "The Constitution and the Bill of Rights," in *Toward a More Perfect Union: Writings of Herbert J. Storing*, edited by Joseph M. Bessette (Washington, D.C.: AEI Press, 1995), 118, 119.

26. William Rehnquist, "The Notion of a Living Constitution," *Texas Law Review* 54 (May 1976): 693–706.

27. Fairness demands noting that Jaffa shared the critical view of *Lochner* well into the 1980s, writing in 1983 that "The most pernicious of these [reactionary interpretations of the Constitution] were like the famous *Lochner* case of 1905." See "The Doughface Dilemma" in Harry V. Jaffa, *American Conservatism and the American Founding* (Durham, N.C.: Carolina Academic Press, 1984), 176. By the 1990s Jaffa was reevaluating some of his views on the constitutionality of economic liberty, and, although he never returned specifically to *Lochner*, he did admit to admiring the revisionist work of Richard Epstein and Roger Pilon.

28. Justice Antonin Scalia, address in Rome, June 27, 1996, *Origins: CNS Documentary Service* 26, no. 6.

29. Scalia Lecture at Texas Wesleyan University School of Law, May 10, 2000; http://www.uhuh.com/constitution/endurco.htm.

30. Antonin Scalia, *A Matter of Interpretation: Federal Courts and the Law* (Princeton, N.J.: Princeton University Press, 1997), 134.

31. "Thomas' Unsettling View of 'Natural Rights'," Editorial, *Human Events*, July 20, 1991, 3.

32. Harry V. Jaffa, Letter to *Human Events*, July 23, 1991, on file with author.

33. Readers interested in this question should see Ralph Rossum, *Understanding Clarence Thomas: The Jurisprudence of Constitutional Restoration* (Lawrence: University Press of Kansas, 2013).

34. Harry V. Jaffa, *Original Intent and the Framers of the Constitution: A Disputed Question* (Washington, D.C.: Regnery Gateway, 1994).

35. For example, in a speech before the Chamber of Commerce, in Elmira, New York, May 3, 1907 (*Addresses and Papers of Charles Evans Hughes, Governor of New York, 1906–1908* [1908], 139), Justice Charles Evans Hughes said, "We are under a Constitution, but *the Constitution is what the judges say it is,* and the judiciary is the safeguard of our liberty and of our property under the Constitution." No.

CHAPTER 8. EXTREMISM IN DEFENSE OF LIBERTY

Epigraph: Harry V. Jaffa, *American Conservatism and the American Founding* (Durham, N.C.: Carolina Academic Press, 1984), 135.

1. George Kateb, "Strange Bedfellows," Review of *Equality and Liberty* by Harry V. Jaffa, *Commentary* (August 1965), https://www.commentarymagazine.com /articles/equality-and-liberty-by-harry-v-jaffa/.

2. Harry V. Jaffa, letter to Henry Regnery, November 1, 1982, copy on file with author.

3. Friedrich Hayek's later work, on the evolutionary character of morality, was more problematic from several points of view, was never fully developed, and was received critically by many of Hayek's colleagues.

4. Jaffa, *American Conservatism and the American Founding,* 59.

5. Harry V. Jaffa, "Required Discrimination," *Wall Street Journal,* September 8, 1992.

6. Jaffa wrote: "Communists and Nazis, I maintain, have no right to the use of free speech in a free society. However, whether it is wise or expedient to deny them its use is another matter. I believe that the United States is a sufficiently civilized and a sufficiently stable community to bear the advocacy of almost anything, whether it be National Socialism, Communism, or Cannibalism. I would take my stand with Jefferson, who in his first inaugural address said, 'If there be any among us who would wish to dissolve this Union or to change its republican form, let them stand undisturbed as monuments of the safety with which error of opinion may be tolerated where reason is left free to combat it.'" From "On the Nature of Civil and Religious Liberty," in *The Conservative Papers,* edited by Ralph de Toledano and Karl Hess (New York: Doubleday Anchor, 1964), 250–268.

7. "A Conversation with Harry Jaffa at Rosary College," in Jaffa, *American Conservatism and the American Founding,* 63–64.

8. Harry V. Jaffa, *Extremism and Moderation: Barry Goldwater's 1964 Acceptance Speech* (Claremont, Calif.: Claremont Institute, 1998), 17.

9. Ibid., 11.

10. It was a pledge he didn't keep. Jack Kemp asked him on several occasions to draft speeches for him, which generally Kemp didn't use, and Jaffa occasionally drafted an unsolicited speech and sent it off to presidential hopefuls, including, in one instance, Vice President George H. W. Bush.

11. David Frum, "The Goldwater Myth," FrumForum, February 27, 2009, http://www.frumforum.com/the-goldwater-myth/.

12. Barry Goldwater, letter to Harry V. Jaffa, August 18, 1994; on file with author.

13. See Jaffa's recollections in "L'Envoi to Woody Hayes," *Claremont Review of Books* online, January 3, 2003, http://www.claremont.org/crb/basicpage/lenvoi-to-woody-hayes/.

CHAPTER 9. THE ADMINISTRATIVE STATE
AND THE END OF CONSTITUTIONAL GOVERNMENT

Epigraph: Harry V. Jaffa, "On the Necessity of a Scholarship of the Politics of Freedom," in *Statesmanship: Essays in Honor of Sir Winston S. Churchill*, edited by Harry V. Jaffa (Durham, N.C.: Carolina Academic Press, 1981), 6.

1. Paul Eidelberg, *A Discourse on Statesmanship: The Design and Transformation of the American Polity* (Urbana: University of Illinois Press, 1974), 299.

2. "I myself seek in vain an expression that exactly reproduces the idea that I form of it for myself and that contains it; the old words despotism and tyranny are not suitable. The thing is new, therefore I must try to describe it, since I cannot name it. . . . Thus, after taking each individual by turns in its powerful hands and kneading him as it likes, the sovereign extends its arms over society as a whole; it covers its surface with a network of small, complicated, painstaking, uniform rules, through which the most original minds and the most vigorous souls cannot clear a way to surpass the crowd; it does not break wills, but it softens them, bends them, and directs them; it rarely forces one to act, but it constantly opposes itself to one's acting; it does not destroy, it prevents things from being born; it does not tyrannize, it hinders, compromises, enervates, extinguishes, dazes, and finally reduces each nation to being nothing more than a herd of timid and industrious animals of which the government is the shepherd. . . . I have always believed that this sort of regulated, mild, and peaceful servitude, whose picture I have just painted, could be combined better than one imagines with some of the external forms of freedom, and that it would not be impossible for it to be established in the very shadow of the sovereignty of the people." Alexis de Toqueville, *Democracy in America*, translated and edited by Harvey C. Mansfield and Delba Winthrop (Chicago: University of Chicago Press, 2000), 663–664. See also Daniel R. Ernst, *Tocqueville's Nightmare: The Administrative State Emerges, 1900–1940* (New York: Oxford University Press, 2014).

3. Some of the more complete and useful treatments include Eidelberg, *A Discourse on Statesmanship*, esp. chap. 8, "The Public Teaching of Woodrow Wilson";

Ronald J. Pestritto, *Woodrow Wilson and the Roots of Modern American Liberalism* (Lanham, Md.: Rowman and Littlefield, 2005); Jean Yarbrough, *Theodore Roosevelt and the American Political Tradition* (Lawrence: University Press of Kansas, 2012). See also Charles R. Kesler, *I Am the Change: Barack Obama and the Crisis of Liberalism* (New York: Broadside Books, 2012), esp. chap. 2, "Woodrow Wilson and the Politics of Progress."

4. Harvey C. Mansfield Jr., *America's Constitutional Soul* (Baltimore, Md.: Johns Hopkins University Press, 1991), 5.

5. Good short accounts of the Progressive teaching on the separation of powers and its relation to the idea of the distinction between politics and administration include John Marini, *The Politics of Budget Control: Congress, the Presidency, and the Growth of the Administrative State* (Washington, D.C.: Crane Russak, 1992), especially 183–203; and Dennis J. Mahoney, "A Newer Science of Politics: The Federalist and American Political Science in the Progressive Era," in *Saving the Revolution: The Federalist Papers and the American Founding*, edited by Charles R. Kesler (New York: Free Press, 1987), 250–264.

6. Woodrow Wilson, *Constitutional Government in the United States* (New York: Columbia University Press, 1908), 56, 60.

7. Cited in Pestritto, *Woodrow Wilson and the Roots of Modern American Liberalism*, 82.

8. Wilson, *Constitutional Government in the United States*, 192.

9. Roscoe Pound, "Spurious Interpretation," *Columbia Law Review* 7 (1907): 384.

10. Frank J. Goodnow, *Politics and Administration: A Study in Government* (New York: MacMillan, 1900), 85–86.

11. See Philip Hamburger, *Is Administrative Law Unlawful?* (Chicago: University of Chicago Press, 2014); and Richard Epstein, *How Progressives Rewrote the Constitution* (Washington, D.C.: Cato Institute, 2006).

12. Gary Lawson, "The Rise and Rise of the Administrative State," *Harvard Law Review* 107, no. 6 (April 1994): 1248–1249.

13. The best account of the idea of Progress is Robert Nisbet's magisterial *History of the Idea of Progress* (New York: Basic Books, 1980).

14. Woodrow Wilson, "What Is Progress?," 1912 campaign speech, later published as chapter 2 of *The New Freedom: A Call for the Emancipation of the Generous Energies of a People* (New York and Garden City: Doubleday, Page, 1918).

15. G. W. F. Hegel, *The Philosophy of History*, translated by J. Sibree (New York: Dover Publications, 1956), 17.

16. Woodrow Wilson, "Leaders of Men," June 17, 1890, http://teaching americanhistory.org/library/document/leaders-of-men/#1R.

17. Condorcet: "Nature has set no term to the perfection of our human faculties, that the perfectibility of man is truly indefinite; and that the progress of this

perfectibility, from now onwards independent of any power that might wish to halt it, has no other limit than the duration of the globe upon which nature has cast us. This progress . . . will never be reversed." (Marie Jean Antoine de Condorect, *Sketch for a Historical Picture of the Progress of the Human Mind*, translated by June Barraclough (London: Weidenfeld and Nicolson, 1955), 4–5.

18. Woodrow Wilson, "The Study of Administration," November 1, 1886, http://teachingamericanhistory.org/library/document/the-study-of-administration/.

19. Max Weber, *From Max Weber: Essays in Sociology*, edited by H. H. Gerth and C. Wright Mills (New York: Oxford University Press, 1944), 233–234.

20. In commenting on that lecture in *Natural Right and History* (Chicago: University of Chicago Press, 1953), Leo Strauss directs our attention to a "more adequate discussion" of Weber's famous dilemma of the "ethic of responsibility" and the "ethic of ultimate ends" by referring readers to specific passages in Lord Charnwood's *Abraham Lincoln* (New York: Henry Holt, 1917) regarding Lincoln's understanding of how a statesman needed to approach the slavery question in the 1850s, and to Churchill's summary in *Marlborough* of how lengthening historical perspective can change our judgments. One notes two things about these "more adequate discussions." First, they are brief—much briefer than Weber's complex abstractions. Second, they are historical—examples of the axiom that "history is philosophy teaching by example." In the latter reference, Churchill writes: "It is not given to princes, statesmen, and captains to pierce the mysteries of the future, and even the most penetrating gaze reaches only conclusions which, however seemingly vindicated at a given moment, are inexorably effaced by time. One rule of conduct alone survives as a guide to men in their wanderings: fidelity to covenants, the honour of soldiers, and the hatred of causing human woe"; *Marlborough: His Life and Times* (Chicago: University of Chicago Press, 2002), 4:600. This was published only a few months before the capitulation at Munich. After the war, Churchill repeated and extended this theme in his account of Munich in *The Gathering Storm*, and it reads like a commentary and refutation of Weber's lecture, even though it is certain Churchill never read Weber. See Churchill, *The Gathering Storm* (Boston: Houghton Mifflin, 1948), 319–321.

21. Herbert J. Storing, "The Achievement of Leo Strauss," in *Toward a More Perfect Union: Writings of Herbert J. Storing*, edited by Joseph M. Bessette (Washington, D.C.: AEI Press, 1995), 446; Edward C. Banfield, "Policy Science as Metaphysical Madness," in *Here the People Rule: Selected Essays* (New York: Plenum Press, 1985), 146; Walter Berns, "The Behavioral Sciences and the Study of Political Things: The Case of Christian Bay's *The Structure of Freedom*," *American Political Science Review* 55, no. 3 (September 1961): 559; and Martin Diamond, "Teaching about Politics as a Vocation," in *As Far as Republican Principles Will Admit: Essays by Martin Diamond*, edited by William A. Schambra (Washington, D.C.: AEI Press, 1992), 304.

22. A good survey of the arc of political science is David M. Ricci, *The Tragedy of Political Science: Politics, Scholarship, and Democracy* (New Haven: Yale University Press, 1984), esp. chaps. 4, 5, and 6.

23. Berns, "The Behavioral Sciences," 557. Berns also directs our attention to Socrates in the *Phaedo*: "It seemed to me necessary to take refuge in speaking and to investigate the truth of existing things in spoken words."

24. Jaffa, "On the Necessity of a Scholarship of the Politics of Freedom," 8.

25. Harry V. Jaffa, "Political Philosophy and Political Reality," lecture delivered at Henry Salvatori Center, Claremont McKenna College, December 3, 1991, http://www.claremont.org/crb/basicpage/political-philosophy-and-political-reality/.

26. John Wettergreen, Jaffa's first graduate student at Ohio State University and then at Claremont, passed away at the untimely age of forty-three in 1989, before finishing a book with the title *Total Regulation*.

27. Jaffa, "On the Necessity of a Scholarship of the Politics of Freedom," 5–6.

28. See in particular Fred Siegel's *Revolt Against the Masses: How Liberalism Has Undermined the Middle Class* (New York: Encounter Books, 2014). On the other hand, see John Adams Wettergreen, "Is Snobbery a Formal Value? Considering Life at the End of Modernity," *Western Political Quarterly* 26, no. 1 (March 1973): 109–129.

29. See in particular Michael Walsh, *The Devil's Pleasure Palace: The Cult of Critical Theory and the Subversion of the West* (New York: Encounter Books, 2015).

30. Leo Strauss, *The City and Man* (Chicago: University of Chicago Press, 1963), 11.

31. I might as well use Wikipedia's description of the runaway trolley thought experiment: "The general form of the problem is this: There is a runaway trolley barreling down the railway tracks. Ahead, on the tracks, there are five people tied up and unable to move. The trolley is headed straight for them. You are standing some distance off in the train yard, next to a lever. If you pull this lever, the trolley will switch to a different set of tracks. However, you notice that there is one person on the side track. You have two options: (1) Do nothing, and the trolley kills the five people on the main track. (2) Pull the lever, diverting the trolley onto the side track where it will kill one person. Which is the correct choice?"

32. Leo Strauss, *What Is Political Philosophy? And Other Studies* (New York: Free Press, 1959), 23.

CHAPTER 10. POLITICAL PHILOSOPHY IN AN ANTI-PHILOSOPHIC AGE

Epigraphs: Margaret Thatcher, in John Blundell, *Margaret Thatcher: Portrait of the Iron Lady* (New York: Algora Publishing, 2008), p. 137. Harry V. Jaffa, "Leo Strauss Remembered," *National Review* 25, no. 49 (1973).

1. Nathan Tarcov and Thomas L. Pangle, "Epilogue: Leo Strauss and the History

of Political Philosophy," in *History of Political Philosophy*, edited by Leo Strauss and Joseph Cropsey, 3rd ed. (Chicago and London: University of Chicago Press, 1987), 928.

2. Leo Strauss, letter to Karl Lowith, August 20, 1946, reprinted in the *Independent Journal of Philosophy* 4 (1983): 111.

3. Harry V. Jaffa, "The Unity of Tragedy, Comedy, and History: An Interpretation of the Shakespearean Universe," in *Shakespeare as a Political Thinker*, edited by John Alvis and Thomas G. West (Durham, N.C.: Carolina Academic Press, 1981), 277.

4. Allan Bloom, "Political Philosophy and Poetry," in *Giants and Dwarfs: Essays 1960–1990* (New York: Simon & Schuster, 1990), 56–67, 58.

5. Jonathan Dollimore, "Shakespeare, Cultural Materialism and the New Historicism," in *Political Shakespeare: New Essays in Cultural Materialism*, edited by Jonathan Dollimore and Alan Sinfield (Manchester, [UK]: Manchester University Press, 1985), 3.

6. Bloom wrote on *Othello*, Jaffa on *King Lear*. These essays were later extended and collected into a book, *Shakespeare's Politics* (Chicago: University of Chicago Press, 1964).

7. Is this idea so outrageous or novel? The modernist artist and critic Wyndham Lewis argued much the same thesis in his 1927 book *The Lion and the Fox: The Role of the Hero in the Plays of William Shakespeare*. "The master figure of Elizabethan drama is Machiavelli. . . . Elizabethan drama . . . was more terrified of Machiavelli than of anybody."

8. See especially Harry V. Jaffa, "Macbeth and the Moral Universe," *Claremont Review of Books* 8, no. 1 (Winter 2007/08), http://www.claremont.org/crb/article /macbeth-and-the-moral-universe/.

9. Ibid.

10. Walter Berns, *For Capital Punishment: Crime and the Morality of the Death Penalty* (New York: Basic Books, 1979).

11. Ibid., 156, 158.

12. Jaffa, "Macbeth and the Moral Universe."

13. Berns, *For Capital Punishment*, 169.

14. Ibid., 165: "It would take me too far afield to attempt to demonstrate that Lincoln, contrary to the legend that he himself helped to write, was the uncommonest of men; and, besides, that demonstration has already been made, and made with a clarity and wisdom that I could not hope to match." See Harry V. Jaffa, *Crisis of the House Divided: An Interpretation of the Issues in the Lincoln-Douglas Debates*, 3rd ed. (Chicago: University of Chicago Press, 1982; originally published 1959).

15. Walter Berns, letter to Harry Jaffa, January 20, 1981. Joseph Cropsey wrote in a similar voice to Jaffa in 1984: "When we were young, I never doubted that I understood you. Now you are a mystery to me. . . . I considered you the best and wisest of my generation. Whenever we met, I learned something from you; it distressed me that I had nothing to teach you in return. . . . From all of this you will

readily understand how little pleasure I have had in watching the best friend of my best years become a pastiche of Don Quixote and Mrs. Grundy."

16. Sigurd Burckhardt, "English Bards and *APSR* Reviewers," *American Political Science Review* 54, no. 1 (March 1960): 162.

17. Walter Berns, *Making Patriots* (Chicago: University of Chicago Press, 2001), 98.

18. Harry V. Jaffa, *A New Birth of Freedom: Abraham Lincoln and the Coming of the Civil War* (Lanham, Md.: Rowman and Littlefield, 2000), 258. See also Jaffa's very different, and typically complicated, view of Lincoln and Christianity in ibid., 351–353.

19. Walter Berns, "Reply to Harry Jaffa," *National Review*, January 22, 1982.

20. Walter Berns, *Freedom, Virtue and the First Amendment* (Baton Rouge: Louisiana State University Press, 1957), 19.

21. Berns, "Reply to Harry Jaffa."

22. Leo Strauss, *Thoughts on Machiavelli* (Chicago: University of Chicago Press, 1958), 299.

23. Harry V. Jaffa, *American Conservatism and the American Founding* (Durham, N.C.: Carolina Academic Press, 1984), 129.

24. Leo Strauss, *The City and Man* (Chicago: University of Chicago Press, 1963), 11.

25. Harvey Mansfield Jr., comments made at the 28:40 mark of his fourth video conversation with Bill Kristol, http://conversationswithbillkristol.org/video/harvey -mansfield-iv/.

26. Steven B. Smith, *Reading Leo Strauss: Politics, Philosophy, Judaism* (Chicago: University of Chicago Press, 2006).

27. Steven B. Smith, "Hidden Truths," *New York Times Book Review*, August 23, 2013, http://www.nytimes.com/2013/08/25/books/review/two-books-about-the -legacy-of-leo-strauss.html.

28. Leo Strauss, "What Can We Learn from Political Theory?," *The Review of Politics* 69, no. 4 (Fall 2007): 515–529.

29. Ibid., 526.

30. Ibid., 527.

31. Ibid., 527–528.

32. Strauss, *Thoughts on Machiavelli*, 13.

33. Ibid., 14.

34. Leo Strauss, "On Classical Political Philosophy," in *What Is Political Philosophy? And Other Studies* (New York: Free Press, 1959), 78–94.

35. Leo Strauss, "Progress or Return?," in *The Rebirth of Classical Political Rationalism: An Introduction to the Thought of Leo Strauss*, edited by Thomas L. Pangle (Chicago: University of Chicago Press, 1989), 227–270.

36. Ibid., 260.

37. Ibid., 233.

38. Leo Strauss, *Natural Right and History* (Chicago: University of Chicago Press, 1953), 323.

39. Harry V. Jaffa, letter to Henry Salvatori, May 9, 1980, on file with author.

40. Paul Gottfried, a strong critic of both Jaffa and Leo Strauss, reports that one of Jaffa's closest friends from boyhood, the late Jesuit Francis Canavan, once told Gottfried that Jaffa said, "Frank, I'm inventing a myth and I'll make people believe it."

41. Thomas L. Pangle, "Patriotism, American Style," *National Review*, November 29, 1985, 31.

42. Alexis de Tocqueville, *Democracy in America*, translated and edited by Harvey C. Mansfield and Delba Winthrop (Chicago: University of Chicago Press, 2000), 227.

43. Steven B. Smith, *Political Philosophy* (New Haven, Conn.: Yale University Press, 2012), 254.